Iterative Methods in Combinatorial Optimization

With the advent of approximation algorithms for NP-hard combinatorial optimization problems, several techniques from exact optimization such as the primal-dual method have proven their staying power and versatility. This book describes a simple and powerful method that is iterative in essence and similarly useful in a variety of settings for exact and approximate optimization. The authors highlight the commonality and uses of this method to prove a variety of classical polyhedral results on matchings, trees, matroids, and flows.

The presentation style is elementary enough to be accessible to anyone with exposure to basic linear algebra and graph theory, making the book suitable for introductory courses in combinatorial optimization at the upper undergraduate and beginning graduate levels. Discussions of advanced applications illustrate their potential for future application in research in approximation algorithms.

LAP CHI LAU is an Assistant Professor in the Department of Computer Science and Engineering at The Chinese University of Hong Kong. Lap Chi's main research interests are in combinatorial optimization and graph algorithms. His paper on Steiner tree packing was given the Machtey award in the IEEE Foundations of Computer Science Conference. His Ph.D. thesis was awarded the doctoral prize from the Canadian Mathematical Society and a doctoral prize from the Natural Sciences and Engineering Research Council of Canada.

R. RAVI is Carnegie Bosch Professor of Operations Research and Computer Science at Carnegie Mellon University. Ravi's main research interests are in combinatorial optimization (particularly in approximation algorithms), computational molecular biology, and electronic commerce.

MOHIT SINGH is an Assistant Professor in the School of Computer Science, McGill University. He completed his Ph.D. in 2008 at the Tepper School of Business, Carnegie Mellon University, where his advisor was Professor R. Ravi. His thesis was awarded the Tucker prize by the Mathematical Programming Society. His research interests include approximation algorithms, combinatorial optimization, and models that deal with uncertainty in data.

CAMBRIDGE TEXTS IN APPLIED MATHEMATICS

All titles listed below can be obtained from good booksellers or from Cambridge University Press. For a complete series listing, visit http://www.cambridge.org/uk/series/sSeries.asp?code=CTAM

Complex Variables: Introduction and Applications (2nd Edition),
MARK J. ABLOWITZ & ATHANASSIOS S. FOKAS
Scaling, G. I. R. BARENBLATT
Introduction to Symmetry Analysis, BRIAN J. CANTWELL
Hydrodynamic Instabilities, FRANÇOIS CHARRU
Introduction to Hydrodynamic Stability, P. G. DRAZIN
A First Course in Continuum Mechanics, OSCAR GONZALEZ & ANDREW M. STUART
Theory of Vortex Sound, M. S. HOWE
Applied Solid Mechanics, PETER HOWELL, GREGORY KOZYREFF, & JOHN OCKENDON
Practical Applied Mathematics: Modelling, Analysis, Approximation, SAM HOWISON
A First Course in the Numerical Analysis of Differential Equations (2nd Edition),
    ARIEH ISERLES
A First Course in Combinatorial Optimization, JON LEE
Finite Volume Methods for Hyperbolic Problems, RANDALL J. LEVEQUE
Bäcklund and Darboux Transformations, C. ROGERS & W. K. SCHIEF
An Introduction to Parallel and Vector Scientific Computation, RONALD W. SHONKWILER &
    LEW LEFTON

Iterative Methods in Combinatorial Optimization

LAP CHI LAU
The Chinese University of Hong Kong

R. RAVI
Carnegie Mellon University

MOHIT SINGH
McGill University

CAMBRIDGE
UNIVERSITY PRESS

CAMBRIDGE
UNIVERSITY PRESS

University Printing House, Cambridge CB2 8BS, United Kingdom

One Liberty Plaza, 20th Floor, New York, NY 10006, USA

477 Williamstown Road, Port Melbourne, VIC 3207, Australia

314-321, 3rd Floor, Plot 3, Splendor Forum, Jasola District Centre, New Delhi - 110025, India

79 Anson Road, #06-04/06, Singapore 079906

Cambridge University Press is part of the University of Cambridge.

It furthers the University's mission by disseminating knowledge in the pursuit of education, learning and research at the highest international levels of excellence.

www.cambridge.org
Information on this title: www.cambridge.org/9781107007512

© Lap Chi Lau, R. Ravi, and Mohit Singh 2011

First published 2011

A catalogue record for this publication is available from the British Library

Library of Congress Cataloging in Publication data
Lau, Lap Chi.
    Iterative methods in combinatorial optimization / Lap Chi Lau, R. Ravi, Mohit Singh.
        p.   cm. – (Cambridge texts in applied mathematics)
    Includes bibliographical references and index.
    ISBN 978-1-107-00751-2 (hardback) – ISBN 978-0-521-18943-9 (pbk.)
    1. Iterative methods (Mathematics)   2. Combinatorial optimization.   I. Ravi, R.
    (Ramamoorthi), 1969–   II. Singh, Mohit.   III. Title.   IV. Series.
    QA297.8.L38 2011
    518′.26–dc22   2011003653

ISBN 978-1-107-00751-2 Hardback
ISBN 978-0-521-18943-9 Paperback

Contents

Preface   *page* ix

1   Introduction   **1**
   1.1   The assignment problem   1
   1.2   Iterative algorithm   3
   1.3   Approach outline   5
   1.4   Context and applications of iterative rounding   8
   1.5   Book chapters overview   8
   1.6   Notes   10

2   Preliminaries   **12**
   2.1   Linear programming   12
   2.2   Graphs and digraphs   19
   2.3   Submodular and supermodular functions   21

3   Matching and vertex cover in bipartite graphs   **28**
   3.1   Matchings in bipartite graphs   28
   3.2   Generalized assignment problem   32
   3.3   Maximum budgeted allocation   35
   3.4   Vertex cover in bipartite graphs   40
   3.5   Vertex cover and matching: duality   43
   3.6   Notes   44

4   Spanning trees   **46**
   4.1   Minimum spanning trees   46
   4.2   Iterative 1-edge-finding algorithm   54
   4.3   Minimum bounded-degree spanning trees   57
   4.4   An additive one approximation algorithm   60
   4.5   Notes   62

5   Matroids   **65**
   5.1   Preliminaries   65
   5.2   Maximum weight basis   67
   5.3   Matroid intersection   71
   5.4   Duality and min–max theorem   74
   5.5   Minimum bounded degree matroid basis   77
   5.6 k matroid intersection   82
   5.7   Notes   85

6   Arborescence and rooted connectivity   **88**
   6.1   Minimum cost arborescence   89
   6.2   Minimum cost rooted k-connected subgraphs   95
   6.3   Minimum bounded degree arborescence   101
   6.4   Additive performance guarantee   106
   6.5   Notes   108

7   Submodular flows and applications   **110**
   7.1   The model and the main result   110
   7.2   Primal integrality   112
   7.3   Dual integrality   116
   7.4   Applications of submodular flows   117
   7.5   Minimum bounded degree submodular flows   124
   7.6   Notes   128

8   Network matrices   **131**
   8.1   The model and main results   131
   8.2   Primal integrality   133
   8.3   Dual integrality   136
   8.4   Applications   139
   8.5   Notes   143

9   Matchings   **145**
   9.1   Graph matching   145
   9.2   Hypergraph matching   155
   9.3   Notes   160

10   Network design   **164**
   10.1   Survivable network design problem   164
   10.2   Connection to the traveling salesman problem   168
   10.3   Minimum bounded degree Steiner networks   172
   10.4   An additive approximation algorithm   175
   10.5   Notes   179

11	**Constrained optimization problems**	**182**
	11.1 Vertex cover	182
	11.2 Partial vertex cover	184
	11.3 Multicriteria spanning trees	187
	11.4 Notes	189
12	**Cut problems**	**191**
	12.1 Triangle cover	191
	12.2 Feedback vertex set on bipartite tournaments	194
	12.3 Node multiway cut	197
	12.4 Notes	200
13	**Iterative relaxation: Early and recent examples**	**203**
	13.1 A discrepancy theorem	203
	13.2 Rearrangments of sums	206
	13.3 Minimum cost circulation	208
	13.4 Minimum cost unsplittable flow	210
	13.5 Bin packing	212
	13.6 Iterative randomized rounding: Steiner trees	220
	13.7 Notes	228
14	**Summary**	**231**
	Bibliography	233
	Index	241

Preface

Audience

As teachers and students of combinatorial optimization, we have often looked for material that illustrates the elegance of classical results on matchings, trees, matroids, and flows, but also highlights methods that have continued application. With the advent of approximation algorithms, some techniques from exact optimization such as the primal-dual method have indeed proven their staying power and versatility. In this book, we describe what we believe is a simple and powerful method that is iterative in essence and useful in a variety of settings.

The core of the iterative methods we describe relies on a fundamental result in linear algebra that the row rank and column rank of a real matrix are equal. This seemingly elementary fact allows us via a counting argument to provide an alternate proof of the previously mentioned classical results; the method is constructive and the resulting algorithms are iterative with the correctness proven by induction. Furthermore, these methods generalize to accommodate a variety of additional constraints on these classical problems that render them NP-hard – a careful adaptation of the iterative method leads to very effective approximation algorithms for these cases.

Our goal in this book has been to highlight the commonality and uses of this method and convince the readers of the generality and potential for future applications. We have used an elementary presentation style that should be accessible to anyone with introductory college mathematics exposure in linear algebra and basic graph theory. Whatever advanced material in these areas we require, we develop from scratch along the way. Some basic background on approximation algorithms such as is provided in the various books and surveys available on this subject will be useful in appreciating the power of the results we prove in this area. Other than the basic definition of an approximation algorithm and the understanding of polynomial-time complexity, no further technical background is required from this typically more advanced subject.

An important secondary goal of the book is to provide a framework and material for introductory courses in combinatorial optimization at the upper-class undergraduate and beginning graduate levels. We hope the common approach across the chapters gives a comprehensive way to introduce these topics for the first time. The more advanced applications are useful illustrations for graduate students of their potential for future application in their research.

History

This book is inspired by the application of the iterative method in the field of approximation algorithms and its recent adaptations to prove performance guarantees for problems with two objectives. This adaptation showed us how the proof technique can be used to reprove several classical results in combinatorial optimization and also in approximation algorithms in a unified way. The book owes its origin to the paper by Jain [75] describing a 2-approximation algorithm for a large class of minimum cost network-design problems in undirected networks. There are other earlier illustrations of the method in the literature, but it is Jain's work that inspired the adaptation that led to the results in this monograph.

Jain's result itself was a breakthrough when it appeared, and demonstrated the power of his *iterative rounding* method to prove this result that was conjectured based on a long line of earlier papers that applied a different primal-dual method to these problems. In this sense, his method was a purely primal attack on the problem. His method was extended by Lau et al. [88] to degree-bounded network design problems. The adaptation of this method by Singh and Lau [125] to the degree-bounded minimum cost spanning tree problem surprisingly involves no rounding at all! Instead, variables whose value are set to one in the linear programming relaxation are selected, and the program is modified carefully to continue to yield this property. This explains the title of this monograph and also hints at how this adaptation now allows one to prove *exact* results since we no longer have to round any variables and lose optimality.

Acknowledgments

We are grateful to the many organizations whose support have enabled this work: US National Science Foundation, Research Grants Council of Hong Kong, Microsoft Research, Kyoto University RIMS, the Qatar Foundation, Carnegie Mellon University – Pittsburgh and Doha, McGill University, and the Chinese University of Hong Kong. We are also grateful to our families for their support of this endeavor. We hope you will enjoy reading this monograph as much as we did writing it.

Dedications

Lau dedicates this work to his parents, his wife Pui Ming, and their children Ching Lam, Sing Chit, and Ching Yiu. Ravi dedicates this work to the memory of his late brother, R. Balasubramaniam, who encouraged him to write a book. Singh dedicates this work to his parents.

1

Introduction

In this first chapter we motivate our method via the assignment problem. Through this problem, we highlight the basic ingredients and ideas of the method. We then give an outline of how a typical chapter in the rest of the book is structured, and how the remaining chapters are organized.

1.1 The assignment problem

Consider the classical assignment problem: Given a bipartite graph $G = (V_1 \cup V_2, E)$ with $|V_1| = |V_2|$ and weight function $w : E \to \mathbb{R}_+$, the objective is to match every vertex in V_1 with a distinct vertex in V_2 to minimize the total weight (cost) of the matching. This is also called the minimum weight bipartite perfect matching problem in the literature and is a fundamental problem in combinatorial optimization. See Figure 1.1 for an example of a perfect matching in a bipartite graph.

One approach to the assignment problem is to model it as a linear programming problem. A linear program is a mathematical formulation of the problem with a system of linear constraints that can contain both equalities and inequalities, and also a linear objective function that is to be maximized or minimized. In the assignment problem, we associate a *variable* x_{uv} for every $\{u, v\} \in E$. Ideally, we would like the variables to take one of two values, zero or one (hence in the ideal case, they are binary variables). When x_{uv} is set to one, we intend the model to signal that this pair is matched; when x_{uv} is set to zero, we intend the model to signal that this pair is not matched. The following is a linear programming formulation of the assignment problem:

$$
\begin{aligned}
\text{minimize} \quad & \sum_{u,v} w_{uv} x_{uv} \\
\text{subject to} \quad & \sum_{v:\{u,v\}\in E} x_{uv} = 1 \quad \forall u \in V_1
\end{aligned}
$$

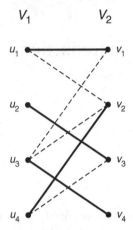

Figure 1.1 The solid edges form a perfect matching in the bipartite graph.

$$\sum_{u:\{u,v\}\in E} x_{uv} = 1 \qquad \forall v \in V_2$$

$$x_{uv} \geq 0 \qquad \forall \{u,v\} \in E$$

The objective function is to minimize the total weight of the matching, while the two sets of linear equalities ensure that every vertex in V_1 is matched to exactly one vertex in V_2 in the assignment and vice-versa.

A fundamental result in the operations research literature [71] is the polynomial time solvability (as well as the practical tractability) of linear programming problems. There is also a rich theory of optimality (and certificates for it) that has been developed (see e.g., the text by Chvatal [29]). Using these results, we can solve the problem we formulated earlier quite effectively for even very large problem sizes.

Returning to the formulation, however, our goal is to find a "binary" assignment of vertices in V_1 to vertices in V_2, but in the solution returned, the x-variables may take fractional values. Nevertheless, for the assignment problem, a celebrated result that is a cornerstone of combinatorial optimization [30] states that for any set of weights that permit a finite optimal solution, there is always an optimal solution to the preceding linear program (LP) that takes binary values in all the x-variables.

Such *integrality* results of LPs are few and far between, but reveal rich underlying structure for efficient optimization over the large combinatorial solution space [121]. They have been shown using special properties of the constraint matrix of the problem (such as total unimodularity) or of the whole linear system including the right-hand side (such as total dual integrality). This book is about a simple and fairly intuitive method that is able to re-prove many (but not all) of the results obtained by these powerful methods. One advantage of our approach is that it can be used to incorporate additional constraints that make the problem computationally hard and allow us to derive good approximation algorithms with provable performance guarantee for the constrained versions.

1.2 Iterative algorithm

Our method is iterative. Using the following two steps, it works inductively to show that the LP has an integral optimal solution.

- If any x_{uv} is set to 1 in an optimal solution to the LP, then we take this pair as matched in our solution, delete them both to get a smaller problem, and proceed to the next iteration.
- If any variable x_{uv} is set to 0 in an optimal solution, we remove the edge (u, v) to again get a smaller problem (since the number of edges reduces by 1) and proceed to the next iteration.

We continue these iterations till all variables have been fixed to either 0 or 1. Given the preceding iterative algorithm, there are two claims that need to be proven. First, the algorithm works correctly (i.e., it can always find a variable with value 0 or 1) in each iteration, and, second, the selected matching is an optimal (minimum weight) matching. Assuming the first claim, the second claim can be proved by a simple inductive argument. The crux of the argument is that in each iteration our solution pays exactly what the fractional optimal solution pays. Moreover, the fractional optimal solution when restricted to the residual graph remains feasible for the residual problem. This allows us to apply an inductive argument to show that the matching we construct has the same weight as the fractional optimal solution and is thus optimal. For the first claim, it is not clear a priori that one can always find a variable with value 1 or 0 at every step. Indeed, the example in Figure 1.2 shows that there might not be such a variable at some fractional optimal solution. However, we use the important concept of the extreme point (or vertex) solutions of linear programs to show that the preceding iterative algorithm works correctly.

Definition 1.2.1 *Let $P = \{x : Ax = b, x \geq 0\} \subseteq \mathbb{R}^n$. Then $x \in \mathbb{R}^n$ is an* **extreme point solution** *of P if there does not exist a nonzero vector $y \in \mathbb{R}^n$ such that $x + y, x - y \in P$.*

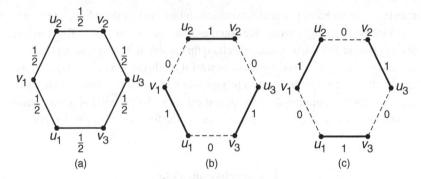

Figure 1.2 (a) The fractional solution which places $\frac{1}{2}$ on all the edges is an optimal fractional solution but not an extreme point solution. The fractional solution in (a) is the convex combination of the integral solutions in (b) and (c).

Extreme point solutions are also known as vertex solutions and are equivalent to basic feasible solutions. These concepts are defined in Chapter 2. Pictorially extreme point solutions are the corner points of the set of feasible solutions. The following basic result shows that there is always an optimal extreme point solution to bounded linear programs.

Lemma 1.2.2 *Let $P = \{x : Ax = b, x \geq 0\}$ and assume that the optimum value $\min\{c^T x : x \in P\}$ is finite. Then for any feasible solution $x \in P$, there exists an extreme point solution $x' \in P$ with $c^T x' \leq c^T x$.*

The following rank lemma is an important ingredient in the correctness proofs of almost all iterative algorithms in this monograph (see Chapter 2).

Lemma 1.2.3 (Rank Lemma) *Let $P = \{x : Ax = b, x \geq 0\}$ and let x be an extreme point solution of P such that $x_i > 0$ for each i. Then the number of variables is equal to the number of linearly independent constraints of A (i.e. the rank of A).*

1.2.1 Contradiction proof idea: Lower bound > upper bound

We give an outline of the proof that at each iteration there exists a variable with value 0 or 1. Suppose for contradiction that $0 < x_{uv} < 1$ for every edge $\{u, v\} \in E$. We use this assumption to derive a lower bound on the number of variables of the linear program. Let n be the number of remaining vertices in V_1 (or V_2, they have the same cardinality) at the current iteration. Then each vertex in V_1 must have two edges incident on it, since $\sum_{v \in V_2 : (u,v) \in E} x_{uv} = 1$ and $x_{uv} < 1$ for each $(u, v) \in E$. Thus, the total number of edges is at least $2n$.

This is a lower bound on the number of variables of the linear program, since we have one variable for each edge.

On the other hand, using the rank lemma, we derive an upper bound on the number of variables of the linear program. In the linear program for bipartite matching, we have only $2n$ constraints (one for each vertex in $V_1 \cup V_2$). Moreover, these $2n$ constraints are dependent since the sum of the constraints for vertices in V_1 equals the sum of the constraints for vertices in V_2. Hence, the number of linearly independent constraints is at most $2n - 1$. By the Rank Lemma, the number of variables is at most $2n - 1$. This provides us an upper bound on the number of variables. Since our upper bound is strictly smaller than the lower bound, we obtain the desired contradiction. Therefore, in an extreme point solution of the linear program for bipartite matching, there must exist a variable with value 0 or 1, and thus the iterative algorithm works. The number of iterations can be simply bounded by the number of edges in the bipartite graph. We give a formal proof of the preceding outline in Chapter 3.

1.2.2 Approximation algorithms for NP-hard problems

The preceding framework can be naturally adapted to provide an approximation algorithm via the iterative method. In particular, for this, the preceding iterative algorithm typically has one or both of two additional steps: *rounding* and *relaxation*.

(i) **Rounding:** Fix a threshold $\alpha \geq 1$. If there is a variable x_i that has a value of at least $\frac{1}{\alpha}$ in the optimal extreme point solution, then pick the corresponding element in the solution being constructed.
(ii) **Relaxation:** Fix a threshold β. If there is a constraint $\sum_i a_i x_i \leq b$ such that $\sum_i a_i \leq b + \beta$, then remove the constraint in the residual formulation.

For the bipartite matching problem, we will see how the iterative algorithm presented here can be adapted to give approximation algorithms for the generalized assignment problem in Chapter 3. Other generalizations include the budgeted allocation problem in Chapter 3 and the hypergraph matching problem in Chapter 9.

1.3 Approach outline

We now give an overview of the structure of the rest of the monograph. Early chapters in the book contain two main components: The first deals with proving the integrality of the LP relaxation of a well-studied problem, while the second shows how the iterative proof of integrality can be extended to design approximation algorithms for NP-hard variants of these basic problems. Both components follow the natural outline described next.

(i) **Linear Programming Formulation:** We start by giving a linear programming relaxation for the optimization problem we study. If the problem is polynomially solvable, this relaxation will be one with integral extreme points, and that is what we will set out to show. If the problem is NP-hard, we state an approximation algorithmic result, which we then set out to prove.

  (a) **Solvability:** Sometimes the linear programming relaxation we start with will be exponential in size. We then show that the linear program is solvable in polynomial time. Usually, this would entail providing a polynomial time *separation oracle* for the program using the formalism of the ellipsoid method [67]. Informally, the separation oracle is a procedure that certifies that any given candidate solution for the program is either feasible or not and, in the latter case, provides a separating hyperplane which is a violated inequality of the formulation. In programs with an exponential number of such inequalities that are implicity described, the design of the separation oracle is itself a combinatorial optimization problem, and we sketch the reduction to one.

(ii) **Characterization of Extreme Point Solution:** We then give a characterization result for the optimal extreme point solutions of the linear program based on the rank lemma (Lemma 1.2.3). This part aims to show that any maximal set of linearly independent tight constraints at this extreme point solution can be captured by a sparse structure. Sometimes the proof of this requires the use of the *uncrossing* technique [30] in combinatorial optimization, which will be introduced in Chapter 4.

(iii) **Iterative Algorithm:** We present an iterative algorithm for constructing an integral solution to the problem from an extreme point solution. The algorithm has two simple steps.

  (a) If there is a variable in the optimal extreme point solution that is set to a value of 1, then include the element in the integral solution.

  (b) If there is a variable in the optimal extreme point solution that is set to a value of 0, then remove the corresponding element.

In each case, at each iteration, we reduce the problem and arrive at a *residual* version, then we recompute an optimal extreme point solution and iterate the above steps until all variables have been set this way. In designing approximation algorithms we also use the rounding and relaxation steps as stated earlier.

(iv) **Analysis:** We then analyze the iterative algorithm. This involves arguing the following two facts. We establish, first, that the algorithm runs correctly and, second, that it returns an optimal solution.

   (a) **Correctness:** We show that the iterative algorithm is correct by arguing that there is always a 1-element or a 0-element to pick in every iteration. This crucially uses the characterization of tight constraints at this optimal extreme point solution. The argument here also follows the same contradiction proof idea (lower bound > upper bound): We assume for a contradiction that there is no 1-element or 0-element and get a large lower bound on the number of nonzero variables in the optimal extreme point solution. On the other side, we use the sparsity of the linearly independent tight constraints to show an upper bound on the number of such constraints. This then contradicts the Rank Lemma that insists that both these numbers are equal, and proves that there is always a 1- or 0-element.

   (b) **Optimality:** We finally show that the iterative algorithm indeed returns an optimal solution using a simple inductive argument. The crux of this argument is to show that the extreme point solution induced on the residual problem remains a feasible solution to this residual problem.

For the NP-hard variants of the problems we study, our goal is to show that the preceding framework can be naturally adapted to provide an approximation algorithm via the iterative method. In particular, recall that this iterative algorithm typically has one or both of two additional steps: *rounding* and *relaxation*.

(i) **Rounding:** Fix a threshold $\alpha \geq 1$. If there is a variable x_i which in the optimal extreme point solution has a value of at least $\frac{1}{\alpha}$ then include the corresponding element in the solution.

   Adding this rounding step does not allow us to obtain optimal integral solution but only near-optimal solutions. Using the above step, typically one obtains an approximation ratio of α for covering problems addressed using this framework.

(ii) **Relaxation:** Fix a threshold β. If there is a constraint $\sum_i a_i x_i \leq b$ such that $\sum_i a_i \leq b + \beta$ then remove the constraint in the residual formulation.

   The iterative relaxation step removes a constraint and hence this constraint can be violated in later iterations. But the condition on the removal of the constraints ensures that the constraint is only violated by an additive amount of β. This step enables us to obtain *additive* approximation algorithms for a variety of problems.

To summarize, for designing approximation algorithms, we first study the exact optimization problem in the above framework. We then use the preceding two steps in various combinations to derive strong approximation algorithms for constrained versions of these exact problems. In the last few chapters, we find a few examples of approximation algorithms that do not strictly fit this framework (e.g., multicriteria versions, cut problems, bin packing), but the overall approach for these problems remains the same.

1.4 Context and applications of iterative rounding

One goal in presenting the collections of results in this book is to convince the reader that iterative rounding is an effective tool in proving results in optimization. As with any tool, a key question is: When is this tool applicable and what are the alternates?

The iterative method for exact optimization used a rank-based argument of the sparsity of the solution to argue integrality of a proposed linear programming formulation of the underlying problem. In Section 13.2, we detail the earliest application we know of this method to prove Steinitz's result on rearrangements.

As we mentioned in the introduction, the iterative method for approximation algorithms was introduced in the work of Jain on the survivable network design problem. For this minimum-cost subgraph selection problem, Jain formulated a covering linear program and showed how any extreme point always has a positive variable of value at least half; he did this by using the sparsity of the extreme point solution, which followed from a rank-based argument. In this context, the iterative method is a specific version of the *deterministic rounding* paradigm applied to LP relaxations for NP-hard problems. Thus, it fits in the broader context of a variety of other LP rounding methods for the design of approximation algorithms including randomized rounding, primal-dual methods, and Lagrangean relaxations. Among these methods, iterative rounding is particularly applicable in solving multiobjective problems where a base problem is complicated by more than one objective function: Examples include the bipartite matching problem complicated by additional load constraints at each node to give the NP-hard generalized assignment problem, or the minimum spanning tree (MST) problem complicated by degree constraints on nodes gives the NP-hard bounded-degree MST problem. An understanding of the iterative method applied to the base problem is then a useful guide to extending its application to the constrained multiobjective versions.

1.5 Book chapters overview

In the next chapter, we develop all the preliminaries needed in the following chapters. We discuss linear programs, and their polynomial time solvability using the separation oracle. We also outline the important rank lemma and other properties about extreme point solutions. Finally, we discuss the LP duality theorem and the complementary slackness conditions, and some basic facts about submodular functions and graphs.

A first stream of chapters study problems in undirected graphs. In Chapter 3, we give the first example to illustrate the iterative method on bipartite matching and vertex cover problems. We also show how the proof for bipartite matching leads to approximation algorithms for the generalized assignment problem and the budgeted allocation problem. In Chapter 4, we study the classical spanning tree problem and its extension to the minimum bounded degree spanning tree problem. This chapter introduces the uncrossing technique in combinatorial optimization. In Chapter 5, we generalize the arguments for undirected spanning trees to bases of matroids as well as to the common bases in the intersection of two matroids, and also to the minimum bounded degree matroid basis problem and the maximum common independent set problem in the intersection of k matroids. We also show integrality of the dual of matroid and matroid intersection problems that lead to certain min–max results.

A second stream of chapters study problems in directed graphs. In Chapter 6, we study the directed rooted spanning tree (or arborescence) problem, along with a degree-bounded version and then generalize the method developed here to a rooted k-connected subgraph problem providing a self-contained proof of a result of Frank and Tardos [46]. This is developed further in Chapter 7 to showing the integrality of submodular flow problems. For this last problem, we again complement the proof of exact LP characterization with a description of an approximation algorithm for the degree-bounded version built upon the proof of the exact counterpart. For the submodular flow problem, we also give a proof of the integrality of its dual.

We then present a few more advanced chapters applying the iterative method. In Chapter 8, we apply the iterative method to general problems involving network matrices as constraint matrices (with integral right-hand sides) and their duals. We then show the application of network matrices to derive integrality of the duals of various linear programs encountered in earlier chapters (such as those for matroid bases, matroid intersection, and submodular flow). In Chapter 9, we address the generalization of perfect and maximum matchings in bipartite graphs to general graphs, and also address higher dimensional matching problems. We then present a common generalization of Jain's 2-approximation algorithm for the survivable network design problem (SNDP), and a result of Boyd and Pulleyblank on 1-edges in the Held-Karp relaxation for the Symmetric Traveling Salesman Problem (STSP) in Chapter 10. This

chapter also generalizes Jain's result to degree bounded network design problems. In Chapter 11, we extend the application of the method to constrained
optimization problems such as partial covering and multicriteria problems. In
Chapter 12, we add the primal-dual complementary slackness conditions to
the iterative method to derive approximation results for some cut problems.
In Chapter 13 we present some early examples of iterative methods, including
the Beck-Fiala theorem on discrepancy and Karmarkar-Karp algorithm for bin
packing. Most chapters contain selected historical notes as well as exercises.

1.6 Notes

Polyhedral combinatorics, the compact polyhedral description of important
combinatorial optimization problems, is a fundamental and unifying tool in
algorithms, combinatorics, and optimization. A highlight of this line of research
is the pioneering work by Jack Edmonds [34]; we refer the reader to the
book [121] and the historical survey [119] by Schrijver for an encyclopedic
treatment of this subject.

Two closely related methods for proving integrality of polyhedra that are
widely covered in Schrijver's book deserve mention: Total Unimodularity (TU)
and Total Dual Integrality (TDI). Informally, TU matrices are constraint matrices such that for integral right-hand sides, the linear programming relaxations
provide integral solutions (whenever the solutions exist and are finite). Alternately, using the relation between extreme points solutions and basic feasible
solutions to LPs developed in the next chapter, these matrices are those for
which every square submatrix has determinant value zero, plus one or minus
one. The class of Network matrices that we will study in Chapter 8 is an important example of such TU matrices. Total Dual Integrality involves both the
constraint matrix and the right-hand side: A system of inequalities defined by a
constraint matrix and right-hand side vector is TDI if, for all integer objective
coefficients, the dual program has an integral solution (whenever it exists and
is finite). If a system is TDI for an integral right-hand side, then the polyhe-
don described by the system is integral hence giving another way of providing
characterizations of integral solutions to combinatorial optimization problems.
A popular example of an integral characterization that arises from a TDI system is the description of matchings in general graphs that we develop using our
alternate iterative method in Chapter 9.

An implicit use of the iterative method is found in the alternate proof of
Steinitz's theorem due to Grinberg and Sevastyanov [10, 65, 127]. Earlier uses
of the iterative relaxation method can be traced back to the proof of a discrepancy
theorem by Beck and Fiala [14] and the approximation algorithm for the bin

packing problem by Karmarkar and Karp [77]. In approximation algorithms, the first explicit use of the iterative rounding method is due to Jain [75].

An iterative approach similar to the one we describe is used in bounding quantities of interest in randomly chosen combinatorial objects and is termed the "semi random method." For more details, see the books by Alon and Spencer [2] or Molloy and Reed [99].

2
Preliminaries

In this chapter we discuss linear programming and basic facts about extreme point solutions to linear programs. We then briefly discuss solution methods for linear programs, particularly stating the sufficiency of finding a separation oracle for the program to be able to solve it. We then state some concepts from graph theory which are used throughout the book. The last part of the chapter discusses submodular and supermodular functions. These functions give a general tool for modeling a variety of optimization problems. Excellent introductory textbooks or surveys in all three areas are available for further reference [17, 73, 131].

2.1 Linear programming

Using matrix notation, a linear program is expressed as follows.

$$
\begin{aligned}
\text{minimize} \quad & c^T x \\
\text{subject to} \quad & Ax \geq b \\
& x \geq 0
\end{aligned}
$$

If x satisfies ($Ax \geq b, x \geq 0$), then x is a *feasible* solution. If there exists a feasible solution to the linear program, it is *feasible*; otherwise, it is *infeasible*. An *optimal* solution x^* is a feasible solution such that $c^T x^* = \min\{c^T x \text{ s.t. } Ax \geq b, x \geq 0\}$. The linear program is *unbounded* (from below) if $\forall \lambda \in \mathbb{R}, \exists$ feasible x such that $c^T x < \lambda$.

There are different forms in which a linear program can be represented. However, all these forms are equivalent to the form we consider above and can be converted into one another by simple linear transformations (see e.g., [29]).

2.1.1 Extreme point solutions to linear programs

In this subsection, we discuss basic properties about extreme point solutions (Definition 1.2.1). First, we have the following definition.

Definition 2.1.1 *Let P be a polytope and let x be an extreme point solution of P, then x is **integral** if each coordinate of x is an integer. The polytope P is called **integral** if every extreme point of P is integral.*

We now show basic properties about extreme point (or vertex) solutions. Most proofs are quite standard and we give a short sketch. The reader is referred to standard texts on linear programming (e.g., Chvatal [29]) for details. We now prove Lemma 1.2.2. We state it again for completeness.

Lemma 2.1.2 *Let $P = \{x : Ax \geq b, x \geq 0\}$ and assume that $\min\{c^T x : x \in P\}$ is finite. Then for every $x \in P$, there exists an extreme point solution $x' \in P$ such that $c^T x' \leq c^T x$, (i.e., there is always an extreme point optimal solution).*

Proof The idea of the proof is to show that we can move from a current optimal solution to one that has more zero components or more tight constraints and is thus closer to being an extreme point solution.

Consider x such that it is optimal but not an extreme point solution. That implies there exists $y \neq 0$ such that $x + y \in P$ and $x - y \in P$. Therefore,

$$A(x + y) \geq b, x + y \geq 0$$

$$A(x - y) \geq b, x - y \geq 0$$

Let $A^=$ be the submatrix of A restricted to rows which are at equality at x, and $b^=$ be the vector b restricted to these rows. Thus, we have $A^= x = b^=$. Hence, we must have $A^= y \geq 0$ and $A^=(-y) \geq 0$. Subtracting, we get $A^= y = 0$. Since x is optimal, the following holds.

$$c^T x \leq c^T (x + y)$$
$$c^T x \leq c^T (x - y)$$
$$\Rightarrow c^T y = 0$$

Moreover, since $y \neq 0$, without loss of generality assume there exists j such that $y_j < 0$ (if not then use $-y$). Consider $x + \lambda y$ for $\lambda > 0$ and increase λ until $x + \lambda y$ is no longer feasible due to the nonnegativity constraints on x. Formally, let

$$\lambda^* = \min \left\{ \min_{j : y_j < 0} \frac{x_j}{-y_j}, \min_{i : A_i x > b_i, A_i y < 0} \frac{A_i x - b_i}{-A_i y} \right\}.$$

We now show that $x + \lambda^* y$ is a new optimal solution with one more zero coordinate or one extra tight constraint. Since $x + y \geq 0$ and $x - y \geq 0$, if $x_i = 0$ then $y_i = 0$. Therefore, the coordinates that were at 0, remain at 0. Moreover $A^=(x + y) = A^= x = b$ since $A^= y = 0$; hence, tight constraints remain tight. Since we assume that $\min\{c^T x : x \in P\}$ is finite, λ^* is finite, and the solution $x + \lambda^* y$ has one more zero coordinate (when $\lambda^* = (x_j)/(-y_j)$) or one extra tight constraint (when $\lambda^* = (A_i x - b_i)/(-A_i y)$).

Proceeding this way, we can convert any optimal solution to one that is also an extreme point solution, proving the claim.   □

The next theorem relates extreme point solutions to corresponding nonsingular columns of the constraint matrix.

Lemma 2.1.3 *Let $P = \{x : Ax \geq b, x \geq 0\}$. For $x \in P$, let $A^=$ be the submatrix of A restricted to rows which are at equality at x, and let $A^=_x$ denote the submatrix of $A^=$ consisting of the columns corresponding to the nonzeros in x. Then x is an extreme point solution if and only if $A^=_x$ has linearly independent columns (i.e., $A^=_x$ has full column rank).*

Proof ($\Leftarrow$) If x is not an extreme point solution, we will show that $A^=_x$ has linearly dependent columns. By the hypothesis, there exists $y \neq 0$ such that $A^= y = 0$ (see the proof of the previous theorem). Therefore, $A^=_y$ (the columns where y has a nonzero coordinate) has linearly dependent columns. By the observation made at the end of the previous proof, $x_j = 0 \Rightarrow y_j = 0$. Therefore, $A^=_y$ is a submatrix of $A^=_x$. Therefore, the columns of $A^=_x$ are linearly dependent.

($\Rightarrow$) We want to show that if $A^=_x$ has linearly dependent columns, then x is not an extreme point solution. By the hypothesis, there exists $y \neq 0$ such that $A^=_x y = 0$. Complete y to an n-dimensional vector by setting the remaining coordinates to 0. Now by construction, $A^= y = 0$. Moreover, by construction, $y_j = 0$ whenever $x_j = 0$. Note that there exists $\epsilon > 0$ such that $x + \epsilon y \geq 0$ and $x - \epsilon y \geq 0$. Also $x + \epsilon y$ and $x - \epsilon y$ are feasible since $A(x + \epsilon y) = Ax + \epsilon Ay \geq b$ and $A(x - \epsilon y) \geq b$ for small enough $\epsilon > 0$. Hence, x is not an extreme point solution.   □

We now prove the important Rank Lemma. We restate the lemma (in canonical form) for completeness.

Lemma 2.1.4 (Rank Lemma) *Let $P = \{x : Ax \geq b, x \geq 0\}$, and let x be an extreme point solution of P such that $x_i > 0$ for each i. Then any maximal number of linearly independent tight constraints of the form $A_i x = b_i$ for some row i of A equals the number of variables.*

Proof Since $x_i > 0$ for each i, we have $A_x^= = A^=$. From Lemma 2.1.3, it follows that $A^=$ has full column rank. Since the number of columns equals the number of nonzero variables in x and row rank of any matrix equals the column rank[†], we have that row rank of $A^=$ equals the number of variables. Then any maximal number of linearly independent tight constraints is exactly the maximal number of linearly independent rows of $A^=$ which is exactly the row rank of $A^=$ and hence the claim follows. $\quad\square$

Next, we highlight various methods of solving linear programs. First, we introduce the concept of *basic feasible solutions* and show their equivalence to extreme point solutions. Basic feasible solutions form a key ingredient in the simplex algorithm which is the most widely used algorithm for solving linear programs in practice.

2.1.1.1 Basic feasible solution

Consider the linear program

$$\begin{array}{ll} \text{minimize} & c^T x \\ \text{subject to} & Ax \geq b \\ & x \geq 0 \end{array}$$

By introducing slack variables s_j for each constraint, we obtain an equivalent linear program in *standard form*.

$$\begin{array}{ll} \text{minimize} & c^T x \\ \text{subject to} & Ax + s = b \\ & x \geq 0 \\ & s \geq 0 \end{array}$$

Henceforth, we study linear program in standard form: $\{\min cx : Ax = b, x \geq 0\}$. Without loss of generality, we can assume that A is of full row rank. If there are dependent constraints, we can remove them without affecting the system or its optimal solution.

A subset of columns B of the constraint matrix A is called a *basis* if the matrix of columns corresponding to B (i.e., A_B), is invertible. A solution x is called *basic* if and only if there is a basis B such that $x_j = 0$ if $j \notin B$ and

---

[†] Important check: If you are rusty on why this statement is true, a crisp proof of the equality of the row rank and column rank can be found in the short note due to Andrea and Wong [4] that is available on the Web.

$x_B = A_B^{-1}b$. If in addition to being basic, it is also feasible (i.e., $A_B^{-1}b \geq 0$), it is called a *basic feasible solution* for short. The correspondence between bases and basic feasible solutions is not one to one. Indeed there can be many bases, which correspond to the same basic feasible solution. The next theorem shows the equivalence of extreme point solutions and basic feasible solutions.

Theorem 2.1.5 *Let A be a m × n matrix with full row rank. Then every feasible x to $P = \{x : Ax = b, x \geq 0\}$ is a basic feasible solution if and only if x is an extreme point solution.*

Proof ($\Rightarrow$) If x is a basic feasible solution, then A_B is invertible. Since A_x is a submatrix of A_B (it is a proper submatrix if some basic variable is at 0), A_x has linearly independent columns. Therefore, by Lemma 2.1.3, x is an extreme point solution.

($\Leftarrow$) If x is an extreme point solution, then by Lemma 2.1.3, A_x has linearly independent columns. Now we can add columns to A_x from A to convert it into an invertible matrix A_B. Note that since $Ax = b$, $A_B x_B + A_N x_N = b$, where A_N and x_N denote the nonbasic parts of A and x, respectively. By construction of A_B, $x_N = 0$ and so $x_B = A_B^{-1}b$. So x is a basic feasible solution with A_B as the basis.   □

2.1.2 Algorithms for linear programming

The *simplex* algorithm solves linear programs to get a basic feasible optimal solution. It works by starting at any basic feasible solution and moving to a *neighboring* basic feasible solution, which improves the objective function. The *convexity* of the linear program ensures that once the simplex algorithm ends at a *local* optimum basic feasible point, it has achieved the global optimum as well. Many variants of the simplex algorithm have been considered, each defined by which neighboring basic feasible solution to move in case there are more than one improving basic feasible points in the neighborhood. Although the simplex algorithm works efficiently in practice, there are examples where each variant of the simplex algorithm runs in exponential time. Again, for more details, see e.g. [29].

Polynomial-time algorithms for solving linear programs fall in two categories: ellipsoid algorithms [78] and interior point algorithms [76]. We refer the reader to Nemhauser and Wolsey [106] and Wright [133] for details about these algorithms. Both these algorithms solve linear programs to obtain *near* optimal solution in polynomial time. Moreover, there are rounding algorithms [106], which, given a sufficiently *near* optimal solution to a linear program, return an optimal extreme point solution.

Theorem 2.1.6 *There is an algorithm that returns an optimal extreme point solution to a linear program. Moreover, the running time of the algorithm is polynomial in the size of the linear program.*

2.1.3 Separation and optimization

In this book, we will also encounter linear programs where the number of constraints is exponential in the size of the problem (e.g., in the spanning tree problem in Chapter 4, we will write linear programs where the number of constraints is exponential in the size of the graph), and it is not obvious that one can enumerate them, let alone solve them in polynomial time. We use the notion of separation to show that many exponentially sized linear programs can be solved in polynomial time.

Definition 2.1.7 *Given $x^* \in \mathcal{R}^n$ and a polytope $P = \{x : Ax \geq b, x \geq 0\}$, the* **separation problem** *is the decision problem whether $x^* \in P$. The solution of the separation problem is the answer to the membership problem and in case $x^* \notin P$, it should return a valid constraint $A_i x \geq b_i$ for P, which is violated by x^* (i.e., $A_i x^* < b_i$).*

The following theorem of Grötschel, Lóvasz, and Schrijver [67] shows that polynomial time separability is equivalent to polynomial time solvability of a linear program; we state it in an informal manner that is convenient for combinatorial optimization problems. The basis of this equivalence is the ellipsoid algorithm.

Theorem 2.1.8 *Given a family of polytopes and a polynomial-time separation oracle for the members of the family one can find an optimal extreme point solution to a linear objective function over a member of the family (assuming it is bounded) via the ellipsoid algorithm that uses a polynomial number of operations and calls to the separation oracle.*

Clearly, one can solve the separation problem by checking each constraint but for problems where the number of constraints is exponential in size such a method is too slow. In this book, as we consider LP formulations with an exponential number of constraints, we will often provide efficient separation oracles showing that the linear program for the problem is solvable in polynomial time.

2.1.4 Linear programming duality

Linear programming duality is a key concept to certify and characterize optimal solutions to linear programs. Consider the following primal linear program in the standard form:

$$\text{minimize} \quad \sum_{j=1}^{n} c_j x_j$$

$$\text{subject to} \quad \sum_{j=1}^{n} a_{ij} x_j \geq b_i \qquad \forall 1 \leq i \leq m$$

$$x_j \geq 0 \qquad \forall 1 \leq j \leq n$$

The corresponding dual program is

$$\text{maximize} \quad \sum_{i=1}^{m} b_i y_i$$

$$\text{subject to} \quad \sum_{i=1}^{m} a_{ij} y_i \leq c_j \qquad \forall 1 \leq j \leq n$$

$$y_i \geq 0 \qquad \forall 1 \leq i \leq m$$

It is not difficult to show that the optimal value of the primal linear program is at least the optimal value of the dual linear program, and thus any dual feasible solution provides a lower bound on the optimal value of the primal program. This is called the weak LP duality theorem, whose proof also follows from the derivation of the complementary slackness conditions below. A fundamental result in linear programming is the strong duality theorem, which shows that the optimal value of the primal linear program is actually equal to that of the dual linear program.

Theorem 2.1.9 (Strong Duality Theorem) *If the primal linear program has an optimal solution, so does its dual, and the respective optimal costs are equal.*

Many combinatorial min–max theorems can be derived from the strong duality theorem. For example, we will see in Chapter 3 the min–max theorem for bipartite matching, and in Chapter 5 for the minmax theorem for matroid intersection. We refer the reader to any textbook on linear programming (e.g., [29]) for the proof of the strong duality theorem.

2.1.4.1 Complementary slackness conditions

The complementary slackness conditions provide a characterization for an optimal primal solution x and an optimal dual solution y. We will use the complementary slackness conditions in Chapter 12.

Primal complementary slackness conditions:

$$\text{Either } x_j = 0 \text{ or } \sum_{i=1}^{m} a_{ij} y_i = c_j.$$

Dual complementary slackness conditions:

$$\text{Either } y_i = 0 \text{ or } \sum_{j=1}^{n} a_{ij} x_j = b_i.$$

These conditions can be derived as follows:

$$\sum_{j=1}^{n} c_j x_j \geq \sum_{j=1}^{n} \left(\sum_{i=1}^{m} a_{ij} y_i \right) x_j$$

$$= \sum_{i=1}^{m} \left(\sum_{j=1}^{n} a_{ij} x_j \right) y_i$$

$$\geq \sum_{i=1}^{m} b_i y_i$$

where the first inequality is by the constraints in the dual linear program, the second equality is by interchanging the order of the summations, and the third inequality is by the constraints in the primal linear program. Note that this shows the weak duality theorem. Since x and y are optimal solutions, by the strong duality theorem, we have that $\sum_{j=1}^{n} c_j x_j = \sum_{i=1}^{m} b_i y_i$, and thus equality must hold throughout. The primal complementary slackness conditions follow from the first inequality holding as an equality, while the dual complementary slackness conditions follow from the last inequality holding as an equality.

2.2 Graphs and digraphs

Most problems addressed in this book are on networks connecting nodes with edges or links. We define graph theoretic concepts, which will be encountered in later chapters. Given an undirected graph $G = (V, E)$ and a set $S \subseteq V$, we denote $\delta_G(S)$ or $\delta_E(S)$ to be the set of edges, which have exactly one endpoint in S. For a vertex $v \in V$, $\delta_G(\{v\})$ is simply denoted by $\delta_G(v)$. We also denote $d_G(v)$ or $d_E(v)$ to be degree of v (i.e., $|\delta_G(v)|$). For sets $X, Y \subseteq V$, we denote $E_G(X, Y)$ to be the set of edges which has exactly one endpoint in X and one in Y. We also denote $E_G(X, X)$ by $E_G(X)$. Observe that $\delta_G(X) = E_G(X, V \setminus X)$.

We also denote $|\delta_G(X)|$ by $d_G(X)$. The subscript G or E is sometimes dropped from the notation if the graph G is clear from the context. A subgraph H of G is *spanning* if it contains all the vertices of G, *connected* if there is a path between any two vertices of H, a *tree* if it is acyclic and connected. An important concept is a *spanning tree*, subgraph which is both spanning and a tree. Observe that a spanning tree is a also a minimally spanning connected subgraph.

Given a directed graph $D = (V, A)$ and a set $S \subset V$, we denote $\delta_D^{in}(S)$ to be the set of arcs whose head is in S but tail is not in S. Similarly, $\delta_D^{out}(S)$ is the set of arcs whose tail is in S but the head is not in S. For a vertex $v \in V$, we denote $\delta_D^{in}(\{v\})$ as $\delta_D^{in}(v)$ and $\delta_D^{out}(\{v\})$ as $\delta_D^{out}(v)$. The in-degree of v, $|\delta_D^{in}(v)|$, is denoted by $d_D^{in}(v)$ and the out-degree of v, $|\delta_D^{out}(v)|$, is denoted by $d_D^{out}(v)$. The degree of v, $d_D(v)$ is the sum of its in-degree and out-degree. For sets $X, Y \subseteq V$, we denote $E_D(X, Y)$ to be the set of arcs whose tail is in X and the head is in Y. Observe that $\delta_D^{out}(X) = E_D(X, V \setminus X)$. We denote $|\delta_D^{in}(X)|$ and $|\delta_D^{out}(X)|$ by $d_D^{in}(X)$ and $d_D^{out}(X)$, respectively. A subgraph H of D is called *strongly connected* if there is a directed path from each vertex of H to every other vertex, *weakly connected* if the underlying undirected graph is connected, acyclic if there is no directed cycle in H. H is called an *arborescence* if the underlying graph is a spanning tree and the graph has only one vertex with no in-edges, which is called the root. If the root of an arborescence is the vertex r, then it is also called an r-arborescence.

Let $e = \{u, v\}$ be an edge. By G/e, we denote the graph obtained from G by *contracting* u, v into a single vertex x, while keeping all the edges in $\delta_G(\{u, v\})$ (an edge in G with an endpoint in $\{u, v\}$ becomes an edge in G/e with an endpoint in x) and removing the edges between u and v. Contracting an arc uv in a directed graph D is defined similarly, while an arc in D with head/tail in $\{u, v\}$ becomes an arc in D/e with head/tail in x.

We will use frequently the following fundamental min–max theorem in graph theory.

Theorem 2.2.1 (Menger's Theorem [98]) *Let $D = (V, A)$ be a directed graph, and $s, t \in V$ be two distinct vertices. The maximum number of arc-disjoint s-t paths in D is equal to the minimum $d_D^{in}(X)$ over all $X \subset V$ with $s \notin X$ and $t \in X$.*

Menger's theorem shows a close connection between disjoint paths and cuts, which will be used in writing linear programs and constructing separation oracles. One can also obtain the corresponding min–max theorems for undirected graphs and for vertex connectivity by simple transformations (see the exercises).

2.3 Submodular and supermodular functions

In this section, we define special classes of set functions with some nice convexity-like properties. Typically, in our applications, these functions are defined over a set of vertices of a graph we will be working with; most of the time, they will also be integer valued and positive. More comprehensive treatments on these topics are available in the monograph by Fujishige [50] and the book by Schrijver [121].

2.3.1 Submodularity

Definition 2.3.1 *A function $f : 2^V \to \mathbb{R}$ is submodular if for every pair A, B of subsets of V, we have*

$$f(A) + f(B) \geq f(A \cap B) + f(A \cup B).$$

A simple example of a submodular set function defined on the vertices of an undirected graph $G = (V, E)$ is cardinality of the cut function $d : 2^V \to \mathbb{Z}_+$ where $d(S) = |\delta(S)|$.

Proposition 2.3.2 *The cut function d of any undirected graph is submodular.*

Proof To see that d is submodular, note that, on the right-hand side, we have

$$d(A \cap B) = |E(A \cap B, A \setminus B)| + |E(A \cap B, B \setminus A)| + |E(A \cap B, V \setminus (A \cup B))|.$$

Similarly, we also have

$$d(A \cup B) = |E(A \cap B, V \setminus (A \cup B))| + |E(A \setminus B, V \setminus (A \cup B))| \\ + |E(B \setminus A, V \setminus (A \cup B))|.$$

On the left-hand side, we have

$$d(A) = |E(A \cap B, V \setminus (A \cup B))| + |E(A \cap B, B \setminus A)| + |E(A \setminus B, V \setminus (A \cup B))| \\ + |E(A \setminus B, B \setminus A)|.$$

Similarly, we get

$$d(B) = |E(A \cap B, V \setminus (A \cup B))| + |E(A \cap B, A \setminus B)| + |E(B \setminus A, V \setminus (A \cup B))| \\ + |E(B \setminus A, A \setminus B)|$$

Comparing the preceding expressions shows that the edges in $E(A \setminus B, B \setminus A)$ are responsible for the inequality (rather than equality). Also see Figure 2.1. $\square$

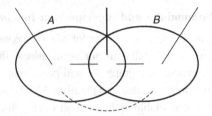

Figure 2.1 In this example the solid edges are counted exactly once in both the LHS $d(A)+d(B)$, and the RHS $d(A \cap B)+d(A \cup B)$, and the bold edge is counted exactly twice on both sides. The dashed edge is counted in the LHS but not in the RHS.

Note that the edge cut function can be extended to the case when nonnegative weights, say $x : E \rightarrow \mathbb{R}_+$ are assigned to the edges. Instead of $d(S) = |\delta(S)|$, we have $x(\delta(S)) = \sum_{e \in \delta(S)} x_e$. The proof also shows that the function x is submodular as well.

Proposition 2.3.3 *The weighted-cut function of any undirected graph is submodular.*

For undirected graphs, since the degree function is symmetric (i.e., $d(S) = d(V - S)$), by applying Proposition 2.3.2 on the complements we have

$$d(A)+d(B) \geq d(A \setminus B)+d(B \setminus A) \qquad (2.1)$$

which can also be verified directly using the same method as above (see Figure 2.2).

Let us define a stronger notion of submodularity.

Definition 2.3.4 *A function $f : 2^V \rightarrow \mathbb{R}$ is strongly submodular if for every pair A, B of subsets of V, we have*

$$f(A) + f(B) \geq f(A \cap B) + f(A \cup B)$$

and

$$f(A) + f(B) \geq f(A \setminus B) + f(B \setminus A).$$

The second property in Definition 2.3.4 has also been referred to as *posimodularity* [101, 102]. The edge cut functions in undirected graphs are strongly submodular. Indeed, if a function is submodular and symmetric, then it is strongly submodular (see exercises).

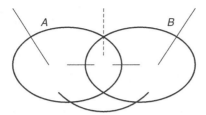

Figure 2.2 In this example, the solid edges are counted exactly once in both the LHS $d(A)+d(B)$ and the RHS $d(A \setminus B)+d(B \setminus A)$, and the bold edge is counted exactly twice on both sides. The dashed edge, however, is counted in the LHS but not in the RHS.

2.3.2 Supermodularity

We move on to a symmetric concept, supermodularity.

Definition 2.3.5 *A function* $f : 2^V \to \mathbb{R}$ *is supermodular if for every pair* A, B *of subsets of* V*, we have*

$$f(A) + f(B) \leq f(A \cap B) + f(A \cup B).$$

As before, a simple example of a supermodular set function defined on the vertices of an undirected graph $G = (V, E)$ is the induced edge function $d : 2^V \to \mathbb{Z}_+$ where $i(S)$ is the number of edges in E with both endpoints in S (i.e., $i(S) = |E(S)|$). A verification similar to the above can be carried out to establish that the induced edge function is supermodular. Also, if nonnegative values, say $x : E \to \mathbb{R}_+$ are assigned to the edges and we consider $x(S) = \sum_{e \in E(S)} x_e$, it follows that this function is supermodular as well.

Proposition 2.3.6 *The induced edge function* $i(.)$ *for any undirected graph is supermodular. This is also true for the weighted version with nonnegative weights.*

2.3.3 Refinements

Definition 2.3.7 *Two subsets* A *and* B *of a ground set* V *are* intersecting *if* $A \cap B \neq \emptyset$, $A - B \neq \emptyset$ *and* $B - A \neq \emptyset$. *A function* $f : 2^V \to \mathbb{R}$ *is* intersecting-submodular *if for every pair* A, B *of intersecting subsets of* V*, we have*

$$f(A) + f(B) \geq f(A \cap B) + f(A \cup B).$$

Definition 2.3.8 *Two subsets* A *and* B *of a ground set* V *are* crossing *if none of the four subsets* $A \cap B, A \setminus B, B \setminus A$ *and* $V \setminus (A \cup B)$ *are empty. A function*

$f : 2^V \to \mathbb{R}$ *is* crossing-submodular *if for every pair* A, B *of crossing subsets of* V, *we have*

$$f(A) + f(B) \geq f(A \cap B) + f(A \cup B).$$

To distinguish the regular submodular functions from the more restricted intersecting and crossing varieties, they are also sometimes dubbed fully submodular. Other important examples of fully submodular functions arise as cut functions of directed graphs $D = (V, A)$. Define $\delta^{in}(S)$ for a subset S of vertices as the set of arcs whose heads are in S and tails are in $V \setminus S$, which we can denote as $A(V \setminus S, S)$. Symmetrically, define $\delta^{out}(S)$ as the set $A(S, V \setminus S)$. Denote $|\delta^{in}(S)|$ and $|\delta^{out}(S)|$ by $d^{in}(S)$, and $d^{out}(S)$, respectively. Both these functions d^{in} and d^{out} defined on vertex subsets are fully submodular (see Figure 2.3). Unlike undirected graphs, however, the functions d^{in} and d^{out} are not strongly submodular.

Proposition 2.3.9 *The cut functions* d^{in} *and* d^{out} *of any directed graph are submodular. This is also true for the weighted directed cut functions with nonnegative weights.*

A broader class of functions generalizing supermodularity is useful in specifying connectivity requirements for network design problems.

Definition 2.3.10 *A function* $f : 2^V \to \mathbb{R}$ *is skew (or weakly) supermodular if for every pair* A, B *of subsets of* V, *at least one of the following inequalities is true.*

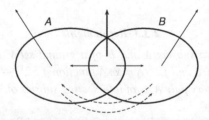

Figure 2.3 In this example the solid arcs are counted exactly once in both the LHS $\delta^{out}(A) + \delta^{out}(B)$ and the RHS $\delta^{out}(A \cup B) + \delta^{out}(A \cap B)$ and the bold edges are counted exactly twice on both sides. The dashed edges are counted in the LHS but not in the RHS.

$$f(A) + f(B) \leq f(A \cap B) + f(A \cup B),$$

$$f(A) + f(B) \leq f(A \setminus B) + f(B \setminus A).$$

In the survivable network design problem on an undirected graph $G = (V, E)$, we are given nonnegative integral edge-connectivity requirements r_{uv} for all pairs of vertices, and we are interested in finding a subgraph with at least r_{uv} edge-disjoint paths between u and v for every pair u, v. If we define the connectivity requirement function f for any set S as $f(S) = \max_{u \in S, v \notin S} r_{uv}$, it is not hard to verify that f is skew supermodular.

Functions that are both submodular and supermoduar are modular – the typical example being the cardinality (or "modulus") function. Furthermore, f is submodular if and only if $-f$ is supermodular, and if f is submodular and g is supermodular, then $f - g$ is submodular. Finally, if f is skew supermodular and g is strongly submodular, then $f - g$ is skew supermodular. These follow directly as a consequence of the definitions.

2.3.3.1 Minimizing submodular function

A rich literature examines the minimization of submodular functions in (strongly) polynomial time given a value oracle for the function – Chapter 45 of the book by Schrijver [121] contains most references on this topic. We mention three important results in this vein: Queyranne [112] gave an algorithm for minimizing symmetric submodular functions, building on earlier work of Nagamochi and Ibaraki for finding a minimum cut in an undirected graph. Grötschel, Lóvasz, and Schrijver [68] gave a polynomial time algorithm for finding the minimum of a general submodular function. They also showed that the minimum among sets of odd cardinality can be computed in polynomial time, building on earlier work of Padberg and Rao [109]. Finally, for the general case of submodular function with only oracle access to values, strongly polynomial time algorithms were first presented by Iwata, Fleischer and Fujishige [74] and also independently by Schrijver [118]. More generally defined submodular function (e.g., on intersecting or cross-free families) can also be minimized in polynomial time – see Chapter 49 in [121].

We will be making use of submodular (and supermodular) functions extensively in this monograph. In a typical application, the set of tight constraints at an extreme point solution corresponds to a set of cuts in a graph for which a (submodular) function value is an integer. Depending on the type of submodular function (full, intersecting, or crossing), these tight constraints can then be *uncrossed* to result in a nicely structured basis for them. For instances, for fully submodular constraints, the basis is a chain; for intersecting submodular constraint forms, the basis is a laminar family representable by the forest capturing set-inclusion relation; for crossing submodular constraint systems, the basis is a cross-free family that can also be turned into a laminar family. Such structured sparse representations of the tight constraints at any extreme point solution are the key to proving integrality for many problems – they pave the way to show the upper bound part of the general argument outlined in the beginning of this chapter, typically by a counting argument that is carried out inductively on a representation of these sparse families.

Exercises

2.1 Consider a bounded linear program. Prove that an LP solution x is a basic feasible solution (or extreme point solution) if and only if there is an objective function c such that x is the unique optimum solution.

2.2 Prove Menger's theorem for undirected graphs: The maximum number of edge-disjoint s-t paths is equal to the minimum $d(X)$ over all sets $X \subset V$ with $s \notin X$ and $t \in X$. (*Hint*: "Bidirect" the edges and apply Theorem 2.2.1.)

2.3 Two directed s-t paths P_1 and P_2 are internally vertex-disjoint if $V(P_1) \cap V(P_2) = \{s, t\}$. A vertex set $U \subset V$ is an s-t cut, if there is no directed s-t paths in $G - U$. Prove Menger's theorem for vertex connectivity: The maximum number of internally vertex-disjoint s-t paths is equal to the minimum size of a vertex s-t cut. (*Hint*: "Split" each vertex appropriately and apply Theorem 2.2.1.)

2.4 Derive a corresponding Menger's theorem for vertex connectivity in undirected graphs.

2.5 Show that if a function is submodular and symmetric then it is strongly submodular. Hence, derive that a cut function of an undirected graph is strongly submodular.

2.6 Verify Proposition 2.3.9 that the in- and out-cut functions d^{in} and d^{out} for a digraph are indeed submodular but not strongly submodular.

2.7 Verify Proposition 2.3.6. Is the induced edges (arcs) function supermodular for digraphs?

2.8 Show that a function $f : 2^V \to R_+$ is (fully) submodular if and only if $f(X + v) - f(X) \geq f(Y + v) - f(Y)$ whenever $X \subseteq Y$ and $v \in V - X$.

2.9 Use the equivalent definition of submodular function in Exercise 2.8 to derive Proposition 2.3.2 and Proposition 2.3.9.

2.10 Show that the connectivity requirement function for the survivable network design problem, $f(S) = \max_{u \in S, v \notin S} r_{uv}$ for all $S \subset V$ is skew supermodular.

2.11 Show that the connectivity requirement function for the k-connected subgraph problem, $f(S) = k$ for every nonempty $S \subset V$ is crossing supermodular.

2.12 Show that the connectivity requirement function for the rooted-connectivity problem, $f(S) = k$ for every nonempty $S \subset V$ with $r \notin S$ for a specified vertex r is intersecting supermodular.

3
Matching and vertex cover in bipartite graphs

In this chapter we consider two very closely related problems, maximum weighted matching and minimum cost vertex cover in bipartite graphs. Linear programming duality plays a crucial role in understanding the relationship between these problems. We will show that the natural linear programming relaxations for both the matching problem and the vertex cover problem are integral, and then use duality to obtain a min–max relation between them. Nevertheless, our proofs of integrality use the iterative method by arguing the existence of 1-elements in an extreme point solution.

In the first section, we show the integrality of the more standard maximization version of the matching problem. In the following sections, we show two applications of the proof technique for integrality to derive approximation results for NP-hard problems. We first present a new proof of an approximation result for the generalized assignment problem and then present an approximation result for the budgeted allocation problem. The proofs of both of these results develop on the integrality result for the bipartite matching problem and introduce the iterative relaxation method. Following this, we discuss the integrality of the bipartite vertex cover problem formulation and conclude with a short section on the duality relation between these problems and some historical notes.

3.1 Matchings in bipartite graphs

In this section, we show that the matching polytope in bipartite graphs is integral. Given a bipartite graph $G = (V_1 \cup V_2, E)$ and a weight function $w : E \to \mathcal{R}$, the maximum matching problem is to find a set of vertex-disjoint edges of maximum total weight.

3.1.1 Linear programming relaxation

The linear programming relaxation for the bipartite matching problem is given by the following $LP_{bm}(G)$.

$$
\begin{aligned}
\text{maximize} \quad & \sum_{e \in E} w_e x_e \\
\text{subject to} \quad & \sum_{e \in \delta(v)} x_e \leq 1 && \forall v \in V_1 \cup V_2 \\
& x_e \geq 0 && \forall e \in E
\end{aligned}
$$

Observe that the linear program $LP_{bm}(G)$ is compact (i.e., the number of constraints and variables is polynomially bounded in the size of the problem). Hence, the linear program can be solved optimally in polynomial time using Theorem 2.1.6.

We prove the following theorem by an iterative algorithm in the next section.

Theorem 3.1.1 *Given any weight function w there exists an integral matching M such that $w(M) \geq w \cdot x$ where x is an optimal solution to $LP_{bm}(G)$.*

Our proof of Theorem 3.1.1 as a corollary implies the following theorem.

Theorem 3.1.2 *The linear programming formulation $LP_{bm}(G)$ is integral.*

3.1.2 Characterization of extreme point solutions

Before we prove Theorem 3.1.1, we give a characterization of extreme point solutions of $LP_{bm}(G)$ for which we need a few definitions.

For a set $F \subseteq E$, let $\chi(F)$ denote the vector in $\mathbb{R}^{|E|}$ that has a 1 corresponding to each edge $e \in F$, and 0 otherwise. This vector is called the *characteristic vector* of F. In the following lemma, which follows by a direct application of the Rank Lemma 2.1.4, we characterize an extreme point solution by a set of tight linearly independent constraints.

Lemma 3.1.3 *Given any extreme point solution x to $LP_{bm}(G)$ such that $x_e > 0$ for each $e \in E$ there exists $W \subseteq V_1 \cup V_2$ such that*

(i) $x(\delta(v)) = 1$ *for each $v \in W$.*
(ii) *The vectors in $\{\chi(\delta(v)) : v \in W\}$ are linearly independent.*
(iii) $|W| = |E|$.

Iterative Bipartite Matching Algorithm

(i) Initialization $F \leftarrow \emptyset$.
(ii) While $E(G) \neq \emptyset$ do
   (a) Find an optimal extreme point solution x to $LP_{bm}(G)$ and remove every edge e with $x_e = 0$ from G.
   (b) If there is an edge $e = \{u,v\}$ with $x_e = 1$, then update $F \leftarrow F \cup \{e\}$ and $G \leftarrow G \setminus \{u,v\}$.
(iii) Return F.

Figure 3.1 Bipartite matching algorithm.

3.1.3 Iterative algorithm

We now give the algorithm that constructs an integral matching of weight at least the optimal solution to $LP_{bm}(G)$ proving Theorem 3.1.1. The algorithm is a simple iterative procedure as shown in Figure 3.1.

3.1.4 Correctness and optimality

We prove the correctness of the algorithm in two steps. First, we show that the algorithm returns a matching of optimal weight if the algorithm *always* finds an edge e with $x_e = 0$ in Step (ii)(a). or an edge e with $x_e = 1$ in Step (ii)(b). In the second part, we show that the algorithm will always find such an edge completing the proof.

Claim 3.1.4 *If the algorithm, in every iteration, finds an edge e with $x_e = 0$ in Step (ii)(a). or an edge e with $x_e = 1$ in Step (ii)(b)., then it returns a matching F of weight at least the optimal solution to $LP_{bm}(G)$.*

Proof The proof will proceed by induction on the number of iterations of the algorithm. The base case is trivial when the algorithm proceeds for only one iteration.

If we find an edge e with $x_e = 0$ in Step (ii)(a). of the algorithm, then the residual problem is to find a matching in the graph $G' = G \setminus \{e\}$, where we remove the edge e from G. The residual solution x_{res}, x restricted to $G \setminus \{e\}$, is a feasible solution to the linear programming relaxation of the residual problem. By induction, the algorithm returns a matching $F' \subseteq E(G')$ with weight at least the optimal solution to $LP_{bm}(G')$. Since $w(F') \geq w \cdot x_{res} = w \cdot x$, the induction hypothesis holds in this case.

In the other case, if we find an edge $e = \{u,v\}$ with $x_e = 1$ in Step (ii)(b). of the algorithm, then the residual problem is to find a matching that contains the edge e. This is exactly the matching problem in graph $G' = G \setminus \{u,v\}$, where we remove the vertices u and v and their incident edges from G. Moreover x_{res}, x restricted to edges in G', is a feasible solution to the linear programming relaxation for the residual problem. Inductively, the algorithm will return a matching F' of weight at least the weight of the optimum solution of $LP_{bm}(G')$, and hence $w(F') \geq w \cdot x_{res}$, as x_{res} is a feasible solution to $LP_{bm}(G')$. The algorithm returns the matching $F = F' \cup \{e\}$, and we have

$$w(F) = w(F') + w_e \text{ and } w(F') \geq w \cdot x_{res}$$

which implies that

$$w(F) \geq w \cdot x_{res} + w_e = w \cdot x$$

since $x_e = 1$. Therefore, the weight of the matching returned by the algorithm is at least the weight of the LP solution x. □

We now complete the proof of Theorem 3.1.1 by showing that the algorithm always finds an edge e with $x_e = 0$ or $x_e = 1$. The proof of the following lemma crucially uses the characterization of extreme point solutions given in Lemma 3.1.3.

Lemma 3.1.5 *Given any extreme point solution x of $LP_{bm}(G)$, there must exist an edge e with $x_e = 0$ or $x_e = 1$.*

Proof Suppose for sake of contradiction $0 < x_e < 1$ for each edge $e \in E$. Lemma 3.1.3 implies that there exists $W \subseteq V_1 \cup V_2$ such that constraints corresponding to W are linearly independent and tight, and $|E| = |W|$.

We claim that $d_E(v) = 2$ for each $v \in W$ and $d_E(v) = 0$ for each $v \notin W$. First, $d_E(v) \geq 2$ for each $v \in W$, since $x(\delta(v)) = 1$ for each v and $0 < x_e < 1$ for each $e \in E$. This implies that

$$2|W| = 2|E| = \sum_{v \in V} d_E(v) \geq \sum_{v \in W} d_E(v) \geq 2|W|.$$

This implies the inequalities must hold as equalities, and thus $d_E(v) = 0$ for each $v \notin W$ by the first inequality and $d_E(v) = 2$ for each $v \in W$ by the second inequality.

Hence, E is a cycle cover on the vertices in W. Let C be any such cycle with all vertices in W. Since C is an even cycle because G is bipartite, we also have

$$\sum_{v \in C \cap V_1} \chi(\delta(v)) = \sum_{v \in C \cap V_2} \chi(\delta(v))$$

which contradicts the independence of constraints in condition (ii) of Lemma 3.1.3. Therefore, any extreme point solution x to $LP_{bm}(G)$ must have an edge e with $x_e = 0$ or $x_e = 1$. □

Thus, we obtain from Lemma 3.1.5 that the algorithm in Figure 3.1 returns a matching with total weight at least the weight of the linear program. This completes the proof of Theorem 3.1.1.

3.2 Generalized assignment problem

In this section, we use the iterative relaxation method to obtain an approximation algorithm for the generalized assignment problem. The generalized assignment problem models the following scheduling problem on unrelated parallel machines with costs. We are given a set of jobs J and machines M; for each job $j \in J$ and machine $i \in M$, there is a processing time p_{ij} and cost c_{ij}. Machine i is available for T_i time units and the objective is to assign each job to some machine such that the total cost is minimized and no machine is scheduled for more than its available time.

Shmoys and Tardos [122] gave an algorithm that returns an assignment of cost at most C and each machine is used for at most $2T_i$ time units, where C is the cost of the optimal assignment that uses machine i for at most T_i time units (if such an assignment is possible). In this section, we prove the result of the Shmoys and Tardos [122] using the iterative relaxation method. This proof develops on the iterative proof of the integrality of the bipartite matching given in Section 3.1. We shall prove the following theorem.

Theorem 3.2.1 *There exists a polynomial time algorithm for the generalized assignment problem, which returns a solution of cost at most C that uses each machine i for at most $2T_i$ time units, where C is the cost of an optimal assignment that uses each machine i for at most T_i time units.*

3.2.1 Linear programming relaxation

Before we write the linear program for the problem, we first model the problem as a bipartite matching problem. We start with a complete bipartite graph G with jobs J and machines M as the two sides of the bipartite graph. The edge between job $j \in J$ and machine $i \in M$ has cost c_{ij}. The generalized assignment problem can be reduced to finding a subgraph F of G such that $d_F(j) = 1$ for each job $j \in J$, and the edge incident at j denotes which machine job j is assigned to. The time constraint at machines can be modeled by restricting that $\sum_{e \in \delta(i) \cap F} p_{ij} \leq T_i$ for each machine i. We strengthen this model by disallowing certain assignments using the following observation: If $p_{ij} > T_i$, then no optimal solution assigns job j to i, and hence we can remove all such edges from graph G.

We model the preceding matching problem by the following natural linear programming relaxation LP_{ga} to prove Theorem 3.2.1. Observe that we do not

place time constraints for all machines but a subset $M' \subseteq M$ which is initialized
to M. We have a variable x_e for each $e = ij$ denoting whether job j is assigned
to machine i.

$$\text{minimize} \quad \sum_{e=(i,j)\in E} c_{ij} x_{ij}$$

$$\text{subject to} \quad \sum_{e\in\delta(j)} x_e = 1 \qquad \forall j \in J$$

$$\sum_{e\in\delta(i)} p_e x_e \leq T_i \qquad \forall i \in M'$$

$$x_e \geq 0 \qquad \forall e \in E$$

3.2.2 Characterization of extreme point solutions

The following lemma follows from a direct application of the rank lemma.

Lemma 3.2.2 *Let x be an extreme point solution to the linear program LP_{ga}
with $0 < x_e < 1$ for each edge e. Then there exist $J' \subseteq J$ and $M'' \subseteq M'$ such
that*

(i) $\sum_{e\in\delta(j)} x_e = 1$ *for each $j \in J'$ and $\sum_{e\in\delta(i)} p_e x_e = T_i$ for each $i \in M''$.*
(ii) *The constraints corresponding to J' and M'' are linearly independent.*
(iii) $|J'| + |M''| = |E(G)|$.

3.2.3 Iterative algorithm

We present a simple iterative procedure that returns an assignment of optimal
cost in Figure 3.2. Observe that the iterative procedure generalizes the iterative
procedure for bipartite matching in Section 3.1. The bipartite graph F with
vertex set in $M \cup J$ returns the assignment found by the algorithm.

This procedure demonstrates our first example of the iterative relaxation
method in Step (ii)(c). Here in addition to the usual step of picking an integral
element in the solution, we identify carefully chosen constraints to relax or
remove. The choice is dictated by ensuring that the removal will allow us to
argue that the final integral solution does not have too much violation; at the
same time, we need to ensure that in the absence of an integral element, such a
constraint can always be found to be removed. The crux of the relaxation method
is to find the right relaxation condition that balances this trade-off nicely.

3.2.4 Correctness and performance guarantee

The following lemma shows that the algorithm makes progress at each step of
the algorithm.

Iterative Generalized Assignment Algorithm

(i) Initialization $E(F) \leftarrow \emptyset$, $M' \leftarrow M$.
(ii) While $J \neq \emptyset$ do
    (a) Find an optimal extreme point solution x to LP_{ga} and remove every variable with $x_{ij} = 0$.
    (b) If there is a variable with $x_{ij} = 1$, then update $F \leftarrow F \cup \{ij\}$, $J \leftarrow J \setminus \{j\}$, $T_i \leftarrow T_i - p_{ij}$.
    (c) **(Relaxation)** If there is a machine i with $d(i) = 1$, or a machine i with $d(i) = 2$ and $\sum_{j \in J} x_{ij} \geq 1$, then update $M' \leftarrow M' \setminus \{i\}$.
(iii) Return F.

Figure 3.2 The generalized assignment algorithm.

Lemma 3.2.3 *Consider any extreme point solution x to LP_{ga}. One of the following must hold.*

(i) *There exists an edge $e \in E$ with $x_e \in \{0, 1\}$.*
(ii) *There exists a machine $i \in M'$ with $d(i) = 1$, or $d(i) = 2$ and $\sum_{j \in J} x_{ij} \geq 1$.*

Proof Suppose for sake of contradiction that both the conditions do not hold. By Step (ii)a and Step (ii)b, we have $0 < x_e < 1$ for each edge e. Each job j has degree at least two since $\sum_{e \in \delta(j)} x_e = 1$ and there is no edge with $x_e = 1$ by Step (ii)b. Moreover, each machine in M' has degree at least two because the constraints for machines with degree one have been removed in Step (ii)c. From Lemma 3.2.2 we have that $|E| = |J'| + |M''|$. This implies that

$$|J'| + |M''| = |E| \geq \frac{\sum_{j \in J} d(j) + \sum_{i \in M'} d(i)}{2} \geq |J| + |M'| \geq |J'| + |M''|$$

and hence all inequalities must hold as equalities. The first inequality implies that each machine $i \in M \setminus M'$ has degree zero; the second inequality implies that each job $j \in J'$ and each machine $i \in M''$ have degree exactly two; the last inequality implies that $J = J'$ and $M' = M''$. Therefore, G is a union of cycles, with vertices in $J' \cup M''$ (tight constraints). Consider any cycle C. The total number of jobs in C is exactly equal to the total number of machines in C. Therefore, since each job $j \in J'$ has $\sum_{i \in M''} x_{ij} = 1$, there must be a machine i with $\sum_{j \in J'} x_{ij} \geq 1$. Hence, this machine i has degree two and $\sum_{j \in J'} x_{ij} \geq 1$, contradicting that Step (2)c. cannot be applied. $\qquad\square$

We now prove Theorem 3.2.1 by a simple inductive argument.

Proof of Theorem 3.2.1 We first prove that the algorithm returns an assignment of optimal cost. We claim that at any iteration of the algorithm the cost of assignment given by F plus the cost of the current linear programming solution to LP_{ga} is at most the cost of the initial linear programming solution. This can be shown by a simple inductive argument on the number of iterations. Observe that the claim holds trivially before the first iteration. In any iteration, if we assign job j to machine i in Step (ii)b then the cost of F increases by c_{ij} and the current linear programming solution decreases by $c_{ij}x_{ij} = c_{ij}$ since $x_{ij} = 1$. Hence, the claim holds. If we remove a constraint in Step (ii)c, then the cost of F remains the same, while the cost of the current linear program can only decrease. Hence, the claim holds in this case as well. Thus, finally when F is a feasible assignment, by induction, the cost of assignment given by F is at most the cost of the initial linear programming solution.

Finally, we show that machine i is used at most $2T_i$ units for each i. Fix any machine i. We first argue the following claim. If $i \in M'$, then at any iteration we must have $T_i' + T_i(F) \leq T_i$, where T_i' is the residual time left on the machine at this iteration and $T_i(F)$ is the time used by jobs assigned to machine i in F. The proof of the claim follows by a simple inductive argument as in the preceding inductive argument for costs. Now consider when the machine i is removed from M'. There are two possibilities. If there is only one job j in machine i, then the total processing time at machine i is at most $T_i + p_{ij} \leq 2T_i$, where the inequality holds because of the pruning step (where we deleted edges assigning a job to machine i if its processing time exceeded T_i). If there are two jobs j_1 and j_2 in machine i, then let x denote the linear programming solution when the constraint for machine i is removed. The total processing time at machine i at most

$$T_i(F) + p_{ij_1} + p_{ij_2}$$
$$\leq T_i - x_{ij_1}p_{ij_1} - x_{ij_2}p_{ij_2} + p_{ij_1} + p_{ij_2}$$
$$\leq T_i + (1 - x_{ij_1})p_{ij_1} + (1 - x_{ij_2})p_{ij_2}$$
$$\leq T_i + (2 - x_{ij_1} - x_{ij_2})T_i$$
$$\leq 2T_i$$

because $p_{ij_1}, p_{ij_2} \leq T_i$ again by the pruning step and $x_{ij_1} + x_{ij_2} \geq 1$ by Step (ii)c. This completes the proof of Theorem 3.2.1. ∎

3.3 Maximum budgeted allocation*

In this section, we consider the maximum budgeted allocation problem, which is similar to the generalized assignment problem but is a maximization problem

---

* This section may be skipped in the first reading without loss of continuity in the first reading.

instead of a minimization problem. There are a set Q of indivisible items and a set A of agents. Each agent $i \in A$ is willing to pay a maximum of b_{ij} dollars for item $j \in Q$, but has a maximum budget B_i on total spending. The maximum budgeted allocation problem is to allocate items to agents to maximize revenue. The main result of this section is the following theorem by Chakrabarty and Goel [23].

Theorem 3.3.1 *There is a 4/3-approximation algorithm for the maximum budgeted allocation problem.*

3.3.1 Linear programming relaxation

This problem can be formulated as an integer linear programming, in which there is a variable x_{ij} for agent i and item j to indicate whether item j is assigned to agent i.

$$\text{maximize} \quad \sum_{i \in A} \min(B_i, \sum_{j \in Q} b_{ij} x_{ij})$$

$$\text{subject to} \quad \sum_{i \in A} x_{ij} \le 1 \qquad \forall j \in Q$$

$$x_{ij} \in \{0, 1\} \qquad \forall i \in A, j \in Q$$

The constraints require that each item is allocated to at most one agent. The objective function can be rewritten as a linear function by adding auxiliary constraints. Thus, we obtain a linear programming relaxation by relaxing the integrality constraints. Observe that by appropriate scaling there is always an optimal fractional solution in which $\sum_{j \in Q} b_{ij} x_{ij} \le B_i$ for all $i \in A$. Henceforth, we consider the following equivalent linear programming relaxation, denoted by LP_{mba}, which is similar to that of the generalized assignment problem. Throughout this section, we assume without loss of generality that $b_{ij} \le B_i$ for each $j \in Q$ (for otherwise, we can reset b_{ij} to B_i) and maintain this invariant in all iterations of the iterative algorithm.

$$\text{maximize} \quad \sum_{i \in A} \sum_{j \in Q} b_{ij} x_{ij}$$

$$\text{subject to} \quad \sum_{j \in Q} b_{ij} x_{ij} \le B_i \qquad \forall i \in A$$

$$\sum_{i \in A} x_{ij} \le 1 \qquad \forall j \in Q$$

$$x_{ij} \ge 0 \qquad \forall i \in A, j \in Q$$

3.3.2 Characterization of extreme point solutions

Given a fractional solution x to LP_{mba}, we construct a bipartite graph $G_x = (A \cup Q, E)$ with $ij \in E$ if and only if $x_{ij} > 0$. The following lemma is a direct application of the Rank Lemma 2.1.4.

Lemma 3.3.2 *Given any extreme point solution x to LP_{mba} with $x_{ij} > 0$ for each $i \in A, j \in Q$, there exist $A' \subseteq A, Q' \subseteq Q$ such that*

(i) $\sum_{j \in Q} b_{ij} x_{ij} = B_i$ *for each $i \in A'$ and $\sum_{i \in A} x_{ij} = 1$ for each $j \in Q'$.*
(ii) *The corresponding row vectors in A' and Q' are linearly independent.*
(iii) $|E| = |A'| + |Q'|$.

Similar to the bipartite matching problem and the generalized assignment problem, Lemma 3.3.2 implies that each connected component of G_x has at most one cycle. With an additional cycle elimination argument that shifts the values of the solution along such a cycle without decreasing the objective value, one can prove that G_x is a forest (see exercises). We call an item a *leaf item* if it is a leaf in G_x. We call an agent i a *leaf agent* if all but one neighbor of i are leaf items (i itself may not be a leaf). Since x is an extreme point solution and G_x is a forest, there is at most one nontight constraint in each component. For an agent that is a leaf of a tree, as its bid to the item is at most the agent's budget, such an agent must be nontight in a tree with at least two agents (if such an agent is tight then the component has only this agent and this item). In particular there cannot be two agents that are leaves of a tree. Hence, every tree in the forest has at least one leaf item and one leaf agent, and if a tree has at least two agents then there is at least one tight leaf agent. The following lemma summarizes the properties of the extreme point solutions that we will use.

Lemma 3.3.3 *[23] Given any extreme point solution x to LP_{mba}:*

(i) *The graph G_x is a forest.*
(ii) *There is at least one leaf agent in each component of G_x.*
(iii) *There is at least one tight leaf agent in a component of G_x with at least two agents.*

3.3.3 An iterative 2-approximation algorithm

We first present in Figure 3.3 a simple iterative 2-approximation algorithm for the problem. In the following, $N(i)$ denotes the set of neighbors (items) of agent i in G_x.

We now prove that the above algorithm is a 2-approximation algorithm. Consider an arbitrary iteration. The increase of the integral solution is at least

Iterative 2-Approximation Algorithm for Maximum Budgeted Allocation

While $Q \neq \emptyset$ do

(i) Find an optimal extreme point solution x to LP_{mba}. Remove all edges with $x_{ij} = 0$.
(ii) Pick a leaf agent i. Let L be the set of leaf items in $N(i)$. Assign each item $l \in L$ to i and then remove L. Modify $B_i' := B_i - \sum_{l \in L} b_{il} x_{il}$.
    (a) If i has a non-leaf item j, modify the bid of i on j to be $b_{ij}' \leftarrow \min(b_{ij}, B_i')$.

Figure 3.3 The Maximum budgeted allocation 2-approximation algorithm.

$\sum_{l \in L} b_{il} x_{il}$. Note that x restricted to the remaining edges is a feasible solution to the residual problem. Let $b_{ij}' = \min(b_{ij}, B_i')$ denote the new bid of agent i to item j. If $b_{ij}' = b_{ij}$, then the decrease of the fractional solution is at most $\sum_{l \in L} b_{il} x_{il}$. Otherwise, if $b_{ij}' = B_i'$, then the decrease of the fractional solution is at most

$$\sum_{l \in L} b_{il} x_{il} + (b_{ij} - b_{ij}') x_{ij} \leq \sum_{l \in L} b_{il} x_{il} + (B_i - B_i') = 2 \sum_{l \in L} b_{il} x_{il}$$

where the first inequality follows because $b_{ij} \leq B_i$ and $b_{ij}' = B_i'$ and $x_{ij} \leq 1$. Hence, in either case, the increase of the integral solution is at least half the decrease of the fractional solution in each iteration. It follows by an inductive argument that the final integral solution is at least half the initial fractional solution.

3.3.4 An iterative $\frac{4}{3}$-approximation algorithm

Here we present an improved iterative approximation algorithm for the problem. In Step (ii)(a) of the algorithm in Figure 3.3, the bid of agent i on item j is decreased by the amount collected from the leaf items, and this is the bottleneck of achieving a better approximation algorithm. The new idea is to keep the new bid slightly higher. The intuition is that there is some "surplus" from the amount collected from the leaf items, since they are collected with "factor one" while we only require an approximate solution. The improved algorithm is presented in Figure 3.4.

Iterative $\frac{4}{3}$-Approximation Algorithm for Maximum Budgeted Allocation

While $Q \neq \emptyset$ do

(i) Find an optimal extreme point solution x to LP_{mba}. Remove all edges with $x_{ij} = 0$.

(ii) If there is a leaf agent i with all the items in $N(i)$ being leaf items, then assign each item $l \in N(i)$ to i and remove $N(i)$ and i.

(iii) Pick a tight leaf agent i. Let L be the set of leaf items in $N(i)$, and j be the unique non-leaf item in $N(i)$. Assign each item in $N(i) \setminus \{j\}$ to i and remove each item in $N(i) \setminus \{j\}$. Modify both

$$B_i, b_{ij} \leftarrow \frac{4}{3} b_{ij} x_{ij}.$$

Figure 3.4 The maximum budgeted allocation 4/3-approximation algorithm.

3.3.5 Correctness and performance guarantee

Lemma 3.3.3 guarantees that the algorithm will terminate successfully. Therefore, it remains to prove that the returned integral solution is at least $\frac{3}{4}$ of the initial fractional solution. As in the proof of the 2-approximation algorithm, we apply the following lemma inductively to complete the proof.

Lemma 3.3.4 *In any iteration the increase of the integral solution is at least $\frac{3}{4}$ of the decrease of the fractional solution.*

Proof Consider any iteration, and first suppose that Step (ii) is applied on a leaf agent i in this iteration. Let x denote the optimal fractional solution at the end of the iteration. Note that B_i is modified at most once throughout the algorithm. Suppose B_i has not been modified before this iteration. Then the increase of the integral solution is at least $\sum_{l \in N(i)} b_{il} x_{il}$. Since the current solution x restricted to the remaining edges is a feasible solution in the residual problem, the decrease of the fractional solution is at most $\sum_{l \in N(i)} b_{il} x_{il}$, and thus the lemma holds.

Now suppose that B_i has been modified before this iteration. In this case, let j be the unique neighbor of i. Let y denote the fractional solution when B_i was modified. Let B_i denote the original budget, b_{ij} denote the original bid, and b'_{ij} denote the current bid. The decrease in the fractional solution in the current step is at most its current bid

$$b'_{ij} = \frac{4}{3} b_{ij} y_{ij}.$$

However, from the iteration when its budget was modified, the unspent "fractional" budget left on agent i is at least $b_{ij} y_{ij}$, and hence the increase of the integral solution is at least

$$b_{ij} y_{ij} \geq \frac{3}{4} \cdot b'_{ij}.$$

Therefore, the lemma holds if Step (ii) is applied.

Now, finally assume that Step (iii)(b) was applied on a tight leaf agent i. Let j be the unique nonleaf item in $N(i)$. Then increase in the integral solution is at least

$$\sum_{l \in N(i)\setminus\{j\}} b_{il} x_{il} = B_i - b_{ij} x_{ij}.$$

The decrease in the fractional solution is at most

$$\sum_{l \in N(i)\setminus\{j\}} b_{il} x_{il} + b_{ij} x_{ij} - b'_{ij} x_{ij} = B_i - b'_{ij} x_{ij} = B_i - \frac{4}{3} b_{ij} x_{ij}^2.$$

Hence, the increase in the integral solution is at least $3/4$ of the decrease of the fractional solution as verified below:

$$\Delta(\text{Integral}) - \frac{3}{4} \Delta(\text{FractionalSolution})$$

$$= B_i - b_{ij} x_{ij} - \frac{3}{4} (B_i - \frac{4}{3} b_{ij} x_{ij}^2)$$

$$= \frac{B_i}{4} - b_{ij} x_{ij} (1 - x_{ij}) \geq \frac{B_i}{4} - \frac{b_{ij}}{4} \geq 0$$

where the second last inequality uses the fact that $x(1 - x) \leq 1/4$ for any $0 \leq x \leq 1$. This completes the proof of the lemma, and thus the proof of Theorem 3.3.1. $\square$

3.4 Vertex cover in bipartite graphs

In this section we study the vertex cover problem in bipartite graphs. Given a graph $G = (V, E)$ with cost function $c : V \rightarrow \mathbb{R}_+$, the vertex cover problem asks for a set of vertices V' such that $e \cap V' \neq \emptyset$ for each $e \in E$ and $c(V') = \sum_{v \in V'} c_v$ is minimized. In this section, we restrict our attention to bipartite graphs.

3.4.1 Linear programming relaxation

We first give the following natural linear programming relaxation $LP_{bvc}(G)$ for the vertex cover problem in bipartite graphs. We have a variable x_v for each vertex v denoting its inclusion in the solution.

$$
\begin{aligned}
\text{minimize} \quad & \sum_{v \in V} c_v x_v \\
\text{subject to} \quad & x_u + x_v \geq 1 && \forall e = \{u, v\} \in E \\
& x_v \geq 0 && \forall v \in V
\end{aligned}
$$

As in the previous two sections, the linear program $LP_{bvc}(G)$ is compact (i.e., the number of constraints and variables is polynomially bounded in the size of the problem). Hence, the linear program can be solved optimally in polynomial time by Theorem 2.1.6.

We prove the following theorem by an iterative algorithm.

Theorem 3.4.1 *Given any cost function c there exists an integral vertex cover U such that $c(U) \leq c \cdot x$ where x is an optimal solution to $LP_{bvc}(G)$.*

As before, our proof of Theorem 3.4.1 as a corollary implies the following theorem.

Theorem 3.4.2 *The linear programming formulation $LP_{bvc}(G)$ is integral.*

3.4.2 Characterization of extreme point solutions

Before we prove Theorem 3.4.1 we give a characterization of extreme points of LP_{bvc}. For a set $W \subseteq V$, let $\chi(W)$ denote the vector in $\mathbb{R}^{|V|}$: The vector has a 1 corresponding to each vertex $v \in W$, and 0 otherwise. This vector is called the *characteristic vector* of W, and is denoted by $\chi(W)$. In the following lemma, which follows by a direct application of the Rank Lemma 2.1.4, we characterize an extreme point solution by a set of tight independent constraints.

Lemma 3.4.3 *Given any extreme point x to $LP_{bvc}(G)$ with $x_v > 0$ for each $v \in V$, there exists $F \subseteq E$ such that*

(i) $x_u + x_v = 1$ *for each* $e = \{u, v\} \in F$.
(ii) *The vectors in* $\{\chi(\{u, v\}) : \{u, v\} \in F\}$ *are linearly independent.*
(iii) $|V| = |F|$.

Iterative Bipartite Vertex Cover Algorithm

(i) Initialization $U \leftarrow \emptyset$.

(ii) While $V(G) \neq \emptyset$ do

    (a) Find an optimal extreme point solution x to $LP_{bvc}(G)$ and remove every vertex v with $x_v = 0$ and $d_E(v) = 0$ from G.

    (b) If there is a vertex $v \in V$ with $x_v = 1$ then update $U \leftarrow U \cup \{v\}$, $V(G) \leftarrow V(G) \setminus \{v\}$ and $E(G) \leftarrow E(G) \setminus \delta(v)$.

(iii) Return U.

Figure 3.5 Bipartite vertex cover algorithm.

3.4.3 Iterative algorithm

We now give the algorithm which constructs an integral vertex cover of cost at most the optimal solution to $LP_{bvc}(G)$ proving Theorem 3.4.1. The algorithm is a simple iterative procedure and shown in Figure 3.5.

3.4.4 Correctness and optimality

Following the approach we used for bipartite matching, we prove the correctness of the algorithm in two steps. First, we show that the algorithm returns a vertex cover of optimal cost if the algorithm *always* finds a vertex v with $x_v = 0$ in Step (2) or a vertex v with $x_v = 1$ in Step (2) . In the second part, we show that the algorithm will always find such an vertex completing the proof.

Claim 3.4.4 *If the algorithm, in every iteration, finds a vertex v with $x_v = 0$ and $d_E(v) = 0$ in Step (ii)(a). or a vertex v with $x_v = 1$ in Step (ii)(b)., then it returns a vertex cover U of cost at most the optimal solution to $LP_{bvc}(G)$.*

The proof of this claim is identical to the proof of Claim 3.1.4. We leave the details to the reader. We now complete the proof of Theorem 3.4.1 by showing that we can always find a vertex v with $x_v = 0$ and $d_E(v) = 0$, or a vertex with $x_v = 1$. The proof of the following lemma crucially uses the characterization of extreme point solutions given in Lemma 3.4.3.

Lemma 3.4.5 *Given any extreme point solution x to $LP_{bvc}(G)$ there must exist a vertex v with $x_v = 0$ and $d_E(v) = 0$, or a vertex with $x_v = 1$.*

Proof Suppose for the sake of contradiction that $x_v < 1$ and $x_v = 0$ implies that $d_E(v) \geq 1$ for each vertex $v \in V$. This implies that there is no vertex v with $x_v = 0$. This follows from the fact that any neighbor u of v must have

$x_u = 1$ since $x_u + x_v \geq 1$. Lemma 3.4.3 implies that there exists $F \subseteq E$ such that constraints corresponding to F are tight and $|F| = |V|$.

We claim that F is acyclic. Suppose for the sake of contradiction $C \subseteq F$ is a cycle. Since G is bipartite C is an even cycle. Then C is the disjoint union of two matchings M_1 and M_2. But then the sum of the constraints corresponding to edges in M_1 equals the sum of the constraints corresponding to edges in M_2, contradicting the independence of constraints for edges in F.

Since F is acyclic, we must have $|F| \leq |V| - 1$, a contradiction. □

Thus, by Lemma 3.4.5, the algorithm in Figure 3.5 returns a vertex cover that costs at most the optimal solution to the linear program $LP_{bvc}(G)$, proving Theorem 3.4.1.

3.5 Vertex cover and matching: duality

In this section we prove the following min–max theorem between the size of minimum vertex covers and maximum matchings in bipartite graphs using the integrality proofs we have seen in previous sections.

Theorem 3.5.1 *Given an unweighted bipartite graph $G = (V, E)$ we have*

$$\max\{|M| : M \text{ is a matching}\} = \min\{|U| : U \text{ is a vertex cover}\}.$$

Proof Let M^* be the maximum weight matching returned by the iterative algorithm in Figure 3.1 when the weight function $w_e = 1$ for all $e \in E$. Also, let U^* denote the minimum cost vertex cover returned by the iterative algorithm in Figure 3.5 when the cost function $c_v = 1$ for each $v \in V$. From Theorems 3.1.1 and 3.4.1 we have that M^* is an optimal solution to $LP_{bm}(G)$ and U^* is an optimal solution to $LP_{bvc}(G)$. But $LP_{bm}(G)$ and $LP_{bvc}(G)$ are duals of each other when w and c are uniformly one (see Section 2.1.4). By the strong duality theorem (Theorem 2.1.9), both the linear programs must have optimal solutions of equal value:

$$|M^*| = \max\{|M| : M \text{ is a matching}\} = \min\{|U| : U \text{ is a vertex cover}\} = |U^*|.$$

□

A weighted generalization of the above theorem is true. It can be similarly shown using duality and the fact that the corresponding linear programming problems have integral optima. For more details, see Chapter 18 of Schrijver's book [121].

3.6 Notes

The bipartite perfect matching problem (also known as the assignment problem) is one of the oldest problems in combinatorial optimization (see e.g., [119]). The first proof of polynomial solvability of maximum weight bipartite matching via the Hungarian method was given by Egerváry [40], sharpened by Kuhn [87] and shown efficient by Munkres [100]. The unweighted case was addressed earlier by Frobenius [48]. Birkhoff [16] was the first to show that the extreme points of the bipartite matching polyhedron (defined by the so-called doubly stochastic constraint matrix) are integral.

The generalized assignment problem was first studied by Shmoys and Tardos [122] following up on a bicriteria approximation algorithms for the problem due to Lin and Vitter [91]. Trick [128] studied the version minimizing the weighted sum of cost and makespan of the underlying scheduling problem, while Lenstra, Shmoys and Tardos [90] study the makespan problem and give the 2-approximation that was generalized in the subsequent work of Shmoys and Tardos [122]. Extensions have been considered by Saha and Srinivasan [116] and Zhang et al. [135]; see exercises.

The maximum budgeted allocation problem is NP-hard. The first approximation algorithm is a $(1 + \sqrt{5})/2$-approximation algorithm given by Garg, Kumar, and Pandit [57]. The approximation ratio was subsequently improved to $e/(e-1)$ by Andelman and Mansour [3] and $3/2$ by Azar et al. [6]. The result presented in this chapter is by Chakrabarty and Goel [23]. The same result is also obtained independently by Srinivasan [126] by a dependent rounding algorithm.

The bipartite minimum vertex cover problem is the linear programming dual to the maximum matching problem. The min–max theorem relating them is due to König [84]. The Hungarian method and LP duality can be used to show the integrality of the weighted vertex cover problem. An alternate approach is to use the total unimodularity (see e.g., the book by Nemhauser and Wolsey [106]) of the constraint matrix which is the edge-node incidence matrix of the bipartite graph, which is also an example of a network matrix that we will study in Chapter 8.

Exercises

3.1 Given a bipartite graph $G = (V, E)$ and a cost function $c : E \rightarrow \mathcal{R}$, a perfect matching is a subgraph with degree exactly one at any node.

   (a) Write a linear programming formulation for the minimum cost perfect matching problem.

(b) Give an iterative proof of integrality of the linear programming formulation for the minimum cost perfect matching problem. (*Hint*: Adapt the proof for maximum weight matchings.)

3.2 Show that $LP_{bm}(G)$ and $LP_{bvc}(G)$ are *not* integral when G is not bipartite.

3.3 Generalize the methods given in this chapter for maximum weight matchings and minimum weight vertex covers in bipartite graphs to the case when the right-hand side of the LP constraints are positive integers (rather than all 1's as we considered). Note that the two resulting integrality proofs, along with strong duality, will imply the general min–max relation between maximum-weight matchings with arbitrary vertex degree bounds and minimum-cost vertex cover with arbitrary coverage requirements at the edges.

3.4 Given a set of intervals $[a_i, b_i]$ for each $1 \le i \le n$ and a weight function w on intervals, the *maximum weight k-interval packing* problem asks for a subset J of intervals of maximum weight such that there are at most k intervals in J at any point on the line.

(a) Formulate a linear program for the maximum weight k-interval packing problem.

(b) Show that only $n - 1$ *point* constraints need to be imposed apart from the bound constraints.

(c) Show that the linear program is integral.

3.5 Can you solve the maximum weight k-interval packing problem for intervals on a tree rather than a path (as was the case in the previous problem) using the same approach? If you can, give an integral description for the problem. If not, argue why natural formulations are not integral.

Consider the case when all the intervals in a tree are monotone, that is, they go from a point in a rooted version of the tree to its ancestor (thus, there are no intervals whose endpoints are two incomparable points in the tree). Can you give an integral LP formulation in this case using the approach of the previous problem?

3.6 (Zhang et al. [135], Saha and Srinivasan [116]) Consider the generalized assignment problem where for each machine i we are also given an upper bound U_i on the number of jobs that the machine i can service. Modify the iterative rounding algorithm to obtain the same guarantee as in Theorem 3.2.1 and also that the number of jobs on machine i is at most U_i.

3.7 Prove Lemma 3.3.3 starting from Lemma 3.3.2. (*Hint*: Use the objective function.)

3.8 (Chakrabarty and Goel [23]) Construct an example for LP_{mba} of the maximum budgeted allocation problem with integrality gap $\frac{4}{3}$.

4

Spanning trees

In this chapter, we will study the spanning tree problem in undirected graphs. First, we will study an exact linear programming formulation and show its integrality using the iterative method. To do this, we will introduce the *uncrossing method*, which is a very powerful technique in combinatorial optimization. The uncrossing method will play a crucial role in the proof and will occur at numerous places in later chapters. We will show two different iterative algorithms for the spanning tree problem, each using a different choice of 1-elements to pick in the solution. For the second iterative algorithm, we show three different correctness proofs for the existence of a 1-element in an extreme point solution: a global counting argument, a local integral token counting argument and a local fractional token counting argument. These token counting arguments will be used in many proofs in later chapters.

We then address the degree-bounded minimum-cost spanning tree problem. We show how the methods developed for the exact characterization of the spanning tree polyhedron are useful in designing approximation algorithms for this NP-hard problem. We give two additive approximation algorithm: The first follows the first approach for spanning trees and naturally generalizes to give a simple proof of the additive two approximation result of Goemans [59]; the second follows the second approach for spanning trees and uses the local fractional token counting argument to provide a very simple proof of the additive one approximation result of Singh and Lau [125].

4.1 Minimum spanning trees

In an instance of the minimum spanning tree (MST) problem we are given an undirected graph $G = (V, E)$, with edge costs given as $c : E \to \mathbb{R}$; the task is to find a spanning tree of minimum total edge cost.

4.1.1 Linear Programming Relaxation

In this section, two formulations of the minimum spanning tree problem are discussed (some more are discussed in the exercises). A spanning tree is a minimal 1-edge-connected subgraph. Thus, a natural formulation (sometimes called the undirected LP or the cut LP) is to require that every pair of vertices has a path connecting them. Or equivalently, we can require that there is at least one edge crossing each proper subset of vertices.

$$\text{minimize} \qquad \sum_{e \in E} c_e x_e$$

$$\text{subject to} \qquad x(\delta(S)) \geq 1 \qquad \forall\, S \subset V$$

$$x_e \geq 0 \qquad \forall\, e \in E$$

There is a variable x_e corresponding to each edge e, to indicate whether e is included in the spanning tree and that c_e denotes the cost of e. For a set F of edges, the shorthand $x(F)$ is used to denote $\sum_{e \in F} x_e$. Recall that $\delta(S)$ is the set of edges with exactly one endpoint in S.

There are exponentially many constraints in the undirected LP. However, from Theorem 2.1.8 in Chapter 1, the undirected LP can still be solved in polynomial time if a polynomial time separation oracle can be constructed. Constructing such a polynomial-time oracle is equivalent to finding a cut of total capacity less than one in the graph with capacities x and can be accomplished using a global minimum-cut algorithm. (In detail, given a solution to this linear program, one needs to determine whether it is a feasible solution and, if not, provides a violating inequality. A polynomial time separation oracle for the undirected LP is easy to construct. Given a fractional solution, check first if every variable is nonnegative. Then, for every pair of vertices, check if the maximum flow between them is at least 1. If this condition is satisfied for every pair, then clearly the given fractional solution is a feasible solution. On the other hand, if for some pair this condition is not satisfied, by the max-flow min-cut theorem, there is a set S with $x(\delta(S)) < 1$, and such a set can be found in polynomial time.) Unfortunately, the undirected LP is not an exact formulation of the minimum spanning tree problem as shown in Figure 4.1.

Another formulation is the subtour elimination LP which is related to the study of the traveling salesman problem (TSP). For $S \subseteq V$, define $E(S)$ to be the set of edges with both endpoints in S. For a spanning tree, there are at most $|S| - 1$ edges in $E(S)$, where $|S|$ denotes the number of vertices in S. Insisting on this for every set by using the constraint (4.2) eliminates all the potential subtours that can be formed in the LP solution: This is how the formulation gets its name.

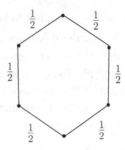

Figure 4.1 Consider a cycle of n vertices, where every edge has the same cost,
say 1. Any spanning tree requires at least $n - 1$ edges, and thus has cost at least
$n - 1$. However, by setting $x_e = 1/2$ for each edge, it can be easily checked that
this is a feasible solution to the undirected LP and has total cost of only $n/2$.

$$\text{minimize} \qquad \sum_{e \in E} c_e x_e \qquad\qquad\qquad\qquad (4.1)$$

$$\text{subject to} \qquad x(E(S)) \le |S| - 1 \qquad \forall\, \emptyset \ne S \subset V \quad (4.2)$$

$$x(E(V)) = |V| - 1 \qquad\qquad\qquad (4.3)$$

$$x_e \ge 0 \qquad\qquad \forall\, e \in E \qquad (4.4)$$

In the next section we will give an iterative algorithm which will prove that
the subtour LP is integral.

Theorem 4.1.1 *Every extreme point solution to the subtour LP is integral and
corresponds to the characteristic vector of a spanning tree.*

Before we give the iterative algorithm and the proof of Theorem 4.1.1, we
show that one can optimize over the subtour LP in polynomial time. We show
this by giving a polynomial time separation oracle for the constraints in subtour
LP. Polynomial time solvability now follows from Theorem 2.1.8.

Theorem 4.1.2 *There is a polynomial time separation oracle for the subtour
LP.*

Proof Given a fractional solution x the separation oracle needs to find a set
$S \subseteq V$ such that $x(E(S)) > |S| - 1$ if such a set exists. It is easy to check
the equality $x(E(V)) = |V| - 1$. Thus, checking the inequality for each sub-
set $S \subset V$ is equivalent to checking $\min_{S \subset V}\{|S| - 1 - x(E(S))\} < 0$. Using
$x(E(V)) = |V| - 1$ we obtain that it is enough to check $\min_S\{|S| - 1 +
x(E(V)) - x(E(S))\} < |V| - 1\}$. We show that solving $2|V| - 2$ min-cut
problems suffice to check the above.

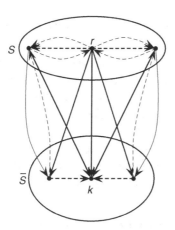

Figure 4.2 The construction for separation of spanning tree constraints. Solid edges are part of the cut, and dashed edges are not part of the cut. Thick edges into k have cost 1 and thick edges from r to any node j cost $\sum_{e \in \delta(j)} \frac{x_e}{2}$. Thin arcs between nodes i and j form a pair of antiparallel edges of cost $\frac{x_{\{i,j\}}}{2}$.

Fix a root vertex $r \in V$. For each $k \in V \setminus \{r\}$, we construct two minimum-cut instances, one that checks the inequality for all subsets S containing r but not k and the other that checks the inequality for all subsets S containing k but not r. We outline the construction in Figure 4.2 for the first one; the second construction follows by changing the roles of r and k.

We construct a directed graph $\hat{G}$ with vertex set V and arcs (i, j) and (j, i) for each edge $\{i, j\}$ in G. We let the weight of edges (i, j) and (j, i) be $\frac{x_{\{i,j\}}}{2}$. We also place arcs from each vertex $v \in V \setminus \{r, k\}$ to k of weight 1 and arcs from r to each vertex $v \in V \setminus \{r\}$ of weight $\sum_{e \in \delta(v)} \frac{x_e}{2} = \frac{x(\delta(v))}{2}$. Consider any cut $(S, V \setminus S)$ which separates r from k. Edges of weight one contribute exactly $|S| - 1$. The edges between i and j of weight $\frac{x_{ij}}{2}$ contribute exactly $\frac{x(\delta(S))}{2}$. The edges from r to rest of the vertices contribute $\sum_{v \notin S} \frac{x(\delta(v))}{2}$. Thus, the total weight of the cut is exactly

$$|S| - 1 + \frac{x(\delta(S))}{2} + \sum_{v \notin S} \frac{x(\delta(v))}{2} = |S| - 1 + x(E(V)) - x(E(S)).$$

Hence, checking whether the minimum cut separating r from k is strictly smaller than $|V| - 1$ checks exactly whether there is a violating set S containing r but not containing k. $\qquad\square$

4.1.2 Characterization of extreme point solutions

In this subsection, we analyze the extreme point solutions to the subtour LP. Recall that an extreme point solution is the unique solution defined by n linearly independent tight inequalities, where n is the number of variables in the linear program. There are exponentially many inequalities in the subtour LP, and an extreme point solution may satisfy many inequalities as equalities. To analyze an extreme point solution, an important step is to find a "good" set of tight inequalities defining it. If there is an edge e with $x_e = 0$, this edge can be removed from the graph without affecting the feasibility and the objective value. So henceforth assume every edge e has $x_e > 0$.

4.1.3 Uncrossing technique

The uncrossing technique is a powerful technique and we shall use it to find a *good* set of tight inequalities for an extreme point solution in the subtour LP. For a set $F \subseteq E$, let $\chi(F)$ denote the characteristic vector in $\mathbb{R}^{|E|}$ that has a 1 corresponding to each edge $e \in F$, and 0 otherwise. The following proposition follows from the supermodularity of $|E(X)|$; see also Proposition 2.3.6.

Proposition 4.1.3 *For $X, Y \subseteq V$,*

$$\chi(E(X)) + \chi(E(Y)) \leq \chi(E(X \cup Y)) + \chi(E(X \cap Y))$$

and equality holds if and only if $E(X \setminus Y, Y \setminus X) = \emptyset$.

Proof Observe that

$$\chi(E(X)) + \chi(E(Y)) = \chi(E(X \cup Y)) + \chi(E(X \cap Y)) - \chi(E(X \setminus Y, Y \setminus X))$$

and proof follows immediately. See Figure 4.3. □

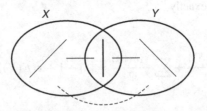

Figure 4.3 In this example, the solid edges are counted exactly once in both the LHS $\chi(E(X)) + \chi(E(Y))$, and the RHS $\chi(E(X \cup Y)) + \chi(E(X \cap Y))$, and the bold edge is counted exactly twice on both sides. The dashed edge, however, is counted in the RHS but not in the LHS.

Given an extreme point solution x to the subtour LP, let $\mathcal{F} = \{S \subseteq V \mid x(E(S)) = |S| - 1\}$ be the family of tight inequalities for x. The following lemma shows that this family is closed under intersection and union.

Lemma 4.1.4 *If $S, T \in \mathcal{F}$ and $S \cap T \neq \emptyset$, then both $S \cap T$ and $S \cup T$ are in $\mathcal{F}$. Furthermore, $\chi(E(S)) + \chi(E(T)) = \chi(E(S \cap T)) + \chi(E(S \cup T))$.*

Proof Observe that

$$
\begin{aligned}
|S| - 1 + |T| - 1 &= x(E(S)) + x(E(T)) \\
&\leq x(E(S \cap T)) + x(E(S \cup T))) \\
&\leq |S \cap T| - 1 + |S \cup T| - 1 \\
&= |S| - 1 + |T| - 1.
\end{aligned}
$$

The first equality follows from the fact that $S, T \in \mathcal{F}$. The second inequality follows from Proposition 4.1.3 (or from Proposition 2.3.6). The third inequality follows from the constraints for $S \cap T$ and $S \cup T$ in the subtour LP. The last equality is because $|S| + |T| = |S \cap T| + |S \cup T|$ for any two sets S, T. Thus, equality must hold everywhere, and we have $x(E(S \cap T)) + x(E(S \cup T)) = |S \cap T| - 1 + |S \cup T| - 1$. Hence, we must have equality for constraints for $S \cap T$ and $S \cup T$ (i.e., $x(E(S \cap T)) = |S \cap T| - 1$ and $x(E(S \cup T)) = |S \cup T| - 1$, which implies that $S \cap T$ and $S \cup T$ are also in $\mathcal{F}$). Moreover, equality holds for Proposition 4.1.3 and thus $\chi(E(S \setminus T, T \setminus S)) = \emptyset$ and $\chi(E(S)) + \chi(E(T)) = \chi(E(S \cap T)) + \chi(E(S \cup T))$. $\square$

Denote by span($\mathcal{F}$) the vector space generated by the set of vectors $\{\chi(E(S)) \mid S \in \mathcal{F}\}$. Recall that two sets X, Y are called *intersecting* if $X \cap Y$, $X - Y$ and $Y - X$ are nonempty. A family of sets is *laminar* if no two sets in the family are intersecting. The following lemma says that an extreme point solution is characterized by tight inequalities whose corresponding sets form a laminar family. This is a crucial structure theorem on the extreme point solutions for the subtour LP.

Lemma 4.1.5 *If $\mathcal{L}$ is a maximal laminar subfamily of $\mathcal{F}$, then span($\mathcal{L}$) = span($\mathcal{F}$).*

Proof Suppose, by way of contradiction, that $\mathcal{L}$ is a maximal laminar subfamily of $\mathcal{F}$ but span($\mathcal{L}$) $\subset$ span($\mathcal{F}$). For any $S \notin \mathcal{L}$, define intersect($S, \mathcal{L}$) to be the number of sets in $\mathcal{L}$ which intersect S (i.e., intersect($S, \mathcal{L}$) = $|\{T \in \mathcal{L} \mid S$ and T are intersecting$\}|$). Since span($\mathcal{L}$) $\subset$ span($\mathcal{F}$), there exists a set S with $\chi(E(S)) \notin$ span($\mathcal{L}$). Choose such a set S with minimum intersect($S, \mathcal{L}$). Clearly, intersect($S, \mathcal{L}$) ≥ 1; otherwise $\mathcal{L} \cup \{S\}$ is also a laminar subfamily, contradicting the maximality of $\mathcal{L}$. Let T be a set in $\mathcal{L}$ which intersects S. Since $S, T \in F$, by Lemma 4.1.4, both $S \cap T$ and $S \cup T$ are in $\mathcal{F}$. Also, both intersect$(S \cap T, \mathcal{L})$ and intersect$(S \cup T, \mathcal{L})$ are strictly smaller than intersect$(S, \mathcal{L})$, which will be proved next in Proposition 4.1.6. Hence, by the minimality of intersect$(S, \mathcal{L})$, both $S \cap T$ and $S \cup T$ are in span$(\mathcal{L})$. By Lemma 4.1.4, $\chi(E(S)) + \chi(E(T)) = \chi(E(S \cap T)) + \chi(E(S \cup T))$. Since $\chi(E(S \cap T))$ and $\chi(E(S \cup T))$ are in span$(\mathcal{L})$ and $T \in \mathcal{L}$, the preceding equation implies that $\chi(E(S)) \in \text{span}(\mathcal{L})$, a contradiction. It remains to prove Proposition 4.1.6.

Proposition 4.1.6 *Let S be a set that intersects $T \in \mathcal{L}$. Then intersect $(S \cap T, \mathcal{L})$ and intersect $(S \cup T, \mathcal{L})$ are strictly smaller than intersect $(S, \mathcal{L})$.*

Proof Since $\mathcal{L}$ is a laminar family, for a set $R \in \mathcal{L}$ with $R \neq T$, R does not intersect T (either $R \subset T$, $T \subset R$ or $T \cap R = \emptyset$). So, whenever R intersects $S \cap T$ or $S \cup T$, R also intersects S. Also, T intersects S but not $S \cap T$ or $S \cup T$. Therefore, intersect$(S \cap T, \mathcal{L})$ and intersect$(S \cup T, \mathcal{L})$ are strictly smaller than intersect$(S, \mathcal{L})$. □

This completes the proof of Lemma 4.1.5. □

The following proposition about the size of a laminar family will be used to bound the number of variables in an extreme point solution.

Proposition 4.1.7 *A laminar family $\mathcal{L}$ over the ground set V without singletons (subsets with only one element) has at most $|V| - 1$ distinct members.*

Proof The proof is by induction on the size of the ground set. If $|V| = 2$, clearly the claim follows. Let $n = |V|$ and the claim be true for all laminar families over ground sets of size strictly smaller than n. Let S be a maximal set in the laminar family, which is not equal to V. Each set in $\mathcal{L}$, except for V, is either contained in S or does not intersect S. The number of sets in $\mathcal{L}$ contained in S (including S itself) is at most $|S| - 1$ by the induction hypothesis. The sets in $\mathcal{L}$ not intersecting with S form a laminar family over the ground set $V \setminus S$ and hence there are at most $|V| - |S| - 1$ such sets. Along with V, this gives a total of at most $(|S| - 1) + (|V| - |S| - 1) + 1 = |V| - 1$ sets. □

The following corollary follows immediately from Proposition 4.1.7.

Corollary 4.1.8 *A laminar family $\mathcal{L}$ over the ground set V (potentially including singletons now) has at most $2|V| - 1$ distinct members.*

Iterative Leaf-finding MST Algorithm

(i) Initialization $F \leftarrow \emptyset$.
(ii) While $|V(G)| \geq 2$ do
    (a) Find an optimal extreme point solution x to the subtour LP and remove every edge e with $x_e = 0$ from G.
    (b) Find a vertex v with at most one edge $e = uv$ incident on it, then update $F \leftarrow F \cup \{e\}$ and $G \leftarrow G \setminus \{v\}$.
(iii) Return F.

Figure 4.4 Iterative leaf-finding MST algorithm.

4.1.4 Leaf-finding iterative algorithm

In this subsection, an iterative procedure to find a minimum spanning tree from an optimal extreme point solution of the subtour LP is presented. The algorithm is shown in Figure 4.4.

4.1.5 Correctness and optimality of leaf-finding algorithm

First, we prove that the algorithm will terminate in the following lemma.

Lemma 4.1.9 *For any extreme point solution x to the subtour LP with $x_e > 0$ for every edge e, there exists a vertex v with $d(v) = 1$.*

Proof Suppose each vertex is of degree at least two. Then $|E| = \frac{1}{2} \sum_{v \in V} d(v) \geq |V|$. On the other hand, since there is no edge e with $x_e = 0$, every tight inequality is of the form $x(E(S)) = |S| - 1$. By Lemma 4.1.5, there are $|\mathcal{L}|$ linearly independent tight constraints of the form $x(E(S)) = |S| - 1$, where $\mathcal{L}$ is a laminar family with no singleton sets. It follows that $|E| = |\mathcal{L}|$ by the Rank Lemma 2.1.4. By Proposition 4.1.7, $|\mathcal{L}| \leq |V| - 1$ and hence $|E| \leq |V| - 1$, a contradiction. $\qquad \square$

Next we show that the returned solution is a minimum spanning tree in the following theorem.

Theorem 4.1.10 *The iterative MST algorithm returns a minimum spanning tree in polynomial time.*

Proof This is proved by induction on the number of iterations of the algorithm. If the algorithm finds a vertex v of degree one (a leaf vertex) in Step (2)b. with an edge $e = \{u, v\}$ incident at v, then we must have $x_e = 1$ since $x(\delta(v)) \geq 1$ is a valid inequality of the LP (subtracting the constraint $x(E(V-v)) \leq |V|-2$ from the constraint $x(E(V)) = |V|-1$. In the iterative leaf-finding algorithm, e is added to the solution F (starting with an initial $F = \emptyset$), and v is removed from the graph. Note that for any spanning tree T' of $G' = G \setminus \{v\}$, we can construct a spanning tree $T = T' \cup \{e\}$ of G. Hence, the residual problem is to find a minimum spanning tree on $G \setminus v$, and the same procedure is applied to solve the residual problem recursively.

Since $x_e = 1$, the restriction of x to $E(G')$, denoted by x_{res}, is a feasible solution to the subtour LP for G'. Inductively, the algorithm will return a spanning tree F' of G' of cost at most the optimal value of the subtour LP for G', and hence $c(F') \leq c \cdot x_{res}$. Therefore,

$$c(F) = c(F') + c_e \text{ and } c(F') \leq c \cdot x_{res}$$

which imply that

$$c(F) \leq c \cdot x_{res} + c_e = c \cdot x$$

as $x_e = 1$. Hence, the spanning tree returned by the algorithm is of cost no more than the cost of an optimal LP solution x, which is a lower bound on the cost of a minimum spanning tree. This shows that the algorithm returns a minimum spanning tree of the graph.   □

Remark 4.1.11 *If x is an optimal extreme point solution to the subtour LP for G, then the residual LP solution x_{res}, x restricted to $G' = G \setminus v$, remains an optimal extreme point solution to the subtour LP for G'. Hence, in the iterative MST algorithm, we only need to solve the original linear program once and none of the residual linear programs.*

Theorem 4.1.10 also shows that the subtour LP is an exact formulation of the minimum spanning tree problem showing the proof of Theorem 4.1.1.

Alternately, note that the proof of Lemma 4.1.9 already showed that $|E| = n - 1$ and since $x(E) = n - 1$ and $x(e) \leq 1$ for all edges $e \in E$ (by considering the constraint $x(E(S)) = |S| - 1$ for the size-two set S defined by the endpoints of the edge), we must have $x_e = 1$ for all edges $e \in E$ proving integrality. Thus, we have that directly either $x_e = 0$ or $x_e = 1$ for all edges e rather than for a single edge. This gives a direct (noniterative) proof of integrality of the subtour LP.

4.2 Iterative 1-edge-finding algorithm

In this section, we give another iterative procedure to find a minimum spanning tree from an optimal extreme point solution to the subtour LP is presented. The

---

Iterative 1-Edge-Finding MST Algorithm

(i) Initialization $F \leftarrow \emptyset$.

(ii) While $|V(G)| \geq 2$ do

    (a) Find an optimal extreme point solution x to the subtour LP and remove every edge e with $x_e = 0$ from G.

    (b) Find an edge $e = \{u, v\}$ with $x_e = 1$ and update $F \leftarrow F \cup \{e\}$, $G \leftarrow G/e$.

(iii) Return F.

Figure 4.5 Iterative 1-edge-finding MST algorithm.

algorithm is shown in Figure 4.5. A key difference is that to create the residual problem, the chosen edge e is contracted from G to identify its endpoints to result in the graph G/e.

4.2.1 Correctness and optimality of 1-edge-finding algorithm

Following the discussion in Section 4.1.5 it is enough to show that the algorithm will terminate. An argument similar to one in proof of Theorem 4.1.10 will show that the output of the algorithm is a minimum spanning tree.

Lemma 4.2.1 *For any extreme point solution x to the subtour LP with $x_e > 0$ for each edge e, there exists an edge f with $x_f = 1$.*

Proof We give three alternate proofs of this lemma mainly to illustrate the three types of counting arguments that can be used to accomplish such proofs.

Proof 1 (Global Counting Argument). This is the proof style of Lemma 4.1.5, which shows by a global degree counting argument over all (nonleaf) nodes that $|E| \geq |V|$, which contradicts the upper bound of $|\mathcal{L}|$ of $|V| - 1$.

Proof 2 (Local Token Counting Argument). By Lemma 4.1.5, there are $|\mathcal{L}|$ linearly independent tight constraints of the form $x(E(S)) = |S| - 1$, and so $|E| = |\mathcal{L}|$. We now show a contradiction to this through a local token counting argument.

We assign one token for each edge e in the support E, for a total of $|E|$ tokens. We will redistribute the tokens so that each set in $\mathcal{L}$ will receive one token and there are some extra tokens left. This implies that $|E| > |L|$, giving us the contradiction. Actually, for the contradiction, we can collect two tokens for each set $S \in \mathcal{L}$. Since $|\mathcal{L}| \geq 1$, this will give the desired extra token and hence the contradiction.

To redistribute the tokens, each edge gives its token to the smallest set containing both of its endpoints. Let S be any set in $\mathcal{L}$ with children $R_1, \ldots, R_k$ (k could be zero). We have

$$x(E(S)) = |S| - 1$$

and for each i,

$$x(E(R_i)) = |R_i| - 1.$$

Subtracting, we obtain

$$x(E(S)) - \sum_{i=1}^{k} x(E(R_i)) = |S| - \sum_{i=1}^{k} |R_i| + k - 1.$$

Let $A = E(S) \setminus (\cup_i E(R_i))$. Observe that S obtains exactly one token for each edge in A. If $A = \emptyset$, then $\chi(E(S)) = \sum_i \chi(E(R_i))$, which contradicts the linear independence of these constraints in $\mathcal{L}$. Moreover, $|A| \neq 1$ as $x(A)$ is an integer, but no single edge in it has an integral value. Hence, $|A| \geq 2$, and thus S receives at least two tokens.

Proof 3 (Local Fractional Token Counting Argument). This is a slight modification of the previous argument but generalizes nicely to the degree-bounded case. As before, we assign one token for each edge e in the support E, for a total of $|E|$ tokens. For each edge e, however, we only redistribute x_e *fractional* token to the smallest set containing both the endpoints. Now, we show that each set in $\mathcal{L}$ can collect at least one token and demonstrate some extra leftover fractional edge tokens as before giving us the contradiction.

Let S be any set in $\mathcal{L}$ with children $R_1, \ldots, R_k$ for some $k \geq 0$. Following the previous proof, we have that

$$x(E(S)) - \sum_i x(E(R_i)) = |S| - \sum_i |R_i| + k - 1$$

$$\implies x(A) = |S| - \sum_i |R_i| + k - 1$$

where $A = E(S) \setminus (\cup_i E(R_i))$. Now S obtains exactly x_e fractional token for each edge e in A. If $A = \emptyset$, then $\chi(E(S)) = \sum_i \chi(E(R_i))$ which contradicts the linear independence of these sets of constraints in $\mathcal{L}$. Moreover, $x(A)$ is an integer and hence it is at least one, giving S the one token it needs.

Since every edge is not integral, we have the extra fractional token of value $(1 - x_e)$ for every edge e as unused tokens giving the contradiction. $\qquad\square$

4.3 Minimum bounded-degree spanning trees

We next turn to the study of the minimum bounded-degree spanning tree (MBDST) problem. In an instance of the MBDST problem, we are given a graph $G = (V, E)$, edge cost given by $c : E \to \mathbb{R}$, a degree upper bound B_v for each $v \in V$ and the task is to find a spanning tree of minimum cost, which satisfies the degree bounds. We prove the following theorem originally due to Singh and Lau [125].

Theorem 4.3.1 *There exists a polynomial time algorithm, which, given a feasible instance of the MBDST problem, returns a spanning tree T such that $d_T(v) \leq B_v + 1$ and cost of the tree T is at most the cost of any tree which satisfies the degree bounds.*

We prove Theorem 4.3.1 using the iterative relaxation technique. However, we first prove a weaker guarantee where the degree bound is violated by an additive factor of two, a result first obtained by Goemans [59] and illustrates a simple extension of the leaf-finding iterative MST algorithm. In Section 4.4, we present the proof of Theorem 4.3.1 that extends the 1-edge-finding iterative MST algorithm.

4.3.1 Linear programming relaxation

We use the following standard linear programming relaxation for the MBDST problem, which we denote by $LP_{mbdst}(G, \mathcal{B}, W)$. In the following we assume that degree bounds are given for vertices only in a subset $W \subseteq V$. Let $\mathcal{B}$ denote the vector of all degree bounds B_v, one for each vertex $v \in W$.

$$\text{minimize} \quad \sum_{e \in E} c_e x_e \qquad (4.5)$$

$$\text{subject to} \quad x(E(V)) = |V| - 1 \qquad (4.6)$$

$$x(E(S)) \leq |S| - 1 \qquad \forall \emptyset \neq S \subset V \qquad (4.7)$$

$$x(\delta(v)) \leq B_v \qquad \forall v \in W \qquad (4.8)$$

$$x_e \geq 0 \qquad \forall e \in E \qquad (4.9)$$

Separation over the inequalities in this linear program can be carried out in polynomial time and follows from Theorem 4.1.2. When the preceding LP relaxation is infeasible, the method signals infeasibility; otherwise, it proceeds to iteratively round and provide an approximate solution. Henceforth, we assume

that we are working with a feasible instance of the problem for which there is
trivially a feasible LP solution.

4.3.2 Characterization of extreme point solutions

We first give a characterization of an extreme point solution to
$LP_{mbdst}(G, \mathcal{B}, W)$. We remove all edges with $x_e = 0$ and focus only on the support of the extreme point solution and the tight constraints from (4.6) through
(4.8). Let $\mathcal{F} = \{S \subseteq V : x(E(S)) = |S| - 1\}$ be the set of tight constraints from
(4.6) to (4.7). From an application of Rank Lemma 2.1.4 and the characterization of extreme point solutions to the spanning tree polyhedron (Lemma 4.1.5),
we have the following characterization.

Lemma 4.3.2 *Let x be an extreme point solution to $LP_{mbdst}(G, \mathcal{B}, W)$ with
$x_e > 0$ for each edge $e \in E$. Then there exists a set $T \subseteq W$ and a laminar family
$\mathcal{L}$ such that*

(i) *$x(\delta(v)) = B_v$ for each $v \in T$ and $x(E(S)) = |S| - 1$ for each $S \in \mathcal{L}$.*
(ii) *The vectors in $\{\chi(E(S)) : S \in \mathcal{L}\} \cup \{\chi(\delta(v)) : v \in T\}$ are linearly
independent.*
(iii) *$|\mathcal{L}| + |T| = |E|$.*

4.3.3 Leaf-finding iterative algorithm

In this section, we give an iterative polynomial-time algorithm, which returns
a tree of optimal cost and violates the degree bound within an additive error of
two. The algorithm is given in Figure 4.6.

Iterative MBDST Leaf-finding Algorithm

(i) Initialization $F \leftarrow \emptyset$.
(ii) While $|V(G)| \geq 2$ do
    (a) Find an optimal extreme point solution x to $LP_{mbdst}(G, \mathcal{B}, W)$ and
        remove every edge e with $x_e = 0$ from G. Let the support of x be E.
    (b) If there exists a vertex $v \in V$ with at most one edge $e = uv$ incident
        on it, then update $F \leftarrow F \cup \{e\}$, $G \leftarrow G \setminus \{v\}$, $W \leftarrow W \setminus \{v\}$, and
        set $B_u \leftarrow B_u - 1$.
    (c) **(Relaxation)** If there exists a vertex $v \in W$ with $d_E(v) \leq 3$, then
        update $W \leftarrow W \setminus \{v\}$.
(iii) Return F.

Figure 4.6 MBDST leaf-finding algorithm.

4.3.4 Correctness and performance guarantee

In the next lemma, we prove by a simple counting argument that in each iteration we can proceed by applying either Step (2)b. or Step (2)c.; this will ensure that the algorithm terminates.

Lemma 4.3.3 *Any extreme point solution x to $LP_{mbdst}(G, \mathcal{B}, W)$ with $x_e > 0$ for each edge $e \in E$ must satisfy one of the following.*

(a) There is a vertex $v \in V$ with $d_E(v) = 1$.
(b) There is a vertex $v \in W$ with $d_E(v) \leq 3$.

Proof We use a global counting argument. Suppose for sake of contradiction that both (a) and (b) are not satisfied. Then every vertex has at least two edges incident on it, and every vertex in W has at least four edges incident on it. Therefore, $|E| = \frac{1}{2} \sum_{v \in V} d(v) \geq \frac{1}{2}(2(n - |W|) + 4|W|) = n + |W|$, where $n = |V|$.

On the other hand, by Lemma 4.3.2, there is a laminar family $\mathcal{L}$ and a set $T \subseteq W$ of vertices such that $|E| = |\mathcal{L}| + |T|$. As $\mathcal{L}$ is a laminar family which contains subsets of size at least two, from Proposition 4.1.7 we have $|\mathcal{L}| \leq n - 1$. Hence, $|E| = |\mathcal{L}| + |T| \leq n - 1 + |T| \leq n - 1 + |W|$, a contradiction. □

We now prove the performance guarantee of the algorithm.

Theorem 4.3.4 *The leaf-finding iterative algorithm in Figure 4.6 returns a tree T of optimal cost with $d_T(v) \leq B_v + 2$ for each $v \in V$.*

Proof The proof that the cost of tree returned is at most the cost of the linear programming solution is identical to the proof of the optimality of the iterative spanning tree algorithm in Section 4.1, and we do not duplicate it here.

We show that the degree of any vertex v is at most $B_v + 2$. At any iteration, let F denote the set of edges selected, and let B'_v denote the current residual degree bound of v. We claim that while the degree constraint of v is present, $d_F(v) + B'_v = B_v$. The proof is by induction on the number of iterations of the algorithm. Clearly, $F = \emptyset$ and $B'_v = B_v$ and the claim holds. At any iteration, whenever we include an edge $e \in \delta(v)$ in F, we reduce B'_v by one and hence the equality holds true.

When the degree bound for the vertex v is removed, then at most three edges are incident at v. In the worst case, we may select all three edges in the solution. Hence,

$$d_T(v) \leq B_v - B'_v + 3 \leq B_v + 2$$

where $B'_v \geq 1$ is the degree bound of v when the degree constraint is removed. $\qquad\qquad\qquad\qquad\qquad\qquad\qquad\qquad\qquad\qquad\qquad\qquad$ $\Box$

4.4 An additive one approximation algorithm

In this section, we give a very simple iterative algorithm, which returns a tree of optimal cost and violates the degree bound within an additive error of one. This algorithm involves no rounding at all (not even picking a 1-edge) – it removes degree constraints one by one and eventually reduces the problem to a minimum spanning tree problem. This can be thought of as an analogue of the 1-edge-finding iterative MST algorithm presented earlier. The algorithm is given in Figure 4.7.

4.4.1 Correctness and performance guarantee

In the next lemma, we prove that in each iteration, the algorithm can find some vertex for which the degree constraint can be removed. Observe that once all the degree constraints are removed we obtain the linear program for the minimum spanning tree problem, which we showed in Section 4.1 to be integral. Hence, the algorithm returns a tree. Moreover, at each step we only relax the linear program. Hence, the cost of the final solution is at most the cost of the initial linear programming solution. Thus, the tree returned by the algorithm has optimal cost. A simple inductive argument also shows that the degree bound is violated by at most an additive one. The degree bound is violated only when we remove the degree constraint, and then $d_E(v) \leq B_v + 1$. Thus, in the worst case, if we include all the edges incident at v in T, the degree bound of v is violated by at most an additive one.

It remains to show that the iterative relaxation algorithm finds a degree constraint to remove at each step. From Lemma 4.3.2, we have that there exists a

---

Iterative Relaxation MBDST Algorithm

(i) While $W \neq \emptyset$ do
  (a) Find an optimal extreme point solution x to $LP_{mbdst}(G, \mathcal{B}, W)$ and remove every edge e with $x_e = 0$ from G. Let the support of x be E.
  (b) **(Relaxation)** If there exists a vertex $v \in W$ with $d_E(v) \leq B_v + 1$, then update $W \leftarrow W \setminus \{v\}$.
(ii) Return E.

Figure 4.7 Additive one MBDST algorithm.

laminar family $\mathcal{L} \subseteq \mathcal{F}$ and $T \subseteq W$ such that $|\mathcal{L}| + |T| = |E|$ and constraints for sets in $\mathcal{L}$ are linearly independent. Observe that if $T = \emptyset$, then only the spanning tree inequalities define the solution x. Hence, x must be integral. In the other case, we show that there must be a vertex in W whose degree constraint can be removed.

Lemma 4.4.1 *Let x be an extreme point solution to $LP_{mbdst}(G, \mathcal{B}, W)$ with $x_e > 0$. Let $\mathcal{L}$ and $T \subseteq W$ correspond to the tight set constraints and the tight degree constraints defining x as given by Lemma 4.3.2. If $T \neq \emptyset$, then there exists some vertex $v \in W$ with $d_E(v) \leq B_v + 1$.*

Proof We use the local fractional token argument as in the integrality proof of the 1-edge-finding iterative MST algorithm we presented earlier.

Suppose for the sake of contradiction, we have $T \neq \emptyset$ and $d_E(v) \geq B_v + 2$ for each $v \in W$. We now show a contradiction by a fractional token argument. We give one token for each edge in E. We then redistribute the token such that each vertex in T and each set in $\mathcal{L}$ gets one token, and we still have extra tokens left. This will contradict $|E| = |T| + |\mathcal{L}|$. The token redistribution is as follows. Each edge $e \in E$ gives as before x_e fractional token to the smallest set in $\mathcal{L}$ containing both endpoints of e, and $(1 - x_e)/2$ fractional token to each of its endpoints for the degree constraints.

We have already argued earlier that the x_e assignment suffices to obtain one token for each member in the laminar family (see the third fractional token argument in the proof of Lemma 4.2.1).

Thus, it suffices to show that each vertex with a tight degree constraint gets one token. Let $v \in W$ be such a vertex. Then v receives $(1 - x_e)/2$ token for each edge incident at v for a total token of value

$$\sum_{e \in \delta(v)} \frac{1 - x_e}{2} = \frac{d_E(v) - B_v}{2} \geq 1$$

where the first equality holds since $\sum_{e \in \delta(v)} x_e = B_v$ and the inequality holds since $d_E(v) \geq B_v + 2$ by Step (1)b. of the algorithm.

To finish the proof, we argue that there is some extra token left for contradiction. If $V \notin \mathcal{L}$, then there exists an edge e that is not contained in any set of $\mathcal{L}$ and the x_e token for that edge gives us the contradiction. Similarly, if there is a vertex $v \in W \setminus T$, then v also collects one token, which it does not need, and we get the desired contradiction. Moreover, if there is a vertex $v \in V \setminus T$, then each edge e incident at v must have $x_e = 1$, else the $(1 - x_e)/2 > 0$ token is extra. Note that $e \in \text{span}(\mathcal{L})$ for each e with $x_e = 1$, since e is a tight set of size two. We have

$$2\chi(E(V)) = \sum_{v \in V} \chi(\delta(v)) = \sum_{v \in T} \chi(\delta(v)) + \sum_{v \in V-T} \chi(\delta(v))$$

$$= \sum_{v \in T} \chi(\delta(v)) + \sum_{v \in V-T} \sum_{e \in \delta(v)} \chi(e).$$

We have argued that $V \in \mathcal{L}$ and $e \in \text{span}(\mathcal{L})$ for each edge $e \in \delta(v)$ for $v \in V - T$. Since $T \neq \emptyset$, this implies the linear dependence of the tight constraints in T and those in $\mathcal{L}$, giving us the contradiction.   □

4.5 Notes

Many variants of the greedy algorithm for finding minimum spanning trees have been obtained starting from Boruvka [18], Kruskal [86], and Prim [111] (Graham and Hell [61] have a useful survey of the history). Edmonds [38] gave the integral linear programming relaxation for minimum spanning tree problem that we presented.

There is a long line of work of successively improving the performance guarantees for the degree-bounded minimum-cost spanning tree problem. The algorithm with additive guarantee of one for the unweighted case was first given by Fürer and Raghavachari [53]. The additive algorithm with violation 2 (with both upper and lower degree bounds) was presented by Goemans [59]. The algorithm with additive violation of 1 was first presented by Singh and Lau [125], also for the case with upper and lower bounds on the degree. The fractional token proof which we used for the additive one proof was first presented by Bansal et al. [8]. Chan et al. [25] consider the degree-bounded spanning tree problem with metric costs and give true approximation by applying splitting off techniques to the solution presented here (see exercises).

Exercises

4.1 **(Partition LP formulation for spanning trees.)** Consider the following partition LP for the minimum spanning tree problem. Let $\pi = \{V_1, \ldots, V_l\}$ be a partition of the vertex set V, and let $|\pi| = l$ denote the *size* of the partition. Define $\Delta(\pi)$ to be the set of edges with endpoints in different sets in the partition π. In any spanning tree, there are at least $|\pi| - 1$ edges in $\Delta(\pi)$ for a partition π of V. Note that the undirected LP is a special case where only partitions of size two are considered. Show that the partition LP is equivalent to the subtour LP.

$$\text{minimize} \qquad \sum_{e \in E} c_e x_e$$

$$\text{subject to} \qquad x(\Delta(\pi)) \geq |\pi| - 1 \qquad \text{for all partitions } \pi \text{ of } V$$

$$x(E(V)) = |V| - 1$$

$$x_e \geq 0 \qquad \qquad \forall\, e \in E$$

4.2 Let $\tau = \{S \subseteq V : x(E(S)) = |S| - 1\}$ where x is an extreme point solution to the spanning tree polyhedron. Solving the linear program using the ellipsoid method enables us to get a set family $\mathcal{F} \subseteq \tau$ such that constraints for sets in $\mathcal{F}$ are linearly independent and span all the tight constraints in τ. But $\mathcal{F}$ need not be laminar. Give a polynomial time algorithm that, given $\mathcal{F}$, returns a laminar family $\mathcal{L} \subseteq \tau$ such that constraints for sets in $\mathcal{L}$ are independent and span all the tight constraints in τ.

4.3 **(Spanning tree formulations.)** Another interesting formulation for the minimum spanning tree problem is the bidirected LP, which models the problem as finding a spanning arborescence (i.e., a directed spanning tree). Given a directed graph D and a *root vertex r*, a *spanning r-arborescence* is a subgraph of D so that there is a directed path from r to every vertex in $V - r$. Given an undirected graph G, we construct a directed graph D by having two opposite arcs (u, v) and (v, u) for each undirected edge uv in G, and the cost of (u, v) and (v, u) in D are the same as the cost of uv in G. Then, pick an arbitrary vertex r as the root vertex, and require that there is a directed path from r to every vertex in $V - r$. Or equivalently, by Menger's theorem, require that there is at least one arc entering every set which does not contain the root vertex. The bidirected LP formulation for the minimum spanning tree problem is shown as follows.

$$\text{minimize} \qquad \sum_{a \in A} c_a x_a$$

$$\text{subject to} \qquad x(\delta^{in}(S)) \geq 1 \qquad \forall\, S \subseteq V - r$$

$$x_a \geq 0 \qquad \qquad \forall\, a \in A$$

It is not clear a priori whether the different spanning tree formulations are exact (i.e., give integer solutions at all extreme points) or not. (For example, consider the bidirected LP, which looks almost the same as the undirected LP.) Also, it is not clear whether they can be solved in polynomial time. The following exercises show that these three formulations are equivalent.

(a) Suppose all edge weights are positive. Then show that the partition LP, the subtour LP, and the bidirected LP are equivalent. That is, any solution of one can be translated into a solution of the other with the same cost.

(b) Using the preceding result, provide separation oracles for these formulations and show that there is a polynomial time separation oracle for the partition LP, the subtour LP, and the bidirected LP.

4.4 Argue that in the iterative relaxation algorithm in Figure 4.7, one only needs to compute an optimal extreme point solution once initially, after that one can modify the current solution to obtain an extreme point solution for the next iteration in a simple way. (*Hint*: After we relax a degree constraint, we only need to find another extreme point solution with cost *no more* than the original solution, and the current solution is an "almost" extreme point solution for the next iteration.)

4.5 (Ghodsi et al. [63]) In an instance of the minimum bounded weighted-degree spanning tree we are given a graph $G = (V, E)$ and cost function $c : E \to \mathbb{R}^+$, a weight function $w : E \to \mathbb{R}^+$, a degree bound B_v on each vertex v, and the task is to find a spanning tree T with minimum cost and $\sum_{e \in \delta_T(v)} w(e) \le B_v$ for all $v \in V$. Give a good bicriteria approximation algorithm for the problem.

4.6 Can you generalize the result in the previous problem to get good bicriteria approximation algorithm for the minimum bounded weighted-degree Steiner tree problem? Why or why not?

4.7 (Chan et al. [25]) Consider the minimum bounded degree spanning tree problem when the cost function $c : E \to \mathbb{Z}$ satisfies triangle inequalities (i.e., $c(uv) + c(vw) \ge c(uw)$ for all $u, v, w \in V$). Given a spanning tree T, denoted by $d_T(v)$ the degree of a vertex v in T and B_v the degree bound for v. Using a minimum-cost flow technique, Fekete et al. [41] showed that the cost of a tree satisfying all degree bounds is at most the cost of T times

$$2 - \min\{\frac{B_v - 2}{d_T(v) - 2} : v \in V, d_T(v) > 2\}.$$

Use this result and Theorem 4.3.1 to prove that there is a $(1 + \frac{1}{B-1})$-approximation algorithm for finding a minimum cost spanning tree with maximum degree B.

5

Matroids

In this chapter, we will study matroids, a combinatorial abstraction, which generalizes spanning trees and a host of other combinatorial structures. After introducing matroids and stating some basic properties, we address the two most important polynomial-time solvable problems in this formalism – finding a maximum weight basis and finding a maximum weight common independent set of two matroids (the so-called two-matroid intersection problem)–and show integral characterizations using an iterative proof. We then consider the duals of these problems and prove a min–max theorem on matroid intersection.

We extend the method developed for the exact characterizations to two NP-hard matroid optimization problems. First, we define a degree-bounded version of the minimum cost basis problem for matroids and adapt our iterative proof method to supply additive approximation algorithms. Then, extending the proof for the two matroid intersection problem, we present a $(k-1)$-approximation algorithm for the unweighted k matroid intersection problem: finding a maximum cardinality common independent set in k matroids defined on the same ground set.

5.1 Preliminaries

Definition 5.1.1 *A pair* $\mathcal{M} = (S, \mathcal{I})$ *is a matroid if* $\mathcal{I}$ *is a* nonempty *collection of subsets of S with the following properties.*

(i) $\emptyset \in \mathcal{I}$.
(ii) $A \in \mathcal{I}$ *and* $B \subseteq A \implies B \in \mathcal{I}$.
(iii) $A, B \in \mathcal{I}$ *and* $|B| > |A| \implies \exists x \in B \setminus A$ *such that* $A \cup \{x\} \in \mathcal{I}$.

S is called the *ground set* of the matroid M. A set $A \subseteq S$ is called *independent* if $A \in \mathcal{I}$ else it is called *dependent*. A maximal set $A \in \mathcal{I}$ is called a *basis* of M. Observe that Property 5.1.1 implies that all bases have the the same cardinality.

65

Examples of Matroids

(i) **Graphic Matroid:** Given an undirected graph $G = (V, E)$, the graphic matroid of G is defined as $\mathcal{M}_G = (E, \mathcal{I}_G)$, where $\mathcal{I}_G = \{F \subseteq E \mid F$ contains no cycles$\}$.

(ii) **Uniform Matroid:** Given a set S and an integer $k \geq 0$, the uniform matroid of rank k is defined as $\mathcal{M}_S^k = (S, \mathcal{I}^k)$, where $\mathcal{I}^k = \{T \subseteq S : |T| \leq k\}$.

(iii) **Partition Matroid:** Given a set $S = \uplus_{i=1}^k S_i$ ($\uplus$ is the operation of disjoint union) and integers $n_1, \ldots, n_k \geq 0$, the partition matroid is defined as $\mathcal{M} = (S, \mathcal{I})$ where $\mathcal{I} = \{\uplus_{i=1}^k T_i \subseteq S_i : |T_i| \leq n_i\}$.

(iv) **Linear Matroid:** Let A be an $m \times n$ matrix and $S = \{1, \ldots, n\}$. For any $1 \leq i \leq n$, let A^i denote the ith column of A. The linear matroid over matrix A is defined as $\mathcal{M}_A = (S, \mathcal{I}_A)$, where $\mathcal{I}_A = \{T \subseteq S : A^i$ for $i \in T$ are linearly independent$\}$.

(v) **Matroid Restriction:** Let $\mathcal{M} = (S, \mathcal{I})$ be a matroid and $T \subseteq S$. Then the matroid restriction of $\mathcal{M}$ to the set T is the matroid $\mathcal{M}_T = (T, \mathcal{I}_T)$, where $\mathcal{I}_T = \{R : R \in \mathcal{I}, R \subseteq T\}$.

It is quite straightforward to verify that these five examples satisfy the properties of matroids, and we leave it as an exercise for the reader.

Definition 5.1.2 (Rank function) *Given a matroid* $\mathcal{M} = (S, \mathcal{I})$*, the rank function* $r_{\mathcal{M}} : 2^S \to \mathbb{Z}$ *of the matroid* $\mathcal{M}$ *is defined as* $r_{\mathcal{M}}(T) = \max_{U \subseteq T, U \in \mathcal{I}} |U|$.

We will drop the subscript $\mathcal{M}$ from the rank function $r_{\mathcal{M}}$ when the matroid $\mathcal{M}$ is clear from the context. Observe that $A \in \mathcal{I}$ if and only if $r(A) = |A|$. We also have the following important property about rank function of matroids. In the terminology introduced in Chapter 2, the property states that the rank function of matroids is (fully) submodular.

Lemma 5.1.3 *Let r be the rank function of matroid $\mathcal{M} = (S, \mathcal{I})$. Then for all $A, B \subseteq S$, we have $r(A) + r(B) \geq r(A \cap B) + r(A \cup B)$.*

Proof Let $r(A \cap B) = k_1, r(A \cup B) = k_2$. This implies that $\exists V \subseteq A \cap B$ such that $r(V) = |V| = k_1$. Similarly, there exists $U \subseteq A \cup B$ such that $r(U) = |U| = k_2$. Moreover, since every independent set can be extended to a basis, we can assume that $V \subseteq U$. Since U is independent, we have $r(A) \geq |U \cap A|$ and $r(B) \geq |U \cap B|$. Now, we have

$$|U \cap A| + |U \cap B| = |U \cap (A \cup B)| + |U \cap (A \cap B)| \geq |U| + |V|$$

$$\implies r(A) + r(B) \geq r(A \cup B) + r(A \cap B)$$

as desired. $\square$

We now define two important operations on matroids.

Definition 5.1.4 (Deletion) *Given a matroid $\mathcal{M} = (S, \mathcal{I})$ and $x \in S$ we define $M \setminus x = (S \setminus \{x\}, \mathcal{I}')$ where $\mathcal{I}' = \{T \setminus \{x\} : T \in \mathcal{I}\}$ to be the matroid obtained by deleting x from M. The rank function of $M \setminus x$, denoted by r_1, is related to the rank function r of M by the formula $r_1(T) = r(T)$ for $T \subseteq S \setminus \{x\}$.*

Definition 5.1.5 (Contraction) *Given a matroid $\mathcal{M} = (S, \mathcal{I})$ and $x \in S$ we define $M/x = (S \setminus x, \mathcal{I}'')$ as the matroid obtained by contracting x in M where $\mathcal{I}'' = \{T \subseteq S \setminus \{x\} : T \cup \{x\} \in \mathcal{I}\}$ if $\{x\}$ is independent, and $\mathcal{I}'' = \mathcal{I}$ if $\{x\}$ is not independent. The rank function of $M/\{x\}$, denoted by r_2, is related to the rank function of M by the formula $r_2(T) = r(T \cup \{x\}) - r(\{x\})$ for $T \subseteq S \setminus x$.*

Note that if $\{x\}$ is not independent, then $M/x = M \setminus x$.

5.2 Maximum weight basis

We now study the maximum weight basis problem in a matroid and give an integral characterization by an iterative argument. Given a matroid $M = (S, \mathcal{I})$ and a weight function $w : S \to \mathbb{R}$, the task is to find a basis of M of maximum weight. In the special case of graphic matroids in connected graphs, this problem reduces to the maximum weight spanning tree problem. If we set edge costs to be the negative of their weights, this is the same as the minimum cost spanning tree problem we studied in Chapter 4.

5.2.1 Linear programming formulation

We begin by giving a linear programming formulation for the problem. Let x_e denote the indicator variable for element e, with the intent that $x_e = 1$ if e is in the solution and 0 otherwise. We obtain the following linear programming relaxation $LP_{mat}(M)$ after relaxing the integrality constraints on the variables x. In the following we use the shorthand $x(T)$ to denote $\sum_{e \in T} x_e$ for any subset T of the ground set S.

$$\text{maximize} \quad \sum_{e \in S} w_e x_e$$

$$\text{subject to} \quad x(S) = r(S)$$

$$x(T) \le r(T) \qquad \forall T \subseteq S$$

$$x_e \ge 0 \qquad \forall e \in S$$

Solving the linear program. Observe that this linear program is exponential in size and hence, an efficient separation routine is needed to separate over

these constraints. The separation routine needs to check that $x(T) \leq r(T)$ for
each $T \subseteq S$. Cunningham [31] provided such a separation routine which as an
input uses the independence oracle for matroid $\mathcal{M}$. Since the rank function of a
matroid is a submodular function, one can also uses an algorithm for minimizing
submodular function [121] to separate over these constraints.

5.2.2 Characterization of extreme point solutions

We now give a characterization of extreme point solutions of the linear program
$LP_{mat}(M)$ by showing that the linearly independent set of tight constraints
associated with it can be chosen to form a special structure.

Definition 5.2.1 (Chain) *A subset $\mathcal{L} \subseteq 2^S$ is a chain if $A \in \mathcal{L}, B \in \mathcal{L}$, then
$A \subseteq B$ or $B \subseteq A$.*

We will use an uncrossing argument to show that the linearly independent
set of tight constraints can be chosen to form a chain. Given an extreme point
solution x to $LP_{mat}(M)$, let $\mathcal{F} = \{T \subseteq S : x(T) = r(T)\}$ be the set of tight
constraints. For a set $T \subseteq S$, let $\chi(T)$ denote the characteristic vector in $\mathbb{R}^{|S|}$
that has a 1 corresponding to each element $e \in T$ and 0 otherwise. We first show
that $\mathcal{F}$ is closed under intersection and union.

Lemma 5.2.2 *If $U, V \in \mathcal{F}$, then both $U \cap V$ and $U \cup V$ are in $\mathcal{F}$. Furthermore,
$\chi(U) + \chi(V) = \chi(U \cap V) + \chi(U \cup V)$.*

Proof

$$r(U) + r(V) = x(U) + x(V)$$
$$= x(U \cap V) + x(U \cup V)$$
$$\leq r(U \cap V) + r(U \cup V)$$
$$\leq r(U) + r(V)$$

The first equality is by the fact that $U, V \in \mathcal{F}$. The second equality follows
from basic set properties. The third inequality follows from the constraints in
the matroid basis $LP_{mat}(M)$. The last equality is because of the submodularity
of the rank function r as shown in Lemma 5.1.3. Moreover, $\chi(U) + \chi(V) =
\chi(U \cap V) + \chi(U \cup V)$ follows from basic set properties.   □

Lemma 5.2.3 *If $\mathcal{L}$ is a maximal chain subfamily of $\mathcal{F}$, then $span(\mathcal{L}) =
span(\mathcal{F})$.*

Proof The proof follows exactly the same argument as in Lemma 4.1.5. We show exactly where the argument differs and why we obtain a chain in this case while we could only argue a laminar structure in Lemma 4.1.5. Lemma 5.2.2 shows that two tight sets A and B can always be uncrossed, not only when A and B intersect as was the case in Lemma 4.1.4. Hence, even if A, B are two tight sets and $A \cap B = \emptyset$, we can uncross them and ensure that no such two sets exist among the constraints defining x. □

Observe that for the spanning tree formulation in Section 4.1, we obtained a laminar family characterizing the extreme point solution in Lemma 4.1.5. For the matroid basis problem, which is a generalization of spanning tree problem, Lemma 5.2.3 implies that the extreme point can be characterized by the chain, which is a simpler structure than a general laminar family. This discrepancy can be explained by the formulation that we chose for the spanning tree problem. Indeed, applying uncrossing on the partition LP does give a characterization such that the extreme point is characterized by a chain, albeit over the edges and not the vertices of the graph (see exercises).

The following lemma follows from Lemma 5.2.3 and the Rank Lemma.

Lemma 5.2.4 *Let x be any extreme point solution to $LP_{mat}(M)$ with $x_e > 0$ for each element $e \in S$. Then there exists a chain $\mathcal{L}$ such that*

(i) $x(T) = r(T)$ *for each* $T \subseteq \mathcal{L}$.
(ii) *The vectors in* $\{\chi(T) : T \in \mathcal{L}\}$ *are linearly independent.*
(iii) $|\mathcal{L}| = |S|$.

5.2.3 Iterative algorithm

We now give an iterative algorithm that constructs an integral solution from the linear program and shows that the linear programming formulation is integral. The algorithm is shown in Figure 5.1.

5.2.4 Correctness and optimality

First, we prove that the algorithm will terminate in the following lemma.

Lemma 5.2.5 *For any extreme point solution x to $LP_{mat}(M)$ with $x_e > 0$ for every element e, there exists an element e with $x_e = 1$.*

Proof We present two proofs for this lemma.

(Global Counting Argument.) Suppose for a contradiction, $0 < x_e < 1$ for each $e \in S$. Then the number of variables is exactly $|S|$. Since there is no element e with $x_e = 0$, every tight inequality is of the form $x(T) = r(T)$.

Iterative Maximum Weight Matroid Basis Algorithm

(i) Initialization $B \leftarrow \emptyset$.

(ii) While B is not a basis do

    (a) Find an optimal extreme point solution x to $LP_{mat}(M)$ and delete every element e with $x_e = 0$ from $\mathcal{M}$, i.e., $M \leftarrow M \setminus e$.

    (b) If there is an element e such that $x_e = 1$, then update $B \leftarrow B \cup \{e\}$ and set $M \leftarrow M/e$.

(iii) Return B.

Figure 5.1 Maximum weight matroid basis algorithm.

By Lemma 5.2.4, there are $|\mathcal{L}|$ linearly independent tight constraints of the form $x(T) = r(T)$ where $\mathcal{L}$ is a chain. Since there is no integral x_e, there is no singleton element in the chain. Thus, every pair of consecutive sets in the chain differ by at least two elements, so $|\mathcal{L}| \leq |S|/2$ which is a contradiction.

(Local Fractional Token Argument.) As in the case of spanning trees, there is a fractional token argument that can be generalized to the degree bounded case. For each $e \in S$, assign one token and distribute x_e fraction of it to the smallest set T in the chain of tight constraints containing it. For every tight set T with child C, the set of fractional tokens assigned to it is $x(T) - x(C) = r(T) - r(C)$, which cannot be zero (due to linear independence of this pair), and hence is at least one. The remaining $(1 - x_e)$ tokens for any element e gives the desired contradiction. $\square$

Next we show that the returned solution is a maximum weight basis, which is proved in the following theorem.

Theorem 5.2.6 *The iterative matroid basis algorithm returns a maximum weight basis in polynomial time.*

Proof This is proved by induction on the number of iterations of the algorithm. The base case is trivial to verify. Let $M = (S, \mathcal{I})$ denote the matroid in the current iteration. If the algorithm finds an element e with $x_e = 0$, we update the matroid to $M \setminus e$. Observe that x restricted to $S \setminus \{e\}$, say x', is a feasible solution to $LP_{mat}(M \setminus e)$. This is easily checked using the rank function of $M \setminus e$, which is identical to the rank function of M on the sets not containing e. By induction, we find a basis B of $M \setminus e$ of weight at least $w \cdot x'$. Observe that B is also a basis of M and costs at least $w \cdot x' = w \cdot x$. Hence, the induction claim is true in this case.

Now, suppose the algorithm selects an element e with $x_e = 1$. Then the algorithm updates the matroid M to M/e and B to $B \cup \{e\}$. Let r denote the rank function of M and r' denote the rank function of M/e. We now claim that x restricted to $S \setminus \{e\}$, say x', is a feasible solution to $LP_{mat}(M/e)$. For any set $T \subseteq S \setminus \{x\}$, we have $x'(T) = x(T \cup \{e\}) - x_e = x(T \cup \{e\}) - 1 \leq r(T \cup \{e\}) - 1 = r'(T)$. By the induction hypothesis, we obtain a basis B' of M/e of weight at least $w \cdot x'$. Then $B' \cup \{e\}$ is a basis of M of weight at least $w \cdot x' + w_e = w \cdot x$ as required. This shows that the algorithm returns a maximum weight integral basis of the matroid M. □

This also shows that the $LP_{mat}(M)$ is an exact formulation of the maximum weight basis problem.

Theorem 5.2.7 *The extreme point solutions of* $LP_{mat}(M)$ *are bases of matroid* M.

5.3 Matroid intersection

Given matroids $M_1 = (S, \mathcal{I}_1)$ and $M_2 = (S, \mathcal{I}_2)$ and a weight function $w : S \rightarrow \mathbb{R}$, the maximum weight two matroid intersection problem is to find a set $T \subseteq S$ of maximum weight, which is independent in both M_1 and M_2 (i.e, T is a maximizer of $\max_{T \subseteq S, T \in \mathcal{I}_1 \cap \mathcal{I}_2} w(T) = \sum_{e \in T} w_e$). This problem generalizes many important problems, including the maximum weight matching in bipartite graphs (Chapter 3) and maximum weight arborescence problem (Chapter 6).
Examples of Matroid Intersection

(i) **Matchings in Bipartite Graph:** Given a bipartite graph $G = (A \cup B, E)$, let $M_A = (E, \mathcal{I}_1)$ be a partition matroid on E where $\mathcal{I}_1 = \{F \subseteq E \mid d_F(v) \leq 1 \ \forall v \in A\}$. Similarly, let $M_B = (E, \mathcal{I}_2)$ be a partition matroid on E where $\mathcal{I}_2 = \{F \subseteq E \mid d_F(v) \leq 1 \ \forall v \in B\}$. Observe that $T \in \mathcal{I}_1 \cap \mathcal{I}_2$ if and only if T is a matching in G. Hence, finding a maximum weight matching in G is equivalent to finding a maximum weight independent set in the intersection of matroids M_A and M_B.

(ii) **Arborescence:** Given a directed graph $G = (D, A)$ with root r, let $M_1 = (A, \mathcal{I}_1)$ be the graphic matroid on the underlying undirected graph of G (where we ignore arc directions). Let $M_2 = (A, \mathcal{I}_2)$ be the partition matroid where $\mathcal{I}_2 = \{B \subseteq A : d_B^{in}(v) \leq 1 \ \forall v \in D \setminus \{r\}$ and $d_B^{in}(r) = 0\}$. Observe that B is a common basis in $\mathcal{I}_1$ and $\mathcal{I}_2$ if and only if B is an arborescence rooted at r.

We now show that an efficient procedure for the maximum weight basis in the intersection of two matroids. In contrast, the matroid intersection problem for three or more matroids is NP-hard in general.

5.3.1 Linear programming relaxation

We now give a linear programming formulation for finding a maximum weight common independent set in the intersection of two matroids and then give an iterative argument to show that it is integral. Let x_e denote the indicator variable for element, with $x_e = 1$ if e is in the common independent set and 0 otherwise. We obtain the following linear programming relaxation $LP_{int}(M_1, M_2)$ after relaxing the integrality constraints on the variables x. Here $r_i(T)$ denotes the rank of the set T in the matroid M_i.

$$\text{maximize} \quad \sum_{e \in S} w_e x_e$$

$$\text{subject to} \quad x(T) \le r_1(T) \qquad \forall T \subseteq S$$

$$x(T) \le r_2(T) \qquad \forall T \subseteq S$$

$$x_e \ge 0 \qquad \forall e \in S$$

Solving the linear program To get a separation oracle for minimum weight matroid basis problem, it suffices to separate over the inequalities in $LP_{int}(M_1, M_2)$. This can be done if we are given as input independence oracles for each of the matroids M_1 and M_2, by using the work of Cunningham [31] as before, or any algorithm for minimizing submodular functions.

5.3.2 Characterization of extreme point solutions

We now give a characterization of extreme points of the linear program $LP_{int}(M_1, M_2)$ by showing that the independent set of tight constraints can be chosen to form a union of two chains. The proof is quite straightforward and uses the characterization of tight inequalities for the matroid basis problem.

Given an extreme point solution x to $LP_{int}(M_1, M_2)$ let $\mathcal{F}_1 = \{T \subseteq S : x(T) = r_1(T)\}$ and $\mathcal{F}_2 = \{T \subseteq S : x(T) = r_2(T)\}$ be the set of tight constraints.

Lemma 5.3.1 *There exist two chains C_1 and C_2 such that $span(C_1 \cup C_2) = span(\mathcal{F}_1 \cup \mathcal{F}_2)$ and constraints in sets C_1 and C_2 are linearly independent.*

Proof Applying Lemma 5.2.3 to families $\mathcal{F}_1$ and $\mathcal{F}_2$ separately, we obtain two chains C_1' and C_2' such that $span(C_1') = span(\mathcal{F}_1)$ and $span(C_2') = span(\mathcal{F}_2)$.

Iterative Matroid Intersection Algorithm

(i) Initialization $I \leftarrow \emptyset$.

(ii) While $S \neq \emptyset$ do

    (a) Find an optimal extreme point solution x to $LP_{int}(M_1, M_2)$ and delete every element e with $x_e = 0$ from M_1 and M_2 (i.e., $M_1 \leftarrow M_1 \setminus e$ and $M_2 \leftarrow M_2 \setminus e$).

    (b) If there is an element e such that $x_e = 1$ then and update $I \leftarrow I \cup \{e\}$, $M_1 \leftarrow M_1/e$ and $M_2 \leftarrow M_2/e$.

(iii) Return I.

Figure 5.2 Matroid intersection algorithm.

Now, picking a maximal independent family from $\mathcal{C}_1' \cup \mathcal{C}_2'$ gives us the desired chains. $\qquad \square$

The following lemma follows from Lemma 5.3.1 and the Rank Lemma.

Lemma 5.3.2 *Let x be any extreme point solution to $LP_{int}(M_1, M_2)$ with $x_e > 0$ for each element $e \in S$. Then there exist two chains $\mathcal{C}_1$ and $\mathcal{C}_2$ such that*

(i) $x(T) = r_i(T)$ *for each $T \subseteq \mathcal{C}_i$ for $i = \{1, 2\}$.*

(ii) *The vectors in $\{\chi(T) : T \in \mathcal{C}_1\} \cup \{\chi(T) : T \in \mathcal{C}_2\}$ are linearly independent.*

(iii) $|\mathcal{C}_1| + |\mathcal{C}_2| = |S|$.

5.3.3 Iterative algorithm

We now give an iterative algorithm, which constructs an integral solution from the linear program and shows that the linear programming formulation is integral. The algorithm is shown in Figure 5.2.

5.3.4 Correctness and optimality

First, we prove that the algorithm will terminate in the following lemma.

Lemma 5.3.3 *For any extreme point solution x to $LP_{int}(M_1, M_2)$ with $x_e > 0$ for every element e, there exists an element e with $x_e = 1$.*

Proof Suppose for a contradiction $0 < x_e < 1$ for each $e \in S$. Then the number of variables is exactly $|S|$. Since there is no element e with $x_e = 0$, every tight inequality is of the form $x(T) = r_1(T)$ or $x(T) = r_2(T)$ for some $T \subseteq S$. By Lemma 5.3.2, we obtain two chains $\mathcal{C}_1$ and $\mathcal{C}_2$ defining x. We now show a contradiction to the fact that $|S| = |\mathcal{C}_1| + |\mathcal{C}_2|$ by a counting argument.

We give two tokens to each element in S for a total of $2|S|$ tokens. Now, we collect two tokens for each member of $\mathcal{C}_1$ and $\mathcal{C}_2$ and an extra token showing the contradiction. This is done as follows. Each element e assigns one token to the smallest set $T_1 \in \mathcal{C}_1$ such that $e \in T_1$ and the other token to the smallest set $T_2 \in \mathcal{C}_2$ such that $e \in T_2$. We now claim that each set in $\mathcal{C}_1 \cup \mathcal{C}_2$ obtains at least two tokens.

The argument is identical for sets in $\mathcal{C}_1$ and $\mathcal{C}_2$. Let $T \in \mathcal{C}_1$ and R be the largest set in $\mathcal{C}_1$ such that $R \subseteq T$. Now, we have $x(T) = r_1(T)$ and $x(R) = r_1(R)$. Subtracting, we obtain $x(T \setminus R) = r_1(T) - r_1(R)$. If $T \setminus R = \emptyset$, then $T = R$, and we have a contradiction to the linear independence of the constraints. Also, since $x(T \setminus R)$ is an integer and $0 < x_e < 1$ for all e, we have that $|T \setminus R| \geq 2$. Thus, T receives one token for each element in $T \setminus R$ for a total of at least two tokens. Therefore, every set in $\mathcal{C}_1 \cup \mathcal{C}_2$ receives at least two tokens. Now, we show that there is at least one extra token. Observe that $S \in \mathcal{C}_1$ or $S \in \mathcal{C}_2$ but not both; say it is in $\mathcal{C}_1$. Hence, there exists an e such that e is not contained in any set in $\mathcal{C}_2$. Hence, one token for e has not been used in the counting argument, giving us the desired extra token for the contradiction. $\square$

It remains to check that the returned solution is optimal. The proof of the following theorem is straightforward and follows from an argument identical to that for Theorem 5.2.6 (and is not duplicated).

Theorem 5.3.4 *The iterative matroid intersection algorithm returns a maximum weight set independent in the intersection of both matroids.*

This also shows that the $LP_{int}(M_1, M_2)$ is an exact formulation of the maximum weight matroid intersection problem.

Theorem 5.3.5 *The extreme point solutions of $LP_{int}(M_1, M_2)$ correspond to independent sets in the intersection of M_1 and M_2.*

5.4 Duality and min–max theorem

In this section, we consider the dual problems of maximum weight basis and maximum weight matroid intersection and show their integrality; we also prove a min–max theorem for matroid intersection. The former results rely on integrality results about covering linear programs where the constraint matrices are network matrices (Chapter 8).

5.4.1 Dual of maximum weight basis

We first consider the dual linear program of the maximum weight basis problem and argue its integrality. The following linear program, which we call

$LP_{dmat}(M)$, is the dual linear program to $LP_{mat}(M)$. We use $y(T)$ to denote the dual variable for a subset T, and we assume that the weights w_e are nonnegative integers.

$$\text{minimize} \quad \sum_{T \subseteq S} r(T)y(T)$$

$$\text{subject to} \quad \sum_{T:e \in T} y(T) \geq w_e \qquad \forall e \in S$$

$$y(T) \geq 0 \qquad \forall T \subseteq S$$

The uncrossing technique can be used to prove the following claim.

Claim 5.4.1 *There is an optimal solution y to $LP_{dmat}(M)$ with the set $\mathcal{C} = \{T \subseteq S : y(T) > 0\}$ being a chain of S.*

Proof Pick an optimal solution that minimizes the number of pairs of sets that are either intersecting or disjoint in the support. We will prove that this number is zero, and this would imply the claim. Suppose for a contradiction that this number is not zero and A and B are such a pair with $\min\{y(A), y(B)\} = \epsilon$. Consider the alternate solution y' with $y'(A) \leftarrow y(A) - \epsilon, y'(B) \leftarrow y(B) - \epsilon, y'(A \cup B) \leftarrow y(A \cup B) + \epsilon$, and $y'(A \cap B) \leftarrow y(A \cap B) + \epsilon$, with $y'(S) \leftarrow y(S)$ for all other sets S. It is easy to see that y' is also a feasible solution to $LP_{dmat}(M)$. Also, by the submodularity of the rank function (Lemma 5.1.3), we have

$$\epsilon(r(A) + r(B)) \geq \epsilon(r(A \cup B) + r(A \cap B)),$$

and thus the objective function value does not increase. Finally, the new solution can easily be checked to have fewer pairs that are disjoint or intersecting in the support, giving the contradiction and finishing the proof. □

Claim 5.4.1 implies that the following restricted linear program, denoted by $LP_{rdmat}(M)$, has the same objective value as $LP_{dmat}(M)$.

$$\text{minimize} \quad \sum_{T \in \mathcal{C}} r(T)y(T)$$

$$\text{subject to} \quad \sum_{T \in \mathcal{C}:e \in T} y(T) \geq w_e \qquad \forall e \in S$$

$$y(T) \geq 0 \qquad \forall T \in \mathcal{C}$$

As $\mathcal{C}$ is a chain, one can show that the constrained matrix of $LP_{rdmat}(M)$ is a *network matrix*: (see Section 8.4.1 in Chapter 8). Then, by the results on LP's with network matrix constraints (Theorem 8.1.1), it follows that $LP_{rdmat}(M)$ is integral. Since we have shown that $LP_{dmat}(M)$ always has integral optimal solutions, we also get the following result.

Theorem 5.4.2 *The linear programming formulation $LP_{dmat}(M)$ is integral.*

5.4.2 Dual of two matroid intersection

Next we prove the integrality of the dual linear program of matroid intersection and obtain a min–max theorem on matroid intersection. The following linear program, denoted by $LP_{dint}(M_1, M_2)$, is the dual linear program to $LP_{int}(M_1, M_2)$ in Section 5.3.

$$\text{minimize} \qquad \sum_{T \subseteq S} r_1(T) y_1(T) + r_2(T) y_2(T)$$

$$\text{subject to} \qquad \sum_{T : e \in T} \big(y_1(T) + y_2(T) \big) \geq w_e \quad \forall e \in S$$

$$y_i(T) \geq 0 \qquad \forall T \subseteq S, 1 \leq i \leq 2$$

The following claim follows by the same uncrossing argument as in Claim 5.4.1.

Claim 5.4.3 *There is an optimal solution y to $LP_{dint}(M_1, M_2)$ where the sets $\mathcal{C}_1 = \{T \subseteq S : y_1(T) > 0\}$ and $\mathcal{C}_2 = \{T \subseteq S : y_2(T) > 0\}$ are both chains of S.*

As in the case of the dual of maximum weight basis, Claim 5.4.3 implies that the following restricted linear program, denoted by $LP_{rdint}(M_1, M_2)$, has the same objective value as $LP_{dint}(M_1, M_2)$.

$$\text{minimize} \qquad \sum_{T \in \mathcal{C}_1} r_1(T) y_1(T) + \sum_{T \in \mathcal{C}_2} r_2(T) y_2(T)$$

$$\text{subject to} \qquad \sum_{T \in \mathcal{C}_1 : e \in T} y_1(T) + \sum_{T \in \mathcal{C}_2 : e \in T} y_2(T) \geq w_e \quad \forall e \in S$$

$$y_i(T) \geq 0 \qquad \forall T \in \mathcal{C}_i, 1 \leq i \leq 2$$

As $\mathcal{C}_1$ and $\mathcal{C}_2$ are chains, one can show that the constrained matrix of $LP_{rdint}(M_1, M_2)$ is a network matrix (see Section 8.4.2 in Chapter 8). Then, by the result on network matrix (Theorem 8.1.1), it follows that $LP_{rdint}(M_1, M_2)$ is integral. As before, since we have shown that $LP_{dint}(M)$ always has integral optimal solutions, we also get the following result.

Theorem 5.4.4 *The linear programming formulation $LP_{dint}(M_1, M_2)$ is integral.*

Using Theorem 5.3.5 and Theorem 5.4.4, we can obtain the following min–max theorem on the maximum cardinality of a common independent set in two matroids M_1 and M_2.

Theorem 5.4.5 *Given matroids $M_1 = (S, \mathcal{I}_1)$ and $M_2 = (S, \mathcal{I}_2)$ with rank functions r_1 and r_2, respectively, the size of a maximum common independent set in $\mathcal{I}_1$ and $\mathcal{I}_2$ is given by*

$$\max_{I \in \mathcal{I}_1 \cap \mathcal{I}_2} |I| = \min_{T \subseteq S} (r_1(T) + r_2(S \setminus T)).$$

Proof The problem of finding a maximum cardinality common independent set is a special case of the maximum weight two matroid intersection problem when $w_e = 1$ for all $e \in S$. By the strong duality theorem of linear programming (Theorem 2.1.9), the objective value of $LP_{int}(M_1, M_2)$ is the same as the objective value of $LP_{dint}(M_1, M_2)$. For the primal program $LP_{int}(M_1, M_2)$, observe that $x_e \le r(\{e\}) \le 1$ since r is the rank function of a matroid. By Theorem 5.3.5, $LP_{int}(M_1, M_2)$ is integral and hence there is an optimal solution with $x_e \in \{0, 1\}$, and thus the optimum value of $LP_{int}(M_1, M_2) = \max_{I \in \mathcal{I}_1 \cap \mathcal{I}_2} |I|$.

For the dual program $LP_{dint}(M_1, M_2)$, since $w_e = 1$ for all $e \in S$ and $r_i(T) \ge 0$ for all $T \subseteq S$, we can assume that $y_i(T) \le 1$ for all $T \subseteq S$. By Theorem 5.4.4, $LP_{dint}(M_1, M_2)$ is integral and hence there is an optimal solution with $y_i(T) \in \{0, 1\}$ for all $T \subseteq S$ and $i = \{1, 2\}$. By Claim 5.4.3, we can assume that the set $\mathcal{C}_1 = \{T \subseteq S : y_1(T) = 1\}$ is a chain. Furthermore, since $w_e = 1$ for all $e \in S$ and $r_i(T) \ge 0$ for all $T \subseteq S$, we can assume that there is only one set T with $y_1(T) = 1$, with T being the largest set in the chain $\mathcal{C}_1$. Similarly, we can assume that there is only one set T' with $y_2(T') = 1$. Since $w_e = 1$ for all $e \in S$ and y is a feasible solution to $LP_{dint}(M_1, M_2)$, we must have $T \cup T' = S$. As the rank function r of a matroid is a monotone function, we can further assume that $T' = S \setminus T$, and thus there is an optimal solution to $LP_{dint}(M_1, M_2)$ with objective value $r_1(T) + r_2(S \setminus T)$ for some $T \subseteq S$, proving the theorem. $\square$

5.5 Minimum bounded degree matroid basis

In this section, we consider the minimum bounded degree matroid basis problem, a generalization of the minimum bounded degree spanning tree problem. We are given a matroid $M = (S, \mathcal{I})$, a cost function c on the ground set S, a hypergraph $H = (S, E)$ on the same ground set, and an upper bound $g(e)$ for each hyperedge $e \in E(H)$. The task is to find a basis B of minimum cost such that $|B \cap e| \leq g(e)$ for each hyperedge $e \in E(H)$.

One motivation for considering the matroid generalization was the following problem posed by Frieze [47]: "Given a binary matroid M_A over the columns of a 0, 1-matrix A and bounds g_i for each row i of A, find a basis B of matroid M_A such that there are at most g_i ones in row i (for all rows i) among the columns in B." The main result of this section is the following theorem.

Theorem 5.5.1 *There is a polynomial time algorithm for the minimum bounded degree matroid basis problem which returns a basis B of cost at most* OPT *such that $|B \cap e| \leq g(e) + \Delta - 1$ for each $e \in E(H)$. Here $\Delta = \max_{v \in S} |\{e \in E(H) : v \in e\}|$ is the maximum degree of the hypergraph H, and* OPT *is the cost of an optimal solution that satisfies all the degree constraints.*

When the hyperedges in H are disjoint, the maximum degree Δ is 1, and the above theorem gives an optimal result. Note that this also follows from the matroid intersection theorem: When the hyperedges induce disjoint sets of the ground set, they define a partition matroid, and the solution we find is a minimum cost common basis of the original matroid and this partition matroid. We mention more applications of Theorem 5.5.1 to approximation algorithms in the last part of this section.

5.5.1 Linear programming relaxation

Let $r : 2^S \rightarrow \mathbb{Z}_+$ denote the rank function of matroid M. We have already argued in Lemma 5.1.3 that r is a monotone submodular function. We denote the following relaxation as $LP_{mat}(M, H)$.

$$
\begin{array}{lll}
\text{minimize} & \displaystyle\sum_{v \in S} c_v x_v & \\[2ex]
\text{subject to} & x(S) = r(S) & \\[1ex]
& x(T) \leq r(T) & \forall T \subseteq S \\[1ex]
& x(e) \leq g(e) & \forall e \in E(H) \\[1ex]
& 0 \leq x_v \leq 1 & \forall v \in S
\end{array}
$$

This linear program is exponential in size but can be separated over in polynomial time as before if given access to an independent set oracle for the underlying matroid.

5.5.2 Characterization of extreme point solutions

The following lemma follows from Lemma 5.2.4 and the Rank Lemma.

Lemma 5.5.2 *Let x be any extreme point solution to $LP_{mat}(M,H)$ with $x_e > 0$ for each element $e \in S$. Then there exists a set $R \subseteq E$ and a chain $\mathcal{L}$ such that x is the unique solution to the following linear system.*

(i) $x(T) = r(T)$ *for each $T \in \mathcal{L}$ and $x(e) = g(e)$ for each $e \in R$.*
(ii) *The vectors in $\{\chi(T) : T \in \mathcal{L}\} \cup \{\chi(e) : e \in R\}$ are linearly independent.*
(iii) $|S| = |\mathcal{L}| + |R|$.

5.5.3 Iterative algorithm

The iterative algorithm in Figure 5.3 is similar to that of the minimum bounded degree spanning tree problem in Chapter 4.

5.5.4 Correctness and performance guarantee

The degree constraint is only violated by at most $\Delta - 1$ in Step 2(c) of the algorithm. Theorem 5.5.1 follows by an inductive argument if the algorithm always terminates successfully, which we will prove in the following lemma.

Lemma 5.5.3 *An extreme point solution x to $LP_{mat}(M,H)$ must satisfy one of the following.*

(i) *There is an element v with $x_v = 1$.*
(ii) *There is a hyperedge e such that $|e| \le g(e) + \Delta - 1$.*

Iterative Minimum Bounded Degree Matroid Basis Algorithm

(i) Initialization $B \leftarrow \emptyset$,
(ii) While B is not a basis do
    (a) Find an optimal extreme point solution x to $LP_{mat}(M,H)$. Delete v with $x_v = 0$. Update each edge $e \in E(H)$ with $e \leftarrow e \setminus \{v\}$. Update matroid $M \leftarrow M \setminus v$.
    (b) For each element v with $x_v = 1$, include v in B and decrease $g(e)$ by 1 for each $e \ni v$. Update $M \leftarrow M/v$.
    (c) For every $e \in E(H)$ with $|e| \le g(e) + \Delta - 1$, remove e from $E(H)$.
(iii) Return B.

Figure 5.3 Minimum bounded degree matroid basis algorithm.

Proof The proof is by a local fractional token argument. Each element is initially assigned Δ tokens, for a total of $\Delta \cdot |S|$ tokens. For each element v, $1 - x_v$ token is redistributed to each hyperedge that contains v, and $\Delta \cdot x_v$ token is redistributed to the smallest set $T \in \mathcal{L}$ which contains e. This is possible since each element is contained in at most Δ hyperedges. We shall show that if neither of the above conditions are satisfied, then each set in $\mathcal{L}$ and each hyperedge constraint in R can collect Δ tokens, and there are still some tokens left. This would imply $|S| > |\mathcal{L}| + |R|$, which contradicts to Lemma 5.5.2.

For each hyperedge e in R, it collects

$$\sum_{v \in e}(1 - x_v) = |e| - \sum_{v \in e} x_v = |e| - g(e) \geq \Delta$$

tokens. The second equality follows because e is tight, and the last inequality follows because the second condition in the lemma is not satisfied. This shows that each hyperedge constraint in R can collect at least Δ tokens.

For each $T \in \mathcal{L}$, let $U \in \mathcal{L}$ be its child in the chain $\mathcal{L}$. Then T collects

$$\Delta \cdot (x(T) - x(U)) = \Delta \cdot (r(T) - r(U)) \geq \Delta \cdot 1 = \Delta$$

tokens. The inequality follows because $\chi(T)$ and $\chi(U)$ are linearly independent and r is an integer monotone function. This shows that each set in $\mathcal{L}$ can collect at least Δ tokens.

It remains to show that there are some unused tokens. If some element is not in exactly Δ hyperedges in R or if $S \notin \mathcal{L}$, then there are some tokens left, which contradicts that $|S| = |\mathcal{L}| + |R|$. Otherwise, we have $\Delta \cdot \chi(S) = \sum_{e \in R} \chi(e)$, which contradicts the linear independence of the characteristic vectors of the sets in R and $S \in \mathcal{L}$. In either case, there is a contradiction implying that one of the conditions in the lemma must be satisfied. $\square$

5.5.5 Applications

We highlight some applications of the bounded degree matroid basis result.

Minimum crossing spanning tree

In the minimum crossing spanning tree problem, we are given a graph $G = (V, E)$ with edge cost function c, a collection of cuts (edge subsets) $\mathcal{C} = \{C_1, \ldots, C_m\}$ and bound g_i for each cut C_i. The task is to find a spanning tree T of minimum cost such that T contains at most g_i edges from cut C_i. The minimum bounded degree spanning tree problem is the special case where $\mathcal{C} = \{\delta(v) : v \in V\}$; note that $\Delta = 2$ for the minimum bounded degree spanning tree problem. The following result can be obtained as a corollary of Theorem 5.5.1.

Corollary 5.5.4 *There exists a polynomial time algorithm for the minimum crossing spanning tree problem that returns a tree T with cost at most* OPT, *and such that T contains at most $g_i + d - 1$ edges from cut C_i for each i, where $d = \max_{e \in E} |\{C_i : e \in C_i\}|$ and* OPT *is the cost of an optimal solution which satisfies all the cut degree constraints.*

Proof Let $M = (E, \mathcal{I})$ denote the graphic matroid over the graph G. The hypergraph H is defined with $V(H) = E(G)$ and $E(H) = \{C_i : 1 \le i \le m\}$. Note that $\Delta = \max_{v \in V(H)} |\{e \in E(H) : v \in e\}| = \max_{e \in E(G)} |\{C_i : e \in C_i\}| = d$. So, using Theorem 5.5.1, we obtain a basis T of matroid M (which is a spanning tree), such that $|T \cap C_i| \le g_i + d - 1$. □

Minimum bounded-ones binary matroid basis

For the minimum bounded-ones binary matroid basis problem, we are given a binary matroid M_A over the columns of a $0, 1$-matrix A and bounds g_i for each row i of A. The task is to find a minimum cost basis B of matroid M_A such that there are at most g_i ones in row i (for all rows i) among the columns in B. The following result is obtained as a corollary of Theorem 5.5.1.

Corollary 5.5.5 *There exists a polynomial time algorithm for the minimum bounded-ones binary matroid basis problem that returns a basis B of cost at most* OPT, *such that there are at most $g_i + d - 1$ ones in any row restricted to columns of B. Here d is the maximum number of ones in any column of A, and* OPT *is the cost of an optimal solution satisfying all the row constraints.*

Proof Let $M = M_A$ be a linear matroid and define a hypergraph H where the vertex set is the columns of A. The hyperedges correspond to rows of A where $e_i = \{A^j : A_{ij} = 1\}$ where A^j is the jth column of A. Note that $\Delta = \max_{v \in V(H)} |\{e \in E(H) : v \in e\}| = \max_j |\{i : a_{ij} = 1\}| = d$, which is the maximum number of ones in any column of A. So, using Theorem 5.5.1, we obtain a basis of $M = M_A$ such that number of ones in any row is at most $g_i + d - 1$. □

Minimum bounded degree spanning tree union

In the minimum bounded degree spanning tree union problem, we are given a graph $G = (V, E)$ with edge cost function c, a positive integer k, and a degree upper bound $g(v)$ for each vertex v. The task is to find a subgraph F which is the union of k edge-disjoint spanning trees and the degree of v in F is at most $g(v)$. The minimum bounded degree spanning tree problem is a special case when $k = 1$. Theorem 5.5.1 implies the following result, which is optimal in terms of the degree upper bounds.

Corollary 5.5.6 *There is a polynomial time algorithm for the minimum bounded degree spanning tree union problem, which returns a subgraph F of cost at most* OPT, *which is the union of k edge-disjoint spanning trees, and the degree of v in F is at most $g(v) + 1$. Here* OPT *is the cost of an optimal solution that satisfies all the degree upper bounds.*

Proof Let $M = (E, \mathcal{I})$ denote the union of k graphic matroids over the graph G, which is a matroid by the matroid union theorem (see e.g., [121]). The hypergraph H is defined with $V(H) = E(G)$ and $E(H) = \{\delta(v) : v \in V(G)\}$. Note that $\Delta = \max_{v \in V(H)} |\{e \in E(H) : v \in e\}| = \max_{e \in E(G)} |\{\delta(v) : v \in V(G) \wedge e \in \delta(v)\}| = 2$. So, using Theorem 5.5.1, we obtain a basis F of matroid M (which is the union of k edge-disjoint spanning trees), such that $|F \cap \delta(v)| \le g(v) + 1$. $\qquad\square$

5.6 k matroid intersection

Given k matroids $M_1 = (S, \mathcal{I}_1), M_2 = (S, \mathcal{I}_2), \ldots, M_k = (S, \mathcal{I}_k)$ on the same ground set S, the maximum k matroid intersection problem is to find a set $T \subseteq S$ of maximum cardinality, which is independent in all matroids $M_1, M_2, \ldots, M_k$. This problem is NP-hard already for $k = 3$ (see the exercises). We will present a 2-approximation algorithm for this problem when $k = 3$, and leave the generalization to general k to the exercises.

5.6.1 Linear programming relaxation

The linear programming relaxation, denoted by $LP_{3int}(M_1, M_2, M_3)$, for three-matroid intersection is a natural extension of $LP_{int}(M_1, M_2)$ for two-matroid intersection. Notice that we only consider the unweighted problem where $w_e = 1$ for all $e \in S$.

$$\text{maximize} \quad \sum_{e \in S} x_e$$

$$\text{subject to} \quad x(T) \le r_1(T) \qquad \forall T \subseteq S$$

$$x(T) \le r_2(T) \qquad \forall T \subseteq S$$

$$x(T) \le r_3(T) \qquad \forall T \subseteq S$$

$$x_e \ge 0 \qquad \forall e \in S$$

There is an efficient separation oracle for this exponential-size linear program, as in the case for two-matroid intersection.

5.6.2 Characterization of extreme point solutions

The proof of the following characterization follows the same lines as the proof of Lemma 5.3.2 for two-matroid intersection.

Lemma 5.6.1 *Let x be any extreme point solution to $LP_{3int}(M_1, M_2, M_3)$ with $x_e > 0$ for each element $e \in S$. Then there exist three chains C_1, C_2, C_3 such that*

(i) $x(T) = r_i(T)$ *for each* $T \subseteq C_i$ *for* $i = \{1, 2, 3\}$.
(ii) *The vectors in* $\{\chi(T) : T \in C_1\} \cup \{\chi(T) : T \in C_2\} \cup \{\chi(T) : T \in C_3\}$ *are linearly independent.*
(iii) $|C_1| + |C_2| + |C_3| = |S|$.

5.6.3 Iterative algorithm

The iterative algorithm is similar to that of two-matroid intersection, except that an element e with $x_e \geq \frac{1}{2}$ will be chosen.

5.6.4 Correctness and performance guarantee

We first show that the iterative algorithm makes progress in each iteration. We then show that the algorithm returns a 2-approximate solution assuming it makes progress in each step. The proof of the former claim is similar to the proof of Lemma 5.3.3, while the proof of the later claim uses some basic results in matroid theory.

Lemma 5.6.2 *For any extreme point solution x to $LP_{3int}(M_1, M_2, M_3)$ with $x_e > 0$ for every element e, there exists an element e with $x_e \geq \frac{1}{2}$.*

Proof Suppose for a contradiction $0 < x_e < \frac{1}{2}$ for each $e \in S$. Then the number of variables is exactly $|S|$. By Lemma 5.6.1, we obtain three chains C_1, C_2, C_3 defining x. We now show a contradiction to the fact that $|S| = |C_1| + |C_2| + |C_3|$ by a counting argument.

We give three tokens to each element in S for a total of $3|S|$ tokens. Now, we collect three tokens for each member of C_1, C_2, C_3 and an extra token showing the contradiction. This is done as follows. Each element e assigns one token to the smallest set $T_i \in C_i$ such that $e \in T_i$ for $i = \{1, 2, 3\}$. We now claim that each set in $C_1 \cup C_2 \cup C_3$ obtains at least three tokens.

Iterative Three-Matroid Intersection Algorithm

(i) Initialization $I \leftarrow \emptyset$.

(ii) While $S \neq \emptyset$ do

    (a) Find an optimal extreme point solution x to $LP_{3int}(M_1, M_2, M_3)$.
Delete every element e with $x_e = 0$ from M_1, M_2, M_3 (i.e., $M_1 \leftarrow M_1 \setminus e$ and $M_2 \leftarrow M_2 \setminus e$ and $M_3 \leftarrow M_3 \setminus e$).

    (b) If there is an element e with $x_e \geq \frac{1}{2}$, then update $I \leftarrow I \cup \{e\}$, $M_1 \leftarrow M_1/e$ and $M_2 \leftarrow M_2/e$ and $M_3 \leftarrow M_3/e$.

(iii) Return I.

Figure 5.4   Three-matroid intersection algorithm.

The argument is identical for sets in C_1, C_2, C_3. Let $T \in C_1$ and R be the largest set in C_1 such that $R \subseteq T$. Now, we have $x(T) = r_1(T)$ and $x(R) = r_1(R)$. Subtracting, we obtain $x(T \setminus R) = r_1(T) - r_1(R)$. If $T \setminus R = \emptyset$, then $T = R$, and we have a contradiction to the linear independence of the constraints. Also, since $x(T \setminus R)$ is an integer and $0 < x_e < \frac{1}{2}$ for all e, we have that $|T \setminus R| \geq 3$. Thus, T receives one token for each element in $T \setminus R$ for a total of at least three tokens. Therefore, every set in $C_1 \cup C_2 \cup C_3$ receives at least three tokens. Now, we show that there is at least one extra token. Observe that the whole set S can be in at most one of the three colections C_1, C_2, or C_3, say it is in C_1. Hence, there exists an e such that e is not contained in any set in C_2. Hence, at least one token for e has not been used in the counting argument, giving us the desired extra token for the contradiction.   □

Theorem 5.6.3 *The algorithm in Figure 5.4 returns a 2-approximate solution to the maximum three-matroid intersection problem in polynomial time.*

Proof This is proved by induction on the number of iterations of the algorithm. The case when the algorithm finds an element e with $x_e = 0$ is handled as in the proof of Theorem 5.2.6. We focus on the case when the algorithm selects an element e with $x_e \geq \frac{1}{2}$. In this case, the algorithm updates the matroid M_i to M_i/e and I to $I \cup \{e\}$. Let $w(x)$ be the objective value of the solution x in the current iteration. To prove the performance guarantee, it suffices to prove that there is a feasible solution in the next iteration with objective value at least $w(x) - 2$. Since we add one element to I and the objective value decreases by at most two, by a standard inductive argument we can prove that the returned independent set has size at least half the objective value of $LP_{3int}(M_1, M_2, M_3)$, and thus the theorem follows.

To prove the claim, we need to demonstrate a feasible solution in the next iteration with objective value at least $w(x) - 2$, after we select the element e and update the matroids M_i to M_i/e. Consider the solution x restricted to $S \setminus e$, denoted by x'. Note that x' has objective value $w(x) - x_e$, but it may not be a feasible solution to $LP_{3int}(M_1/e, M_2/e, M_3/e)$, the linear program in the next iteration. In the next paragraph we will show how to modify x' to satisfy all the constraints defined by matroid M_i/e, by decreasing the objective value by at most $1 - x_e$. By performing this modification to each of the three matroids, we will have a feasible solution to $LP_{3int}(M_1/e, M_2/e, M_3/e)$ with objective value at least $w(x) - x_e - 3(1 - x_e) = w(x) - 3 + 2x_e \geq w(x) - 2$ since $x_e \geq \frac{1}{2}$, as desired.

It remains to show how to modify the solution x' to satisfy all the constraints defined by M_i/e, while decreasing the objective value by at most $1 - x_e$. Since x is a feasible solution to $LP_{3int}(M_1, M_2, M_3)$, it is obviously a feasible solution to $LP_{mat}(M_i)$, the independent set polytope of matroid M_i. Since the independent set polytope of a matroid is integral, the solution x can be written as a convex combination of independent sets in M_i (i.e., $x = \sum_{j=1}^{N} \lambda_j \chi(I_j)$ for some N), where $\sum_{j=1}^{N} \lambda_j = 1$ for nonnegative λ_j's and I_j is an independent set of M_i for each j. Assume that $e \notin I_j$ for $1 \leq j \leq N'$ and $e \in I_j$ for $N' < j \leq N$. Then, by definition, $\sum_{j=1}^{N'} \lambda_i = 1 - x_e$. For each $1 \leq j \leq N'$, let $f_j \neq e$ be an element in the unique circuit (if exists) in $I_j \cup \{e\}$. Since $I_j + e - f_j$ is an independent set in M_i, it follows by definition that $I_j - f_j$ is an independent set in M_i/e. Similarly, $I_j - e$ is an independent set in M_i/e for $N' < j \leq N$. Thus,

$$x^* = \lambda_1 \chi(I_1 - f_1) + \cdots + \lambda_{N'} \chi(I_{N'} - f_{N'}) + \lambda_{N'+1} \chi(I_{N'+1} - e)$$
$$+ \cdots + \lambda_N \chi(I_N - e)$$

is a feasible solution to $LP_{mat}(M_i/e)$, since it is a convex combination of independent sets in M_i/e. Furthermore, $w(x^*) \geq w(x') - \sum_{j=1}^{N'} \lambda_i = w(x') - (1 - x_e)$, proving the theorem. $\qquad \square$

5.7 Notes

Matroids were introduced by Whitney in the 1930s and a comprehensive review of related concepts that led to this as well as the rich literature on it is reviewed by Schrijver in his book [121]. The work of Edmonds [37, 38] first showed the polyhedral characterization results we presented in this chapter. The result for the minimum bounded degree matroid basis problem is by Király, Lau, and Singh [80].

Exercises

5.1 Show that the five examples of matroids in Section 5.1 are indeed matroids by verifying the three matroid properties for each of them.

5.2 Verify that the deletion and contraction matroids defined in Section 5.1 are indeed matroids by checking the two properties of matroids for them. Also prove that their rank function is correctly defined. Finally, convince yourself that for any element x of the matroid, if $\{x\}$ is not independent, then $M \setminus x = M/x$.

5.3 Given a matroid $M = (S, \mathcal{I})$ with rank function r, let $M^* = (S, \mathcal{I}^*)$ be the dual matroid where $\mathcal{I}^* = \{I \subseteq S : S \setminus I$ contains a basis of $M\}$.

(a) Show that M^* is a matroid.

(b) Show that the rank r^* of a set T in the dual matroid M^* is given by
$$r^*(T) = |T| - r(S) + r(S \setminus T).$$

5.4 Let $M = (S, \mathcal{I})$ be a matroid with rank function r, and let $T \subseteq S$. Matroid $M_T = (T, \mathcal{I}_T)$ is defined by $\mathcal{I}_T = \{R \cap T : R \in \mathcal{I}\}$.

(a) Show that M_T is a matroid.

(b) What is the rank function r_T of M_T?

5.5 Given two matroid $M_1 = (S, \mathcal{I}_1)$ and matroid $M_2 = (S, \mathcal{I}_2)$, let $M_{12} = (S_1 \cup S_2, \mathcal{I}_1 \vee \mathcal{I}_2)$ where S_1 and S_2 are two copies of S such that $S_1 \cap S_2 = \emptyset$ and $\mathcal{I}_1 \vee \mathcal{I}_2 = \{A \cup B : A \in \mathcal{I}_1, B \in \mathcal{I}_2\}$. Let $M' = (S_1 \cup S_2, \mathcal{I}')$ be the partition matroid such that $I \in \mathcal{I}'$ if and only if I contains at most one copy of each element in S (remember there are two copies of each element, one in S_1 and the other in S_2).

(a) Show that M_{12} is a matroid.

(b) Show that matroid union $M_1 \cup M_2$ is isomorphic to matroid intersection $M_{12} \cap M'$.

(c) Derive the rank function of matroid union of two matroids using the size of maximum size of an independent set in the intersection of these two matroids.

5.6 Let $D = (V, A)$ be a directed graph and subsets U, S of V. For $X, Y \subseteq V$, call X linked to Y if $|X| = |Y|$ and D has $|X|$-vertex disjoint $X - Y$ paths. (X is the set of starting vertices of these paths, and Y is the set of ending vertices.)

Let $\mathcal{I}$ be the collection of subsets I of S such that some subset of U linked to I. Prove that $M = (S, \mathcal{I})$ is a matroid.

5.7 Show that finding a maximum cardinality independent set in the intersection of *three* matroids is NP-hard.

5.8 Apply uncrossing to the partition LP for the spanning tree problem to obtain a characterization such that characteristic vectors for edge sets corresponding to linearly independent tight constraints form a chain.

5.9 Consider the degree bounded minimum cost spanning tree problem where the degree bounds are imposed only on an independent subset of the nodes of the underlying graph. Show that this problem can be solved optimally in polynomial time.

5.10 Show that Theorem 5.6.3 can be generalized to give a $(k - 1)$-approximation algorithm for the maximum k matroid intersection problem.

6

Arborescence and rooted connectivity

In this chapter we study problems in directed graphs and see how the techniques developed in previous chapters generalize to problems on directed graphs. We first consider exact formulations for the *arborescence* problem and a vertex connectivity problem in directed graphs. For the latter, we demonstrate the iterative method in the more sophisticated uncrossing context which is applied to biset families instead of set families as in previous chapters. We then extend these results to degree bounded variants of the problems and use the iterative method to obtain bicriteria results unlike previous chapters where the algorithm would be optimal on the cost and only violate the degree constraints.

Given a directed graph $D = (V, A)$ and a root vertex $r \in V$, a spanning r-arborescence is a subgraph of D so that there is a directed path from r to every vertex in $V - r$. The minimum spanning arborescence problem is to find a spanning r-arborescence with minimum total cost. We will show an integral characterization using iterative proofs, and extend this result in two directions. Given a directed graph D and a root vertex r, a rooted k-connected subgraph is a subgraph of D so that there are k *internally vertex-disjoint* directed paths from r to every vertex in $V - r$. The minimum rooted k-connected subgraph problem is to find a rooted k-connected subgraph with minimum total cost. We extend the proofs in the minimum arborescence problem to show an integral characterization in this more general setting.

As in the previous chapters, we extend the method developed for the exact characterization to the degree bounded version of the problem. However, unlike in the undirected case, the resulting approximation algorithms have a multiplicative guarantee (rather than an additive guarantee) on the degree and the cost. We also show how additive guarantees on the degree can be recovered in the case of unweighted arborescence where arc costs are not considered.

6.1 Minimum cost arborescence

This problem is studied using the same framework as before: First, formulate the problem as a linear program, then characterize the extreme point solutions of this linear program, and finally use an iterative algorithm to find a minimum spanning r-arborescence.

6.1.1 Linear programming relaxation

It is easy to formulate the minimum spanning arborescence problem as a linear program. There is a natural choice that we call the directed LP, and this is an exact formulation. The directed LP requires that there is a directed path from the root r to every vertex in $V - r$. Or equivalently, by Menger's theorem (Theorem 2.2.1), the formulation requires that there is at least one arc entering every set which does not contain the root vertex. This directed LP formulation, originally due to Edmonds [36], for the minimum spanning arborescence problem is shown below.

Just like earlier formulations, c_a is the cost of choosing arc a, and x_a is a binary variable to denote whether arc a is chosen in the arborescence or not. For a set $S \subseteq V$, the corresponding inequality $x(\delta^{in}(S)) \geq 1$ relates to a vector in $\mathbb{R}^{|A|}$: The vector has a 1 corresponding to each arc $a \in \delta^{in}(S)$, and 0 otherwise (recall that $\delta^{in}(S)$ is the set of all arcs incoming to a vertex $v \in S$ from any vertex outside S). This vector is called the characteristic vector of $\delta^{in}(S)$ and is denoted by $\chi(\delta^{in}(S))$. The term $x(\delta^{in}(S))$ just means the sum $\sum_{a \in \delta^{in}(S)} x_a$.

$$
\begin{aligned}
\text{minimize} \quad & \sum_{a \in A} c_a x_a \\
\text{subject to} \quad & x(\delta^{in}(S)) \geq 1 && \forall\, S \subseteq V - r \\
& x_a \geq 0 && \forall\, a \in A
\end{aligned}
$$

The preceding formulation actually captures all subgraphs containing an arborescence or equivalently, it is the *up-hull* of the arborescence polytope. The arborescence polytope can be obtained by adding the equality $\sum_{a \in A} x_a = |V| - 1$.

Although the number of constraints is exponential in the number of vertices, the availability of an efficient separation oracle ensures the polynomial-time solvability of this LP. Given any solution x, the separation oracle first constructs a graph with arc capacities as x_a. It then computes the minimum cuts from the root vertex r to every other vertex. If all the minimum cuts have value of at least 1, it is easy to see that the solution is feasible. If there exists a minimum cut of value less than 1, the violated constraint is precisely the set of vertices that this cut separates.

One can also write a compact formulation for the directed LP, using the equivalence of flows and cuts. This compact formulation provides an alternative way to solve the directed LP in polynomial time. For each vertex $v \in V - r$, there is a variable f_a^v for each arc a, representing the flow value from r to v through the arc a. The proof of the equivalence of the linear programs is deferred to the exercises.

$$
\begin{aligned}
\text{minimize} \quad & \sum_{a \in A} c_a x_a && \\
\text{subject to} \quad & \sum_{a \in \delta^{in}(v)} f_a^v = 1 && \forall v \in V - r \\
& \sum_{a \in \delta^{in}(u)} f_a^v - \sum_{a \in \delta^{out}(u)} f_a^v = 0 && \forall v \in V - r, \forall u \in V - r - v \\
& \sum_{a \in \delta^{out}(r)} f_a^v = 1 && \forall v \in V - r \\
& x_a \geq f_a^v && \forall a \in A, \forall v \in V - r \\
& f_a^v \geq 0 && \forall a \in A, \forall v \in V - r \\
& x_a \geq 0 && \forall a \in A
\end{aligned}
$$

6.1.2 Characterization of extreme point solutions

As in minimum spanning trees, the uncrossing technique is used to find a *good* set of tight inequalities that defines an extreme point solution to the directed LP. Let $\mathcal{F} = \{S \mid x(\delta^{in}(S)) = 1\}$ be the family of tight inequalities for an extreme point solution x in the directed LP. The next claim follows from the submodularity of the $d^{in}(S)$ function noted earlier in Proposition 2.3.9 (see also Figure 2.3).

Proposition 6.1.1 *For $X, Y \subseteq V$,*

$$
x(\delta^{in}(X)) + x(\delta^{in}(Y)) \geq x(\delta^{in}(X \cup Y)) + x(\delta^{in}(X \cap Y))
$$

and the equality holds if and only if $E(X \setminus Y, Y \setminus X) = \emptyset$.

The following lemma shows that the family $\mathcal{F}$ is closed under intersection and union.

Lemma 6.1.2 *If $S, T \in \mathcal{F}$ and $S \cap T \neq \emptyset$, then both $S \cap T$ and $S \cup T$ are in $\mathcal{F}$. Furthermore, $\chi(\delta^{in}(S)) + \chi(\delta^{in}(T)) = \chi(\delta^{in}(S \cap T)) + \chi(\delta^{in}(S \cup T))$.*

Proof

$$
\begin{aligned}
1 + 1 &= x(\delta^{in}(S)) + x(\delta^{in}(T)) \\
&\geq x(\delta^{in}(S \cap T)) + x(\delta^{in}(S \cup T)) \\
&\geq 1 + 1.
\end{aligned}
$$

The equality follows from the fact that $S, T \in \mathcal{F}$. The first inequality follows from Proposition 6.1.1. The second inequality follows from the constraints for $S \cap T$ and $S \cup T$ in the directed LP. Equality must hold everywhere and thus $x(\delta^{in}(S \cap T)) + x(\delta^{in}(S \cup T)) = 2$. Therefore, we must have equality for constraints for $S \cap T$ and $S \cup T$ (i.e., $x(\delta^{in}(S \cap T)) = 1$ and $x(\delta^{in}(S \cup T)) = 1$, which imply that $S \cap T$ and $S \cup T$ are also in $\mathcal{F}$). Moreover, equality holds for Proposition 6.1.1 and thus $E(S \setminus T, T \setminus S) = \emptyset$ and $\chi(\delta^{in}(S)) + \chi(\delta^{in}(T)) = \chi(\delta^{in}(S \cap T)) + \chi(\delta^{in}(S \cup T))$. □

Denote by span($\mathcal{F}$) the vector space generated by the set of characteristic vectors $\{\chi(\delta^{in}(S)) \mid S \in \mathcal{F}\}$. The following lemma says that an extreme point solution is characterized by tight inequalities whose corresponding sets form a laminar family. The proof follows the same steps as in the case of undirected spanning trees (see Lemma 4.1.5), and we do not duplicate it here.

Lemma 6.1.3 *If $\mathcal{L}$ is a maximal laminar subfamily of $\mathcal{F}$, then span($\mathcal{L}$) = span($\mathcal{F}$).*

Lemma 6.1.3 and the Rank Lemma imply the following.

Corollary 6.1.4 *Let x be any extreme point solution to the directed LP. Then there exists a laminar family $\mathcal{L}$ such that*

(i) $x(\delta^{in}(S)) = 1$ *for all $S \in \mathcal{L}$.*
(ii) *The vectors in $\{\chi(\delta^{in}(S)) : S \in \mathcal{L}\}$ are linearly independent.*
(iii) $|A| = |\mathcal{L}|$.

A laminar family $\mathcal{L}$ defines naturally a forest L as follows (see Figure 6.1): Each node of L corresponds to a set in $\mathcal{L}$, and there is an edge from set R to set S if R is the smallest set containing S. R is called the *parent* of S, and S is called the *child* of R. A node with no parent is called a *root*, and a node with no children is called a *leaf*. Given a node R, the *subtree rooted at R* consists of R and all its descendants. The forest L corresponding to the laminar family $\mathcal{L}$ will be used to perform the token counting arguments inductively.

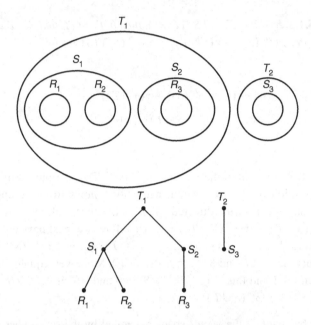

Figure 6.1 A laminar family and its corresponding forest.

6.1.3 Iterative algorithm

We present an iterative algorithm to find a minimum spanning arborescence from an optimal extreme point solution to the directed LP. The algorithm is similar to the Iterative 1-edge-finding Algorithm in Figure 4.5 for finding minimum spanning trees. Again, we use the notation $D/\{uv\}$ to denote the digraph obtained from D by contracting the arc uv.

6.1.4 Correctness and optimality

As in minimum spanning trees, assuming the algorithm terminates successfully, it is easy to show that the returned solution is a minimum spanning arborescence. The proof of the following result is identical to that of Theorem 4.1.10.

Theorem 6.1.5 *The Iterative minimum spanning arborescence algorithm in Figure 6.2 returns a minimum spanning arborescence in polynomial time.*

The key step is to prove that the algorithm will terminate. In the following lemma, we show that there is an arc a with either $x_a = 1$ or $x_a = 0$ at each stage of the algorithm.

Iterative Minimum Spanning Arborescence Algorithm

(i) Initialization $F \leftarrow \emptyset$.

(ii) While $|V(D)| \geq 2$ do

    (a) Find an optimal extreme point solution x to the directed LP and remove every arc a with $x_a = 0$ from D.

    (b) Find an arc $a = uv$ with $x_a = 1$, and update $F \leftarrow F \cup \{a\}$, $D \leftarrow D/\{uv\}$.

(iii) Return F.

Figure 6.2 Minimum arborescence algorithm.

Lemma 6.1.6 *For any extreme point solution x to the directed LP, either there is an arc with $x_a = 0$ or there is an arc with $x_a = 1$.*

Before we begin the proof, let us recall that there exists a laminar family $\mathcal{L}$ such that it represents a linearly independent set of tight constraints (Corollary 6.1.4). The proof, by contradiction, is based on the token argument used in earlier proofs. The idea of the argument is to assume that there is no arc with $x_a = 0$ and $x_a = 1$, and then derive a contradiction by showing that the number of constraints (that is, the number of sets in $\mathcal{L}$) is smaller than the number of nonzero variables (i.e., the number of arcs)–contradicting the Rank Lemma (i.e., Corollary 6.1.4).

As in the undirected case, we present three different counting arguments. While the first argument is the simplest for the minimum arborescence problem, the second argument can be generalized to the minimum cost rooted k-connected subgraph problem, and the third proof can be generalized to the degree-bounded version of the minimum arborescence problem.

Proof 1 (global counting argument) Suppose for sake of contradiction $0 < x_a < 1$. As we have $x(\delta^{in}(v)) \geq 1$ for each $v \in V \setminus \{r\}$; hence, we must have $|\delta^{in}(v)| \geq 2$ for each $v \in V \setminus \{r\}$. Thus,

$$|A| = \sum_{v \in V} |\delta^{in}(v)| \geq \sum_{v \in V \setminus \{r\}} 2 = 2|V| - 2.$$

On the other hand, from Lemma 6.1.4, we have the maximal linearly independent constraints form a laminar family over the ground set $V \setminus \{r\}$. From Corollary 4.1.8, we have that $|\mathcal{L}| \leq 2(|V| - 1) - 1 = 2|V| - 3$, but this contradicts Corollary 6.1.4 since $|A| \geq 2|V| - 2 > |\mathcal{L}|$.

Proof 2 (local token counting argument) For each arc, one token is assigned to its head. So the total number of tokens assigned is exactly $|A|$. These tokens will be redistributed such that each subset $S \in \mathcal{L}$ is assigned one token, and there are still some tokens left. This will imply $|A| > |\mathcal{L}|$ and thus contradicts Corollary 6.1.4. The following lemma shows that the redistribution is possible by an inductive argument on the forest L corresponding to the laminar family $\mathcal{L}$.

Lemma 6.1.7 *For any rooted subtree of the forest $L \neq \emptyset$ with root S, the tokens assigned to vertices inside S can be distributed such that every node in the subtree gets at least one token, and the root S gets at least two tokens.*

Proof The proof is by induction on the height of the subtree. The base case is when S is a leaf. Since $x(\delta^{in}(S)) = 1$ and there is no arc with $x_a = 1$, there are at least two arcs in $\delta^{in}(S)$, and so S gets at least two tokens.

For the induction step, let S be the root and $R_1, \ldots, R_k$ be its children. By the induction hypothesis, each node in the subtree rooted at R_i gets at least one token and R_i gets at least two tokens. Since R_i only needs to keep one token, it can give one token to S. Suppose $k \geq 2$, then S can collect two tokens by taking one token from each of its children, as required. So suppose $k = 1$. If there is an arc a that enters S but not R_1, then S can collect two tokens by taking one token from R_1 and one token from the head of a. Suppose such an arc does not exist, then $\delta^{in}(S) \subseteq \delta^{in}(R)$. Since $x(\delta^{in}(S)) = x(\delta^{in}(R)) = 1$ and there is no arc with $x_a = 0$, this implies $\delta^{in}(S) = \delta^{in}(R)$. Hence $\chi(\delta^{in}(S)) = \chi(\delta^{in}(R))$, but this contradicts the linear independence of the characteristic vectors for sets in $\mathcal{L}$ (recall that $\mathcal{L}$ can be chosen to satisfy the properties in Corollary 6.1.4). Therefore, such an arc must exist, and S can collect two tokens, as required. This completes the proof of the induction step.   □

From Lemma 6.1.7, the number of tokens is at least $|\mathcal{L}| + 1$, which implies that $|A| > |\mathcal{L}|$, contradicting Corollary 6.1.4.

Proof 3 (local fractional token counting argument) The third counting argument also starts from a laminar family $\mathcal{L}$, which satisfies the properties in Corollary 6.1.4. Instead of assigning tokens integrally, we assign tokens fractionally based on the following two rules.

(i) For every arc a, we assign x_a token to the smallest set in $\mathcal{L}$ containing its head.
(ii) For every arc a, we assign $1 - x_a$ token to the smallest set in $\mathcal{L}$ containing its tail.

Thus, the total number of tokens assigned is exactly $|A|$. To derive a contradiction, we show that each subset $S \in \mathcal{L}$ has been assigned at least one token, and there are still some tokens left. This will imply $|A| > |\mathcal{L}|$ and thus contradicts Corollary 6.1.4.

Lemma 6.1.8 *Let S be any set in the $\mathcal{L}$. Then S receives at least one token by the above assignment.*

Proof Let S be any set in $\mathcal{L}$ and let $R_1, \ldots, R_k$ be the children of S where $k \geq 0$ ($k = 0$ implies S is a leaf). We have $x(\delta^{in}(S)) = 1$, and for each R_i we have $x(\delta^{in}(R_i)) = 1$. Subtracting, we obtain $x(\delta^{in}(S)) - \sum_{i=1}^{k} x(\delta^{in}(R_1)) = 1 - k$. Let $A_S = \delta^{in}(S) \setminus (\cup_i \delta^{in}(R_i))$ and $A_R = (\cup_i \delta^{in}(R_i)) \setminus \delta^{in}(S)$. Then the preceding equation can be rewritten as $x(A_S) - x(A_R) = 1 - k$. Observe that the tokens received by S are exactly x_a tokens for each arc $a \in A_S$ and exactly $1 - x_a$ tokens for each arc in A_R. Hence, S receives exactly $x(A_S) + |A_R| - x(A_R)$ tokens, which is an integer since $x(A_S) - x(A_R) = 1 - k$ is an integer. If the tokens received by S is zero, then we must have $A_S = \emptyset$ and $A_R = \emptyset$, and then we have that $\chi(\delta^{in}(S)) = \sum_i \chi(\delta^{in}(R_i))$, contradicting the linear independence of constraints. Thus, S receives at least one token.   □

Therefore each set is assigned one token. To complete the argument, we need to show that there are still some extra tokens. This follows from observing that for any arc incident at the root, the $1 - x_a > 0$ token is still unassigned as there is no set in $\mathcal{L}$ containing its tail. This completes the counting argument.

6.2 Minimum cost rooted *k*-connected subgraphs

It is easy to see that the problem of finding a rooted k-arc-connected subgraph of minimum cost (requiring k arc-disjoint paths from r to every other vertex), generalizes the minimum arborescence problem. In fact, the LP for this problem is very similar to the directed LP for the arborescence (all the constraints require at least k instead of 1 on the right-hand side). The separation oracle, the iterative algorithm, and the counting argument are all similar for this problem as well. We leave the details to the exercises.

We therefore shift our focus to the vertex connectivity problem, giving an LP formulation in the following.

6.2.1 Linear programming relaxation

A natural formulation of the minimum rooted k-connected subgraph problem is to require that there are k internally vertex-disjoint paths from the root to every other vertex. As usual, an equivalent formulation as a "cut covering" problem is considered. For vertex-connectivity, it is not enough to just have k arcs entering

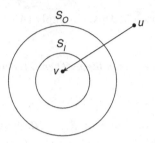

Figure 6.3 In this example the biset $S = (S_O, S_I)$ is shown and the arc (u, v) enters S.

a set, and a more sophisticated notion, biset, is needed. See Figure 6.3 for an example.

Definition 6.2.1 *A* **biset** $S = (S_O, S_I)$ *is a pair of subsets* S_O, S_I *of* V *for which* $\emptyset \subset S_I \subset S_O \subset V$. S_O *is the outer member, and* S_I *is the inner member. An arc* $a = (u, v)$ *is said to enter* $S = (S_O, S_I)$ *if* $u \in V - S_O$ *and* $v \in S_I$, *which is denoted by* $x_a \in \delta^{in}(S)$.

Let us intuitively explain the role of bisets for this problem. A graph is rooted k-connected if upon removal of $l \leq k$ vertices, there are still at least $k - l$ vertex disjoint paths from r to other vertices. This is precisely the reason we count arcs coming in from $V - S_O$ to S_I – corresponding to the case where the vertices in $S_O - S_I$ are deleted.

Let $\mathcal{R}$ be the set of all bisets S for which $S_O \subseteq V - r$. We have the following biset LP formulation for the minimum rooted k-connected subgraph problem. Note that, by Menger's theorem, a 0–1 solution to the biset LP corresponds to a rooted k-connected subgraph (see Exercise 2.2.3).

$$\text{minimize} \quad \sum_{a \in A} c_a x_a$$

$$\text{subject to} \quad x(\delta^{in}(S)) \geq k - (|S_O| - |S_I|) \qquad \forall \text{ bi-sets } S \in \mathcal{R}$$

$$x_a \geq 0 \qquad\qquad\qquad\qquad \forall a \in A$$

We can use a minimum cut algorithm to design a separation oracle for the biset LP. Given a solution x for this problem, we can construct an auxiliary graph D' by expanding each vertex to an arc of capacity 1. All other arc capacities are the values of x_a. It is easy to see that the solution x is a feasible solution to the biset LP if and only if the minimum cut separating the root from a vertex of $V - r$ in D' has outgoing capacity at least k.

It is tempting to try to extend the solution technique motivated by the arbores-cence case for this problem. This actually works to some extent, when we actually complete an iteration in the iterative algorithm, we pick an arc if its value was 1. However, this changes some of the constraints of the LP (the residual problem is no longer an instance of the rooted k vertex-connectivity problem), and therefore even the separation oracle could change in theory (in reality, all that is needed is a small addition to the previously mentioned oracle). To apply the iterative method, we generalize the bi-set LP to the following.

$$\text{minimize} \quad \sum_{a \in A} c_a x_a$$

$$\text{subject to} \quad x(\delta^{in}(S)) \geq g(S) \qquad \forall \text{ bisets } S \in \mathcal{R}$$

$$x_a \geq 0 \qquad \forall \, a \in A$$

Initially $g(S)$ is $k - (|S_O| - |S_I|)$. The function g is required to satisfy a specific supermodularity property, which we shall soon define. We are now in a position to explain the iterative algorithm for the rooted k-connected subgraph problem.

6.2.2 Iterative algorithm

The iterative algorithm to find an optimal rooted k-connected subgraph is given in Figure 6.4.

Note that at each iteration, the separation oracle is exactly the one mentioned earlier where, as a preprocessing step, we expand every vertex to an arc with x value of 1 in the graph and also add in the arcs set to 1 so far by the algorithm, and look for a cut of value k as before. Details are left to the exercises.

Iterative Rooted k-Connected Subgraph Algorithm

(i) Initialization $F \leftarrow \emptyset$, $g' \leftarrow g$.

(ii) While $g' \not\equiv 0$ do

    (a) Find an optimal extreme point solution x to the biset LP with the requirement function g'. Remove every arc a with $x_a = 0$ from D.

    (b) Find an arc $a = uv$ with $x_a = 1$, and update $F \leftarrow F \cup \{a\}$, $D \leftarrow D \setminus \{uv\}$, and set $g'(S) \leftarrow \max\{g(S) - d_F^{in}(S), 0\}$.

(iii) Return F.

Figure 6.4 Rooted k-connected subgraph algorithm.

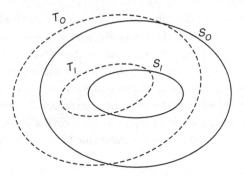

Figure 6.5 In this example, the biset $S = (S_O, S_I)$ and biset $T = (T_O, T_I)$ intersect.

6.2.3 Characterization of extreme point solutions

The uncrossing technique can also be applied to bisets. For a biset $S = (S_O, S_I)$, the corresponding inequality $x(\delta^{in}(S)) \geq g(S)$ defines the characteristic vector $\chi(\delta^{in}(S))$ in $\mathbb{R}^{|A|}$: The vector has a 1 corresponding to each arc $a \in \delta^{in}(S)$, and 0 otherwise. Let $\mathcal{F} = \{S \mid x(\delta^{in}(S)) = g(S)\}$ be the family of tight inequalities for an extreme point solution x to the biset LP. The following lemma shows that this family is closed under intersection and union. Before stating the lemma, we define biset intersections and unions (see Figure 6.5).

Definition 6.2.2 *Given two bisets S, T, define $S \cap T := (S_O \cap T_O, S_I \cap T_I)$ and $S \cup T := (S_O \cup T_O, S_I \cup T_I)$. Two bisets S, T are intersecting if $S_I \cap T_I$, $S_I - T_I$ and $T_I - S_I$ are nonempty, or $S_I \cap T_I$, $S_O \cap T_O$, $S_O - T_O$ and $T_O - S_O$ are nonempty.*

Lemma 6.2.3 *If bisets $S, T \in \mathcal{F}$ and S and T are intersecting, then both $S \cap T$ and $S \cup T$ are in $\mathcal{F}$. Furthermore, $\chi(\delta^{in}(S)) + \chi(\delta^{in}(T)) = \chi(\delta^{in}(S \cap T)) + \chi(\delta^{in}(S \cup T))$.*

Proof

$$g(S) + g(T) = x(\delta^{in}(S)) + x(\delta^{in}(T))$$
$$\geq x(\delta^{in}(S \cap T)) + x(\delta^{in}(S \cup T))$$
$$\geq g(S \cap T) + g(S \cup T)$$
$$\geq g(S) + g(T)$$

The equality is by the fact that $S, T \in \mathcal{F}$. The first inequality follows from the submodularity of the biset function $d^{in}(S)$, which can be shown in a manner similar to the corresponding submodularity of the set function $d^{in}(S)$ in the arborescence problem (see the exercises). The second inequality follows from the constraints in the biset LP. The last inequality is because of the property we require the function g to satisfy *intersecting bisupermodularity*. We will prove in Proposition 6.2.7 that the function g' is intersecting bisupermodular at each stage of the iterative algorithm.

Definition 6.2.4 *A function g is intersecting bisupermodular if for all intersecting bisets S and T, $g(S) + g(T) \leq g(S \cup T) + g(S \cap T)$.*

Therefore, equality holds everywhere, and thus $x(\delta^{in}(S \cap T)) = g(S \cap T)$ and $x(\delta^{in}(S \cup T)) = g(S \cup T)$, which implies that $S \cap T$ and $S \cup T$ are also in $\mathcal{F}$. Moreover, since $x_a > 0$ for every arc a, we have $\chi(\delta^{in}(S)) + \chi(\delta^{in}(T)) = \chi(\delta^{in}(S \cap T)) + \chi(\delta^{in}(S \cup T))$. $\qquad\square$

Denote by span($\mathcal{F}$) the vector space generated by the set of characteristic vectors $\{\chi(\delta^{in}(S)) \mid S \in \mathcal{F}\}$. A family of bi-sets is *bilaminar* if no two bi-sets are intersecting. In a bilaminar family, the inner members form a laminar family, and if $X_I \subseteq Y_I$ then $X_O \subseteq Y_O$ or $Y_O \subseteq X_O$ (see the exercises). The following lemma says that an extreme point solution is characterized by tight inequalities whose corresponding sets form a bilaminar family. The proof is similar to the corresponding proof for the spanning tree problem (see Lemma 4.1.5) and is omitted here.

Lemma 6.2.5 *If $\mathcal{L}$ is a maximal bilaminar subfamily of $\mathcal{F}$, then $span(\mathcal{L}) = span(\mathcal{F})$.*

Lemma 6.2.5 and the Rank Lemma imply the following.

Corollary 6.2.6 *Let x be any extreme point solution to the biset LP. Then there exists a bilaminar family $\mathcal{L}$ such that*

(i) $x(\delta^{in}(S)) = g(S)$ *for all $S \in \mathcal{L}$.*
(ii) *The vectors in $\{\chi(\delta^{in}(S)) : S \in \mathcal{L}\}$ are linearly independent.*
(iii) $|A| = |\mathcal{L}|$.

6.2.4 *Correctness and optimality*

First, for the inductive procedure to work, we want g to be bisupermodular initially. Recall that we initialized $g(S)$ as $k - (|S_O| - |S_I|)$. It is not too difficult to verify that this g is indeed bisupermodular.

Proposition 6.2.7 *The function g' is an intersecting bisupermodular function.*

Proof Let S and R be two intersecting bisets.

$$
\begin{aligned}
g(S) + g(R) &= (k - |S_O| + |S_I|) + (k - |R_O| + |R_I|) \\
&= (k - |S_O \cap R_O| + |S_I \cap R_I|) + (k - |S_O \cup R_O| + |S_I \cup R_I|) \\
&= g(S \cap R) + g(S \cup R)
\end{aligned}
$$

Since g is an intersecting bisupermodular function, and g' is obtained from g by subtracting an intersecting bisubmodular function $d_F^{in}(S)$ (the subset of arcs set to 1 in each iteration), g' is also an intersecting bisupermodular function. □

Assuming the algorithm terminates successfully, the returned solution is a minimum rooted k-connected subgraph – the proof of optimality is by now a standard induction argument which we omit here.

Theorem 6.2.8 *The iterative rooted k-connected subgraph algorithm in Figure 6.4 returns a rooted k-connected subgraph of minimum cost in polynomial time.*

The key to prove the correctness is to show that the algorithm will terminate. This is very similar to a counting argument we employed for minimum arborescences.

Lemma 6.2.9 *For any extreme point solution x to the biset LP, either there is an arc with $x_a = 0$ or there is an arc with $x_a = 1$.*

Suppose for a contradiction that there is no arc with $x_a = 0$ or $x_a = 1$. The proof starts from a bilaminar family $\mathcal{L}$, which satisfies the properties of Corollary 6.2.6. A bilaminar family $\mathcal{L}$ also naturally defines a forest L as follows: Each node of L corresponds to a biset in $\mathcal{L}$, and there is an edge from biset R to biset S if R is the smallest set containing S, where a biset R contains a biset S if $S_I \subseteq R_I$ and $S_O \subseteq R_O$. The goal of the counting argument is the same – assuming there is no arc with $x_a = 0$ and $x_a = 1$, derive a contradiction by showing that the number of inequalities (i.e., the number of sets in $\mathcal{L}$) is smaller than the number of variables (i.e., the number of arcs).

For each arc, one token is assigned to its head. So the total number of tokens assigned is exactly $|A|$. To derive a contradiction, these tokens will be redistributed such that each biset $S \in \mathcal{L}$ is assigned one token, and there are still some excess tokens left. This will imply $|A| > |\mathcal{L}|$ and thus contradict Corollary 6.2.6. The following lemma shows that such a redistribution is possible.

Lemma 6.2.10 *For any rooted subtree of the forest $L \neq \emptyset$ with root S, the tokens assigned to vertices inside S_I can be distributed such that every node in the subtree gets at least one token and the root S gets at least $g(S) + 1$ tokens.*

Proof The proof is by induction on the height of the subtree. The base case is when S is a leaf. Since $x(\delta^{in}(S)) = g(S)$ and there is no arc with $x_a = 1$, there are at least $g(S) + 1$ arcs in $\delta^{in}(S)$, and so S gets at least $g(S) + 1$ tokens.

For the induction step, let S be the root and $R_1, \ldots, R_k$ be its children. By the induction hypothesis, each node in the subtree rooted at R_i gets at least one token and R_i gets at least $g(R_i) + 1$ tokens. Since R_i only needs to keep one token, it can give $g(R_i)$ tokens to S. Let $g(R) = \sum_{i=1}^{k} g(R_i)$. Three cases are considered.

(i) $g(S) < g(R)$. Then S can collect $g(R) \geq g(S) + 1$ tokens from its children.
(ii) $g(S) > g(R)$. Since there is no arc with $x_a = 1$, there must be at least $g(S) - g(R) + 1$ arcs entering S but not its children. So S can take $g(R)$ tokens from its children and $g(S) - g(R) + 1$ tokens from the heads of those arcs. Therefore, S can collect at least $g(S) + 1$ tokens, as required.
(iii) $g(S) = g(R)$. If there is an arc a that enters S but not any of its children, then S can collect $g(S) + 1$ tokens by taking $g(S) = g(R)$ tokens from its children and at least one more token from the head of such arc, as required. Suppose such an arc does not exist, then $\delta^{in}(S) \subseteq \cup_{i=1}^{k} \delta^{in}(R_i)$. Since $x(\delta^{in}(S)) = \sum_{i=1}^{k} x(\delta^{in}(R_i))$ and there is no arc with $x_a = 0$, this implies that $\delta^{in}(S) = \cup_{i=1}^{k} \delta^{in}(R_i)$. Hence, $\chi(\delta^{in}(S)) = \sum_{i=1}^{k} \chi(\delta^{in}(R_i))$, but this contradicts the linear independence of the characteristic vectors for bisets in $\mathcal{L}$. Therefore, such an arc must exist, and thus S can collect $g(S) + 1$ tokens, as required.

This completes the proof of the induction step. $\square$

From Lemma 6.2.10, the number of tokens is at least $|\mathcal{L}| + 1$, which implies that $|A| > |\mathcal{L}|$, contradicting Corollary 6.2.6. This completes the proof of Lemma 6.2.9, and hence Theorem 6.2.8 follows.

6.3 Minimum bounded degree arborescence

The minimum bounded degree arborescence (MBDA) problem is defined as follows: Given a directed graph $G = (V, A)$, a cost function $c : A \rightarrow \mathbb{R}$ and an out-degree upper bound B_v for each vertex $v \in V$, the task is to find an arborescence of minimum cost which satisfies all the out-degree bounds.

First, we present a $(2, 2B_v + 2)$-approximation algorithm for the minimum bounded degree arborescence problem. By this, we mean that the algorithm outputs an arborescence whose cost is twice that of the LP relaxation for the original problem and whose out-degree at any node v is at most $2B_v + 2$. Thus, it is a pseudo-approximation or bicriteria approximation algorithm that both violates the degree bounds as well as delivers a suboptimal cost solution. In the next section, we will present an algorithm with only an additive error of 2 on the degree bounds, but when there are no costs on arcs (the unweighted case).

6.3.1 Linear programming relaxation

The following is a natural extension of the directed LP for this degree-bounded problem where the degree bounds are imposed only on a subset W of the vertices.

$$
\begin{aligned}
\text{minimize} \quad & \sum_{a \in A} c_a x_a \\
\text{subject to} \quad & x(\delta^{in}(S)) \geq 1 && \forall\, S \subseteq V - r \\
& x(\delta^{out}(v)) \leq B_v && \forall\, v \in W \\
& x_a \geq 0 && \forall\, a \in A
\end{aligned}
$$

This linear program can be solved by using a minimum cut algorithm as a separation oracle as in the case of the directed LP for minimum cost arborescences.

To make the formalism sufficiently general to handle residual problems arising in the iterative procedure, we use an LP for a generalization of arborescences to more general cut functions $f : S \to \mathbb{Z}^+$. Recall that a pair of sets $A, B \subset V$ are intersecting if $A \cap B \neq \emptyset$, $A - B \neq \emptyset$ and $B - A \neq \emptyset$. A function f is intersecting supermodular if for every pair of intersecting sets $A, B \subset V$ we have

$$
f(A) + f(B) \leq f(A \cup B) + f(A \cap B).
$$

In the following $f(S)$ is a 0–1 intersecting supermodular function. By setting $f(S) = 1$ for all subsets S that do not contain the root r (this is intersecting supermodular, see Exercise 2.2.12), we get an LP relaxation, denoted by $LP_{mbda}(G, f, \mathcal{B}, W)$, for the arborescence problem. Here $\mathcal{B}$ denotes the vector of out-degree bounds on the subset of vertices W.

$$\text{minimize} \quad \sum_{a \in A} c_a x_a$$

$$\text{subject to} \quad x(\delta^{in}(S)) \geq f(S) \qquad \forall \, S \subseteq V - r$$

$$x(\delta^{out}(v)) \leq B_v \qquad \forall \, v \in W$$

$$x_a \geq 0 \qquad \forall \, a \in A$$

To find a separation oracle for this problem, we need to check whether $x(\delta^{in}(S)) - f(S) \geq 0$ for each $S \subseteq V - r$. For general supermodular function f, we can use an efficient algorithm for submodular function minimization to check this, since $x(\delta^{in}(S)) - f(S)$ is a submodular function. For the function f arising from the minimum bounded degree arborescence problem, we can use an efficient minimum cut algorithm for this task, as we did for the minimum rooted k-connected subgraph problem.

6.3.2 Characterization of extreme point solutions

The proof of the following lemma follows from standard uncrossing arguments as in the minimum arborescence problem.

Lemma 6.3.1 *For any extreme point solution x to LP_{mbda}, there exist a set $T \subseteq W$ and a laminar family $\mathcal{L}$ such that*

(i) $x(\delta^{out}(v)) = B_v$ *for each $v \in T$ and $x(\delta^{in}(S)) = 1$ for each $S \in \mathcal{L}$.*
(ii) *The vectors in $\{\chi(\delta^{out}(v)) : v \in T\} \cup \{\chi(\delta^{in}(S)) : S \in \mathcal{L}\}$ are linearly independent.*
(iii) $|A| = |\mathcal{L}| + |T|$.

6.3.3 Iterative algorithm

The iterative algorithm is similar to that for the minimum bounded degree spanning tree problem in Chapter 4, except that it has a relaxation step as well as a rounding step, in which we choose an arc a even though $x_a < 1$.

6.3.4 Correctness and performance guarantee

We first prove that the algorithm has the claimed performance guarantee, assuming that it terminates successfully.

Theorem 6.3.2 *The iterative algorithm in Figure 6.6 is a $(2, 2B_v + 2)$ approximation algorithm for the minimum bounded degree arborescence problem.*

Iterative Minimum Bounded Degree Arborescence Algorithm

(i) Initialization $F \leftarrow \emptyset$, $f' = f$.

(ii) While $f' \not\equiv 0$ do

    (a) Compute an optimal extreme point solution x to LP_{mbda} $(G, f', \mathcal{B}, W)$. Remove every arc a with $x_a = 0$.

    (b) **(Rounding):** If there is an arc $a = (u, v)$ with $x_a \geq \frac{1}{2}$, then update $F \leftarrow F \cup \{a\}$ and set $B_u \leftarrow B_u - \frac{1}{2}$.

    (c) **(Relaxation):** If there exists a vertex $v \in W$ with $d^{out}(v) < B_v + 3$, then set $W \leftarrow W - v$.

    (d) Update $f'(S) \leftarrow \max\{f(S) - d_F^{in}(S), 0\}$.

(iii) Return F.

Figure 6.6 Minimum bounded degree arborescence algorithm.

Proof First we prove that the cost of the arborescence returned by the algorithm is at most twice the cost of the initial LP solution. The proof is by induction on the number of iterations executed by the algorithm. For the base case that requires only one iteration, the theorem follows since it rounds up a single arc a with $x_a \geq \frac{1}{2}$. For the induction step, let a' be the arc with $x_{a'} \geq \frac{1}{2}$ in the current iteration. Let f' be the residual requirement function after this iteration, and let F' be the set of arcs picked in subsequent iterations for satisfying f'. The key observation is that the current solution x restricted to $A - a'$ is a feasible solution for satisfying f' (by checking the connectivity constraints and also the degree constraints), and thus by the induction hypothesis, the cost of F' is at most $2\sum_{a \in A - a'} c_a x_a$. Consider $F := F' \cup a'$, which satisfies f (by the definition of f'). The cost of F is

$$\text{cost}(F) = \text{cost}(F') + c_{a'} \leq 2\sum_{a \in A - a'} c_a x_a + c_{a'} \leq 2\sum_{a \in A} c_a x_a$$

where the last inequality follows because $x_{a'} \geq \frac{1}{2}$. This implies that the cost of F is at most twice the cost of an optimal fractional solution.

Next we show that the degree of any vertex v is at most $2B_v + 2$. At any iteration, let F denote the set of edges selected, and let B'_v denote the current residual degree bound of v. While the degree constraint of v is present, $d_F(v) = 2(B_v - B'_v)$. This is because, at any iteration, whenever we include an edge $e \in \delta(v)$ in F, we reduce B'_v by half, and hence the equality holds true. When the degree bound for the vertex v is removed, then less than $B'_v + 3$ edges are incident at v. In the worst case, we may select all these edges in the solution.

Hence,

$$d_F(v) < 2(B_v - B'_v) + B'_v + 3 < 2B_v + 3.$$

Since $d_F(v)$ and B_v are integers, this implies that $d_F(v) \leq 2B_v + 2$, as required.   □

We now focus on using a counting argument to prove the following lemma, which guarantees that the algorithm terminates successfully.

Lemma 6.3.3 *An extreme point solution x to LP_{mbda} must satisfy one of the following.*

(i) *There is an arc a with $x_a \geq \frac{1}{2}$.*
(ii) *There is a vertex v with $d^{out}(v) < B_v + 3$.*

Proof The proof uses the local fractional token argument. Each arc is assigned two tokens, for a total of $2|A|$ tokens. For each arc a, $1 - x_a$ token is assigned to its tail, and $1 + x_a$ token is assigned to its head. We shall show that if none of the preceding conditions are satisfied, then each set in $\mathcal{L}$ and each degree constraint in T can collect two tokens, and there are some tokens left. This would imply $|A| > |\mathcal{L}| + |T|$, which contradicts Lemma 6.3.1.

For each tight vertex v in T, it collects

$$\sum_{a \in \delta^{out}(v)} (1 - x_a) = d^{out}(v) - \sum_{a \in \delta^{out}(v)} x_a = d^{out}(v) - B_v \geq 3$$

tokens; the second equality follows because v is tight, and the last inequality follows because the condition in the lemma is not satisfied. This shows that each degree constraint in T can collect at least three tokens. Hence, each degree constraint has at least one extra token. In the following, each node with a degree constraint will contribute its extra token to the smallest set in the laminar family containing it.

For a leaf node $S \in \mathcal{L}$, it collects

$$\sum_{a \in \delta^{in}(S)} (1 + x_a) = d^{in}(S) + \sum_{a \in \delta^{in}(S)} x_a = d^{in}(S) + 1 \geq 4$$

tokens; the second equality follows because S is tight and so $x(\delta^{in}(S)) = 1$, and the last inequality follows because there are no arcs with value at least $1/2$, and hence $d^{in}(S) \geq 3$. This shows that each leaf node in $\mathcal{L}$ can collect at least four tokens. Hence each leaf node has at least two extra tokens to start us off in the bottom-up induction over the laminar family.

We argue by induction going bottom-up in the laminar family $\mathcal{L}$ that we can assign the tokens in the subtree of S so that every set gets at least two tokens and the root gets two extra tokens. We proved the base case for leaves in the previous paragraph. Consider a nonleaf node $S \in \mathcal{L}$, and let its children be $R_1, \ldots, R_l$. If $l \geq 2$, then S can collect two extra tokens from each child by the induction hypothesis, and hence S has at least two extra tokens, as required. So assume S has only one child R_1, and S can collect two tokens from R_1 and needs two more tokens. Since $x(\delta^{in}(S)) = x(\delta^{in}(R_1)) = 1$ and $\chi(\delta^{in}(S)) \neq \chi(\delta^{in}(R_1))$, there are arcs $p \in P := \delta^{in}(S) - \delta^{in}(R_1)$ and $q \in Q := \delta^{in}(R_1) - \delta^{in}(S)$. Every arc $p \in P$ can contribute $1 + x_p$ token to S. If the tail of $q \in Q$ is in T (the set of vertices with tight degree constraint), then its tail contributes 1 token to S since it has a degree constraint, and by the preceding redistribution, every such node gives its one extra token to the smallest set in the laminar family containing it. If the tail of q is not in T, then q can contribute $1 - x_q$ token to S. In this case, note that since $x(\delta^{in}(S)) = x(\delta^{in}(R_1)) = 1$, we have $\sum_{p \in P} x_p = \sum_{q \in Q} x_q$, and thus, S can collect two more tokens from arcs in P and Q, and this completes the induction step. There are always some tokens left at the root node in $\mathcal{L}$, and this completes the proof. $\square$

6.4 Additive performance guarantee

In this section, we present an algorithm for the unweighted problem (without arc costs) that outputs an arborescence that violates the out-degrees by at most two. However, as opposed to the minimum bounded degree spanning tree problem, to achieve an additive guarantee on the degrees, the cost of the solution is no longer bounded. In fact, this tradeoff is shown to be unavoidable using this linear programming relaxation for the problem [8].

6.4.1 Iterative algorithm

The iterative algorithm is similar to the additive one approximation for the minimum bounded degree spanning tree problem. The algorithm removes degree constraint one by one, and include *all* arcs incident on these vertices as candidates for the final solution, and remove them from the graph. In the end a subset of arcs that make up an arborescence among the candidates is output. The algorithm is presented in Figure 6.7.

The degree constraint is violated only in Step (ii)(c) by at most two. So if the algorithm terminates successfully, then the algorithm is an additive two approximation algorithm for the unweighted bounded degree arborescence problem.

Iterative Additive Arborescence Algorithm

(i) Initialization $F \leftarrow \emptyset$, $f' = f$.

(ii) While $A \setminus F \neq \emptyset$ do

    (a) Find an optimal extreme point solution x to $LP_{mbda}(G, f', \mathcal{B}, W)$. Remove every arc a with $x_a = 0$.

    (b) **(Relaxation):** If there exists a vertex $v \in W$ with $d^{out}(v) \leq B_v + 2$, then set $W \leftarrow W - v$ and update $F \leftarrow F \cup \{\delta^{out}(v)\}$.

    (c) Update $f'(S) \leftarrow \max\{f(S) - d_F^{in}(S), 0\}$ and $A \leftarrow A - F$.

(iii) Return any arborescence in F.

Figure 6.7 Additive arborescence algorithm.

6.4.2 Correctness and performance guarantee

The following lemma shows that the algorithm always terminates successfully. The proof uses the characterization of the extreme point solutions of LP_{mbda}.

Lemma 6.4.1 *In any extreme point solution x to LP_{mbda}, there is a vertex $v \in W$ with out-degree at most $B_v + 2$.*

Proof The proof uses a local fractional token argument. Each arc is assigned one token, for a total of $|A|$ tokens. For each arc a, $1 - x_a$ token is assigned to its tail, and x_a token is assigned to its head. We shall show that if the above condition is not satisfied, then each set in $\mathcal{L}$ and each degree constraint in T can collect one token, and there are some tokens left. This would imply $|A| > |\mathcal{L}| + |T|$, contradicting Lemma 6.3.1.

Each vertex v with nonzero out-degree must be in W. Hence it collects

$$\sum_{a \in \delta^{out}(v)} (1 - x_a) = d^{out}(v) - x(\delta^{out}(v)) \geq d^{out}(v) - B_v \geq 3$$

tokens; the first inequality follows because of the out-degree constraint at v, and the last inequality follows because the condition in the lemma is not satisfied. This shows that each vertex with nonzero out-degree has at least two extra tokens. Each such vertex with an out-degree constraint distributes its two extra tokens to the smallest set in $\mathcal{L}$ containing it.

A leaf node $S \in \mathcal{L}$ collects $x(\delta^{in}(v)) = 1$ token. Furthermore, S has at least one extra token if $d^{out}(S) \geq 1$ (actually at least two extra tokens but we only need one extra token for the induction to work). We call S with $d^{out}(S) = 0$ a *sink* node. Note that when S is a leaf node, it gets at least one token if it is a sink node and at least two if it is a nonsink node. We prove inductively (going

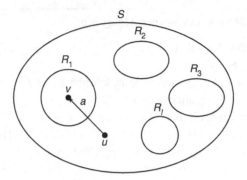

Figure 6.8   In this figure, set S has children $R_1, \ldots, R_l$ where all except R_1 are leaf as well as sink nodes. Thus, the tail u of arc $a \in \delta^{in}(R_1) \setminus \delta^{in}(S)$ must have two extra tokens, which it gives to S.

bottom-up in $\mathcal{L}$) that we can redistribute the tokens in the subtree of any nonleaf node $S \in \mathcal{L}$ so that every set gets at least one token and the root S gets at least two tokens. For the induction step, consider a nonleaf node $S \in \mathcal{L}$, and let its children be $R_1, \ldots, R_l$. If S has at least two children that are nonleaf nodes or are leaf nodes that are nonsink nodes, then S can collect one extra token from each such child by the induction hypothesis, and hence S has at least two tokens, as required. So assume S has at most one child R_1 that is a nonleaf node or a leaf node that is a nonsink node.

Since $x(\delta^{in}(S)) = x(\delta^{in}(R_1)) = 1$ and $\chi(\delta^{in}(S)) \neq \chi(\delta^{in}(R_1))$, there is an arc $a \in \delta^{in}(R_1) - \delta^{in}(S)$. Since $R_2, \ldots, R_l$ are sink nodes, the tail of a is not contained in $R_1 \cup R_2 \cup \cdots \cup R_l$ but is in S. Furthermore, since the tail of a has positive out-degree in the support, it has two extra tokens by the argument in the previous paragraph that it assigns to S, as required. The roots of $\mathcal{L}$ have extra tokens left, completing the proof.   □

6.5 Notes

The directed LP formulation for the minimum spanning arborescence problem is due to Edmonds [36]. The first polynomial-time algorithm for the minimum rooted k-connected subgraph problem was given by Frank and Tardos [46] via the use of submodular flows (which we will introduce in Chapter 7). Recently Frank [45] showed that the minimum rooted k-connected subgraph problem can actually be reduced to the matroid intersection problem, and that the biset LP for this problem is totally dual integral. The bicriteria approximation algorithm for the minimum bounded degree arborescence problem is by Lau et al. [88], while the additive approximation algorithm for the unweighted problem is due to Bansal, Khandekar, and Nagarajan [8].

Exercises

6.1 Show the equivalence of the directed LP and the flow-based LP in Section 6.1.1.

6.2 Write a compact formulation for the spanning tree problem. (*Hint*: Use the compact formulation for the arborescence problem.)

6.3 Show the application of the iterative method to formulate an integral LP for the rooted k-arc-connected subgraph problem. Use the same outline we have used as in the earlier chapters: LP formulation, properties of extreme point solutions, iterative algorithm, and its correctness and optimality.

6.4 Work out the details of the separation oracle for the biset LP relaxation for this problem. Also, show how the separation oracle can be adapted for the LP formulations that arise when some of the arcs are already chosen in a current solution.

6.5 A function g on bisets is intersecting bisubmodular if $g(S) + g(T) \geq g(S \cap T) + g(S \cup T)$ holds for any two intersecting bi-sets S and T. Prove that the biset function $d^{in}(S)$ is intersecting bisubmodular.

6.6 Show that in a bilaminar family, the inner members form a laminar family, and if $X_I \subseteq Y_I$, then $X_O \subseteq Y_O$ or $Y_O \subseteq X_O$.

6.7 Prove Lemma 6.2.5.

6.8 Can the approximation algorithms for the minimum bounded degree arborescence problem be extended to the minimum bounded degree rooted k-edge-connected subgraph problem?

7

Submodular flows and applications

Quoting Lovász from his paper "Submodular Functions and Convexity" [94]:

> Several recent combinatorial studies involving submodularity fit into the following pattern. Take a classical graph-theoretical result (e.g. the Marriage Theorem, the Max-flow-min-cut Theorem etc.), and replace certain linear functions occurring in the problem (either in the objective function or in the constraints) by submodular functions. Often the generalizations of the original theorems obtained this way remain valid; sometimes even the proofs carry over. What is important here to realize is that these generalizations are by no means l'art pour l'art. In fact, the range of applicability of certain methods can be extended tremendously by this trick.

The submodular flow model is an excellent example to illustrate this point. In this chapter, we introduce the submodular flow problem as a generalization of the minimum cost circulation problem. We then show the integrality of its LP relaxation and its dual using the iterative method. We then discuss many applications of the main result. We also show an application of the iterative method to an NP-hard degree bounded generalization and show some applications of this result as well.

The crux of the integrality of the submodular flow formulations will be the property that a maximal tight set of constraints form a *cross-free* family. This representation allows an inductive token counting argument to show a 1-element in an optimal extreme point solution. We will see that this representation is precisely the one we will eventually encounter in Chapter 8 on network matrices.

7.1 The model and the main result

7.1.1 Minimum-cost flows and minimum-cost circulations

Given a directed graph $D = (V, A)$, a source vertex $s \in V$, a sink vertex $t \in V$, a *capacity* function $c : A \to \mathbb{Q}_+$, a *cost* function $w : A \to \mathbb{Q}$, and a value k, the minimum cost s-t flow problem is to find an s-t flow of value k with $x_a \leq c_a$ that minimizes $cost(x) := \sum_{a \in A} w_a \cdot x_a$.

Recall that a flow function x assigns nonnegative flow values to each arc that obeys flow conservation constraints at all nodes except the source s and the sink t. The flow conservation insists that the flow coming via the in-arcs equals that going via the out-arcs. With these constraints at all nodes except s and t, the net out-flow from s equals the net in-flow into t, which is the value of this $s - t$ flow. The capacity constraints mentioned previously insist that the flow routes through an arc not exceed its capacity to carry flow.

Related to this classical problem is the minimum cost circulation problem, where each arc a has a lower bound d_a and an upper bound c_a, and the goal is to find a minimum cost circulation (i.e., a flow function that is conserved at all nodes including s and t) that satisfies capacity lower and upper bounds: $d_a \leq x_a \leq c_a$.

The problem of finding a minimum-cost s-t flow of value k can be easily reduced to a minimum-cost circulation problem: Just add an arc $a_0 = (t, s)$ with $d_{a_0} = c_{a_0} = k$, and $w_{a_0} = 0$. Also let $d_a = 0$ for each arc $a \neq a_0$. Then a minimum cost circulation in the extended directed graph gives a minimum cost flow of value k in the original directed graph.

Also the problem of finding a maximum value s-t flow can be easily reduced to a minimum-cost circulation problem in the extended directed graph: just define $d_{a_0} = 0$, $c_{a_0} = \infty$, and $w_{a_0} = -1$. Moreover, set $w_a = 0$ for each $a \neq a_0$. Then a minimum cost circulation gives a maximum value s-t flow.

Edmonds and Karp showed that the minimum cost circulation problem is solvable in polynomial time. One can now generalize this problem by extending the flow conservation constraints at each node in the circulation from singleton nodes to a collection $\mathcal{C}$ of node subsets. Also, the right-hand side of these constraints, which are all zero for the circulation problem can be generalized to be a submodular function $f(S)$ for the constraint for set S. These two generalizations of the circulation problem give the submodular flow problem.

7.1.2 Generalizing to submodular functions

Let $D = (V, A)$ be a directed graph, and let $\mathcal{C}$ be a *crossing family* of subsets of V (that is, if $T, U \in \mathcal{C}$ with $T \cap U \neq \emptyset$, $T \cup U \neq V$, $T - U \neq \emptyset$ and $U - T \neq \emptyset$, then $T \cap U, T \cup U \in \mathcal{C}$). Recall that a function $f : \mathcal{C} \to \mathbb{R}$ is called crossing submodular, if for all $U, T \in \mathcal{C}$ with $U \cap T \neq \emptyset$, $U \cup T \neq V$, $U - T \neq \emptyset$ and $T - U \neq \emptyset$ one has

$$f(U) + f(T) \geq f(U \cap T) + f(U \cup T).$$

Given such D, C, f, a *submodular flow* is a function $x \in \mathbb{R}^A$ satisfying

$$x(\delta^{in}(U)) - x(\delta^{out}(U)) \leq f(U) \text{ for each } U \in C$$

where $x(\delta^{in}(U))$ is a shorthand for $\sum_{a \in \delta^{in}(U)} x_a$ and similarly for $x(\delta^{out}(U))$. The set P of all submodular flows with the bound constraints $d_a \leq x_a \leq c_a$ is called the *submodular flow polyhedron*.

Note that the minimum-cost circulation, which we generalized from, can easily be seen to be a special case of a maximum-cost version of the submodular flow problem where the costs are -1 for every arc. Take $C = \{\{v\} \mid v \in V\}$; trivially C is a crossing family. Set $f = 0$; obviously f is a crossing submodular function. The maximum-cost submodular flow problem becomes

$$\text{maximize} \qquad \sum_{a \in A} w_a x_a$$

$$\text{subject to} \qquad x(\delta^{in}(v)) - x(\delta^{out}(v)) \leq 0 \qquad \forall v \subseteq V$$

$$d_a \leq x_a \leq c_a \qquad \forall a \in A$$

Note that no inequality at a vertex can be a strict inequality, and so the solution must be a maximum cost circulation. We refer to the above constraint system as constituting the submodular flow polyhedron.

The main result of this chapter is the following theorem.

Theorem 7.1.1 *If f is a crossing submodular function, then both the primal and the dual of the submodular flow polyhedron are integral.*

The result has myriad consequences many of which we will describe in Section 7.4.

7.2 Primal integrality

In this section, the integrality of the submodular flow polyhedron will be derived via an iterative method. We derive the result for the special case when the bound functions are $d_a = 0$ and $c_a = 1$ for all arcs a. The extension to more general integral bounds will be immediate and the subject of the exercises. We only use integral submodular function f in the sequel (but not necessarily nonnegative).

7.2.1 Linear programming relaxation

The linear programming formulation $LP_{smf}(D, f, w)$ is restated as follows.

$$\text{maximize} \qquad \sum_{a \in A} w_a x_a$$

$$\text{subject to} \qquad x(\delta^{in}(S)) - x(\delta^{out}(S)) \leq f(S) \qquad \forall S \subseteq V$$

$$0 \leq x_a \leq 1 \qquad \forall a \in A$$

As you might have expected by now, this linear program can be solved by the ellipsoid method, using the polynomial time algorithm for minimizing submodular functions as a separation oracle. To see this, note that the function $x(\delta^{in}(S)) - x(\delta^{out}(S))$ is modular since this is exactly $\sum_{v \in S}(x(\delta^{in}(v)) - x(\delta^{out}(v)))$. Thus, the function $g(S) = f(S) - (x(\delta^{in}(S)) - x(\delta^{out}(S)))$ is submodular and the separation problem is equivalent to checking whether the minimum of $g(S)$ is negative or not.

7.2.2 Characterization of extreme point solutions

As in previous problems, the uncrossing technique is used to find a "good" set of tight inequalities that defines an extreme point solution to the submodular flow LP. For a set $S \subseteq V$, the corresponding inequality $x(\delta^{in}(S)) - x(\delta^{out}(S)) \leq f(S)$ defines a characteristic vector $\chi(S)$ in $\mathbb{R}^{|A|}$: the vector has value 1 corresponding to each incoming arc $a \in \delta^{in}(S)$, value -1 corresponding to each outgoing arc $a \in \delta^{out}(S)$, and 0 otherwise. Let $\mathcal{F} = \{S \mid x(\delta^{in}(S)) - x(\delta^{out}(S)) = f(S)\}$ be the family of tight inequalities for an extreme point solution x in the submodular flow LP. The following lemma shows that this family is a crossing family. The proof is by now standard – you should work out the details to see how nicely the submodular constraint fits with our usual proof approach (e.g., Sections 4.1.4 and 5.2.2) for this lemma.

Lemma 7.2.1 *If $S, T \in \mathcal{F}$ and $S \cap T \neq \emptyset$ and $S \cup T \neq V$, then both $S \cap T$ and $S \cup T$ are in $\mathcal{F}$. Furthermore, $\chi(S) + \chi(T) = \chi(S \cap T) + \chi(S \cup T)$.*

Denote by span($\mathcal{F}$) the vector space generated by the set of vectors $\{\chi(S) \mid S \in \mathcal{F}\}$. Recall that two sets X, Y are *crossing* if $X \cap Y$, $X - Y$, $Y - X$ and $V - (X \cup Y)$ are nonempty. A family of sets is *cross-free* if no two sets are crossing. The following lemma says that an extreme point solution is characterized by tight inequalities whose corresponding sets form a cross-free family. The proof follows the same lines as in Lemma 4.1.5.

Lemma 7.2.2 *If C is a maximal cross-free subfamily of $\mathcal{F}$, then $span(C) = span(\mathcal{F})$.*

Lemma 7.2.2 and the Rank Lemma imply the following characterization of extreme point solutions.

Lemma 7.2.3 *Let x be any extreme point solution to $LP_{smf}(D, f, w)$ with $0 < x_a < 1$ for each arc $a \in A(D)$. Then there exists a cross-free family C such that*

(i) $x(\delta^{in}(S)) - x(\delta^{out}(S)) = f(S)$ *for each $S \in C$.*
(ii) *The vectors in $\{\chi(S) : S \in C\}$ are linearly independent.*
(iii) $|C| = |A(D)|$.

7.2.3 Iterative algorithm

An iterative procedure is used to find a minimum cost submodular flow from an optimal extreme point solution to $LP_{smf}(D, f, w)$. We fix the values of the arcs with $x_a = 0$ or $x_a = 1$, and update the submodular function accordingly. The algorithm is described in Figure 7.1.

7.2.4 Correctness and optimality

One nice feature of the submodular flow problem is self-reducibility: After an arc $a = uv$ with $x_a = 1$ is picked and the submodular function is modified appropriately, the residual problem is still a submodular flow problem. Assuming the algorithm terminates successfully, the returned solution is a maximum cost submodular flow using the by-now standard induction argument.

Theorem 7.2.4 *The iterative submodular flow algorithm in Figure 7.1 returns a minimum cost submodular flow in polynomial time.*

Iterative Submodular Flow Algorithm

(i) Initialization $F = \emptyset$, $f' \leftarrow f$.
(ii) While $A \neq \emptyset$ do
    (a) Find an optimal extreme point solution x to $LP_{smf}(D, f', w)$. Delete every arc a with $x_a = 0$ from D.
    (b) For each arc $a = uv$ with $x_a = 1$, delete a from D, add a to F, and update $f'(S) \leftarrow f(S) - d_F^{in}(S) + d_F^{out}(S)$ for each $S \subseteq V$.
(iii) Return the solution x.

Figure 7.1 Submodular flow algorithm.

The following lemma shows that the algorithm will terminate.

Lemma 7.2.5 *For any extreme point solution x to $LP_{smf}(D, f, w)$, either there is an arc with $x_a = 0$ or there is an arc with $x_a = 1$.*

The proof of Lemma 7.2.5 starts from a cross-free family C, which satisfies the properties of Lemma 7.2.3. From a cross-free family, a laminar family $\mathcal{L}$ is constructed as follows. Let $r \in V$ be an arbitrary vertex.

$$\mathcal{L} := \{X \subseteq V - r \; : \; X \in C\} \cup \{X \subseteq V - r \; : \; V - X \in C\}.$$

The first set includes the members of C, which does not contain r, and so is laminar. The second set includes the members of C, which contain r, and so their complements form a laminar family. Also it can be checked that a member in the first set does not intersect a member in the second set (otherwise they are crossing in C), and so $\mathcal{L}$ is a laminar family. Note that since the constraints in C are linearly independent, there are no repeated sets in the laminar family $\mathcal{L}$.

As usual, a counting argument will be used to derive a contradiction – assuming there is no arc with $x_a = 0$ or $x_a = 1$, then the number of inequalities is smaller than the number of variables. For each arc, one token is assigned to its head, and one token is assigned to its tail. So the total number of tokens assigned is exactly $2|A|$. These tokens will be redistributed such that each set $S \in \mathcal{L}$ is assigned two tokens, and there are still some excess tokens left. This will imply $|A| > |\mathcal{L}|$ and yield a contradiction. Let L be the forest corresponding to the laminar family $\mathcal{L}$. The following lemma shows that the redistribution is possible.

Lemma 7.2.6 *For any rooted subtree of the forest $L \neq \emptyset$ with root S, the tokens assigned to vertices inside S can be distributed such that every node in the subtree (including the root S) gets at least two tokens.*

Proof The proof is by induction on the height of the subtree. The base case is when S is a leaf. Since $x(\delta^{in}(S)) - x(\delta^{out}(S)) = f(S)$ and there is no arc with $x_a = 1$ or $x_a = 0$, either there are at least two incoming arcs, or there are at least two outgoing arcs, or there are at least one incoming and one outgoing arc. In any case, S can collect two tokens.

For the induction step, let S be the root and $R_1, \ldots, R_k$ be its children. By the induction hypothesis, each node in the subtree rooted at R_i gets at least two tokens, and R_i gets at least two tokens. To prove the induction step, S needs to collect two more tokens. If there is an arc that enters S but not any R_i, or there is an arc that leaves S but not any R_i, then S can collect one token from this arc. Suppose, to the contrary, that such an arc does not exist. Then

$$\text{sign}(S)(\delta^{in}(S) - \delta^{out}(S)) = \sum_{i=1}^{k} \text{sign}(R_i)(\delta^{in}(R_i) - \delta^{out}(R_i))$$

where $\text{sign}(U) = 1$ if the set $U \in \mathcal{C}$ and $\text{sign}(U) = -1$ if the set $V - U \in \mathcal{C}$, since each arc with the tail in R_i and the head in R_j with $i \neq j$ is canceled out in the summation. This implies that

$$\text{sign}(S) \cdot \chi(S) = \sum_{i=1}^{k} \text{sign}(R_i) \cdot \chi(R_i)$$

contradicting the linear independence of the characteristic vectors. Therefore, there must be at least an arc that has an endpoint belonging to S but not $R_1, \ldots, R_k$. If a is the only such arc, then

$$x(a) = \text{sign}(S) \cdot (x(\delta^{in}(S)) - x(\delta^{out}(S)))$$

$$- \sum_{i=1}^{k} \text{sign}(R_i) \cdot (x(\delta^{in}(R_i)) - x(\delta^{out}(R_i)))$$

$$= \text{sign}(S) \cdot f(S) - \sum_{i=1}^{k} \text{sign}(R_i) \cdot f(R_i).$$

Since f is an integer-valued function, then $x(a)$ must be an integer, a contradiction. So there must be at least two such arcs, and therefore S can collect two extra tokens, as required. $\qquad\square$

It remains to show that there are some unused tokens. Consider the roots $S_1, \ldots, S_l$ in the laminar family $\mathcal{L}$. If there is an arc with one endpoint not in any S_i, then the token in that endpoint is unused, as required. Otherwise, if no such arc exists, then the characteristic vectors of S_i are linearly dependent since $\sum_{i=1}^{l} \text{sign}(S_i)(\delta^{in}(S_i) - \delta^{out}(S_i)) = 0$, a contradiction. This completes the proof of Lemma 7.2.5.

7.3 Dual integrality

Consider the dual linear program for the submodular flow problem. We first write the dual linear program of the submodular flow linear program without the upper bound constraints on the arcs. The argument can be simply extended to deal with upper bounds on arcs and is left as an exercise. Denote the LP below by $LP_{dsmf}(D, f, w)$.

$$\text{minimize} \qquad \sum_{S \subseteq V} f(S)\, y(S)$$

$$\text{subject to} \qquad \sum_{S:a \in \delta^{in}(S)} y(S) - \sum_{S:a \in \delta^{out}(S)} y(S) \geq w_a \qquad \forall a \subseteq A$$

$$y(S) \geq 0 \qquad \forall S \subseteq V$$

The uncrossing technique can be used to prove the following claim, whose proof is similar to that of Claim 5.4.1 and Claim 5.4.3.

Claim 7.3.1 *There is an optimal solution y to $LP_{dsmf}(D, f, w)$ with the set $C = \{S \subseteq V(D) : y(S) > 0\}$ being a cross-free family of $V(D)$.*

Claim 7.3.1 implies the following restricted linear program, denoted by $LP_{rdsmf}(D, f, w)$, has the same objective value as $LP_{dsmf}(D, f, w)$.

$$\text{minimize} \qquad \sum_{S \in C} f(S)\, y(S)$$

$$\text{subject to} \qquad \sum_{S \in C: a \in \delta^{in}(S)} y(S) - \sum_{S \in C: a \in \delta^{out}(S)} y(S) \geq w_a \qquad \forall a \in A$$

$$y(S) \geq 0 \qquad \forall S \in C$$

As C is a cross-free family, one can show that the constrained matrix of $LP_{rdsmf}(D, f, w)$ is a network matrix (see Section 8.4.1). Since this is true for any set of costs w, by the result on LPs with network matrix constraints (Theorem 8.1.1), it follows that $LP_{rdsmf}(D, f, w)$ is integral, and hence the following result.

Theorem 7.3.2 *The linear program $LP_{dsmf}(D, f, w)$ is integral for any vector $w \in \mathcal{Z}^m$.*

7.4 Applications of submodular flows

In this section, we show some applications of Theorem 7.1.1, including the Lucchesi–Younger's theorem on directed cut cover, the polymatroid intersection theorem, and Nash-Williams' theorem on graph orientations. We remark that the main result in Section 6.2 about minimum cost rooted k-connected subgraphs was first proved by using Theorem 7.1.1.

7.4.1 Directed cut cover and feedback arc set

Let $D = (V, A)$ be a directed graph. A subset C of A is called a *directed cut* if there exists a nonempty proper subset U of V with $\delta^{in}(U) = C$ and $\delta^{out}(U) = \emptyset$.

Note that if a graph is strongly connected, then there is no directed cut in it. A *directed cut cover* (also known as a *dijoin* in the literature) is a set of arcs intersecting each directed cut.

Lucchesi and Younger proved the following min–max theorem for the minimum size of a directed cut cover, which was conjectured by N. Robertson and by Younger.

Theorem 7.4.1 (Lucchesi–Younger Theorem). *Suppose $D = (V, A)$ is not a strongly connected graph. Then the minimum size of a directed cut cover is equal to the maximum number of arc-disjoint directed cuts.*

We will derive the Lucchesi–Younger theorem from Theorem 7.1.1. The starting point is this simple observation.

Proposition 7.4.2 *Let C consists of all sets U such that the collection of arcs entering U forms a directed cut (i.e., $C := \{U \subseteq V \mid \emptyset \neq U \neq V$ and $\delta^{out}(U) = \emptyset\}$). Then C is a crossing family of subsets.*

To model the minimum directed cut cover problem as a submodular flow problem, we set $f(U) = -1$ for each $U \in C$ and $d(a) = -\infty$, $c(a) = 0$, $w(a) = 1$ for each arc. Note that since $\delta^{out}(U) = \emptyset$ for each $U \in C$, the linear program $LP_{smf}(D, f, w)$ simplifies to the following (after replacing the negation of the original flow variables by x below, hence transforming the maximization to a minimization problem):

$$\text{minimize} \quad \sum_{a \in A} x_a$$

$$\text{subject to} \quad x(\delta^{in}(U)) \geq 1 \qquad \forall U \subseteq C$$

$$x_a \geq 0 \qquad \forall a \in A$$

In this linear program, an optimal integer solution corresponds to a minimum directed cut cover, as the constraints ensure that every directed cut has an arc selected. On the other hand, the dual is

$$\text{maximize} \quad \sum_{U \in C} y(U)$$

$$\text{subject to} \quad \sum_{U \in C : a \in \delta^{in}(U)} y(U) \leq 1 \qquad \forall a \subseteq A$$

$$y(U) \geq 0 \qquad \forall U \in C$$

An optimal integer solution to the dual linear program corresponds to a maximum collection of disjoint directed cuts, as the constraints force the directed

cuts to be arc-disjoint. By Theorem 7.1.1, both the primal and the dual programs have integral optimal solutions, and thus the Lucchesi–Younger theorem
follows by the strong duality theorem of linear programming (Theorem 2.1.9).
Furthermore, an efficient separation oracle for the minimum directed cut cover
problem can be constructed via standard flow techniques, and thus the problem
can be solved in polynomial time.

7.4.1.1 Feedback arc set in directed planar graphs

An interesting corollary of the Lucchesi–Younger theorem is a min–max relation
for the minimum size of a feedback arc set in a directed planar graph. A *feedback
arc set* in a directed graph $D = (V, A)$ is a set of arcs intersecting every directed
cycle. The problem of finding a minimum feedback arc set is NP-complete in
general digraphs. For planar digraphs, however, the problem of computing
a minimum feedback arc set can be reduced to the problem of computing a
minimum directed cut cover.

Given a directed planar graph D, its *(directed) planar dual* D^* is constructed
as follows. Let G_D be the underlying undirected graph of D, and let G_D^* be
its planar dual (a vertex in G_D^* is a face of G_D, and two vertices in G_D^* are
adjacent if and only if the corresponding faces in G_D are adjacent). For each
arc wx of D, let yz be the corresponding dual arc in G_D^*. The direction of yz is
chosen so that it crosses the arc wx *from left to right*. Intuitively, the direction of
yz is obtained by rotating the arc wx clockwise. The resulting directed planar
graph is the planar dual D^*. It can be easily seen that the directed cycles of D
correspond to the directed cuts of D^*. See Figure 7.2. Recall that a feedback
arc set in D intersects every directed cycle in D. This corresponds to a set of
arcs in the planar dual D^* that intersects every directed cut in D^*, which is
by definition a directed cut cover in D^*. Therefore, by computing a minimum
directed cut cover in D^*, a minimum feedback arc set can be constructed in
D. Hence the minimum feedback arc set problem can be solved in polynomial
time in directed graphs. Moreover, the Lucchesi–Younger theorem translates
to the following beautiful min–max theorem.

Theorem 7.4.3 *Let $D = (V, A)$ be a planar directed graph. Then the minimum
size of a feedback arc set is equal to the maximum number of arc-disjoint
directed cycles.*

7.4.2 Polymatroid intersection

Recall that a matroid is characterized by its rank function: In fact, it can be
shown that r is the rank function of a matroid if and only if r is an integer-valued
nonnegative submodular function and $r(T) \leq r(U) \leq |U|$ if $T \subseteq U$. Given a

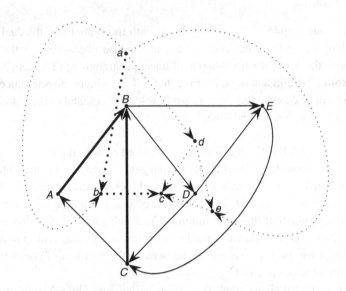

Figure 7.2 In this example, the directed planar graph D is shown in solid edges and its dual D' is dotted edges. The arcs (A, B) and (C, B) form a feedback arc set, and the corresponding dual edges (a, b) and (b, c) form a directed cut cover in the dual graph.

matroid M, we have already seen (in Chapter 5) Edmonds' characterization of the independent set polytope of M, as well as that of the common independent sets in the intersections of two different matroids.

The previous results can be generalized to arbitrary submodular function starting from the observation that the rank function of a matroid is a specific submodular function. Given a submodular set function f on a ground set V, the polytope defined below is called the *polymatroid associated with* f, which is an integral polytope if f is an integer-valued function.

$$x_s \geq 0 \ \text{ for } s \in S,$$

$$x(U) \leq f(U) \ \text{ for } U \subseteq S.$$

Similarly, for two submodular set functions f_1, f_2 on S, the following system characterizes the *polymatroid intersection polytope LP_{pmi}*:

$$x_s \geq 0 \ \text{ for } s \in S,$$

$$x(U) \leq f_1(U) \ \text{ for } U \subseteq S,$$

$$x(U) \leq f_2(U) \ \text{ for } U \subseteq S.$$

Notice that matroid intersection is a special case since the rank function of a matroid is submodular. The following theorem is due to Edmonds.

Theorem 7.4.4 *If f_1 and f_2 are submodular, then the polymatroid intersection polytope and its dual are integral.*

This result can be derived from Theorem 7.1.1. First, a directed graph $D = (V, A)$ is constructed as follows. Let S' and S'' be two disjoint copies of S, let $V = S' \cup S''$, and $A = \{s''s' \mid \text{for } s \in S\}$. Note that $D = (V, A)$ is a directed matching, where each arc in A corresponds to an element in the ground set S. Define $\mathcal{C} = \{U' \mid U \subseteq S\} \cup \{S' \cup U'' \mid U \subseteq S\}$ where U' and U'' denote the sets of copies of elements of U in S' and S'', and define $f : \mathcal{C} \to \mathbb{R}_+$ by

$$
\begin{aligned}
f(U') &:= f_1(U) && \text{for } U \subseteq S, \\
f(V \setminus U'') &:= f_2(U) && \text{for } U \subseteq S, \\
f(S') &:= \min\{f_1(S), f_2(S)\}
\end{aligned}
$$

Then $\mathcal{C}$ and f satisfy the crossing submodular condition. That is, $\mathcal{C}$ is a crossing family and f is a crossing submodular function since f_1 and f_2 are submodular functions. See Figure 7.3. If we take $d = 0$ and $c = \infty$, the submodular flow problem becomes the polymatroid intersection problem (for each U, the constraint for U' ensures that $x(U) \leq f_1(U)$ and the constraint for $V \setminus U''$ ensures that $x(U) \leq f_2(U)$). So Theorem 7.4.4 follows from Theorem 7.1.1. As

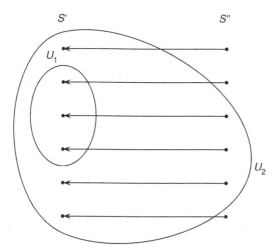

Figure 7.3 In this example, the graph D is shown along with two typical sets U_1 and U_2 in $\mathcal{C}$.

in the case of matroid intersection, a min–max theorem on polymatroid intersection follows from Theorem 7.4.4. The proof is the same as in the proof of Theorem 5.4.5.

Theorem 7.4.5 *Let f_1 and f_2 be submodular set functions on S with $f_1(\emptyset) = f_2(\emptyset) = 0$. Then*

$$\max_{x \in LP_{pmi}} x(U) = \min_{T \subseteq U}(f_1(T) + f_2(U \setminus T)).$$

Furthermore, the following *discrete separation theorem* can be proved, using a similar construction as in the proof of Theorem 7.4.4. We defer the details to the exercises.

Theorem 7.4.6 *Let S be a ground set, $p : 2^S \to \mathbb{Z} \cup \{-\infty\}$ a supermodular function and $b : 2^S \to \mathbb{Z} \cup \{\infty\}$ a submodular function for which $p(\emptyset) = b(\emptyset) = 0$ and $p \leq b$. Then there exists an integer-valued modular function m for which $p \leq m \leq b$.*

7.4.3 Graph orientation

Recall that a directed graph is strongly k-arc-connected if there are k arc-disjoint paths between every ordered pair of vertices. Given an undirected graph, when does it have a strongly k-arc-connected orientation? Nash-Williams proved the following necessary and sufficient condition.

Theorem 7.4.7 *An undirected graph G has a k-strongly-connected orientation if and only if G is $2k$-edge-connected.*

We derive Nash-Williams theorem using Theorem 7.1.1. The submodular flow problem is defined on directed graphs; to reduce graph orientation to submodular flow, we first choose an arbitrary orientation D of G. If D is strongly k-arc-connected, then there is nothing to prove. Otherwise, the task is to reverse the orientations of some arcs to obtain a strongly k-arc-connected orientation. For each arc a, there is a variable x_a, where $x_a = 1$ means that the direction of a will be reversed, while $x_a = 0$ means that the direction of a will be retained from the arbitrary initial orientation.

Let $\emptyset \neq U \subset V$ be an arbitrary subset. After reversing the directions of some arcs, the target is to have k arcs entering each set U (and thus by Menger's theorem, the resulting directed graph is strongly k-arc-connected). Before reversing, there are $d_D^{in}(U)$ arcs entering U. The number of new arcs entering U after reversing is $x(\delta^{out}(U)) - x(\delta^{in}(U))$. Therefore, to have k arcs entering U after reversing, the constraint is $d_D^{in}(U) - x(\delta^{in}(U)) + x(\delta^{out}(U)) \geq k$, and thus the goal is to find an integral vector x satisying

$$x(\delta^{in}(U)) - x(\delta^{out}(U)) \leq d_D^{in}(U) - k,$$

$$0 \leq x_a \leq 1.$$

Note that the right-hand side $d_D^{in}(U) - k$ is a crossing submodular function, and thus this "re-orientation" problem is a submodular flow problem. Observe that when G is $2k$-edge-connected, $x \equiv \frac{1}{2}$ is a feasible fractional solution to this submodular flow problem, since

$$d_D^{in}(U) + x(\delta_D^{out}(U)) - x(\delta_D^{in}(U)) = d_D^{in}(U) + \frac{1}{2}d_D^{out}(U) - \frac{1}{2}d_D^{in}(U)$$

$$= \frac{1}{2}d^{in}(U) + \frac{1}{2}d^{out}(U)$$

$$\geq \frac{1}{2}(2k - d_D^{out}(U)) + \frac{1}{2}d^{out}(U)$$

$$= k.$$

By Theorem 7.1.1, the linear program for the submodular flow problem is integral. Since there is a feasible solution when G is $2k$-edge-connected, there is also an integral solution when G is $2k$-edge-connected, proving Nash-Williams Theorem 7.4.7.

Note that by formulating the orientation problem as a submodular flow problem, many generalizations can be solved consequently. One example is the weighted version where the two possible orientations of an arc may have different costs, and the goal is to find the minimum cost strongly k-arc-connected orientation. This also includes a special case of orientating *mixed graphs*, where the directions of some edges are fixed.

Another example is the degree-constrained version where the indegree (and thus the outdegree) of each vertex is fixed. To see this, consider the following extra constraints:

$$x(\delta^{in}(v)) - x(\delta^{out}(v)) \leq d(v),$$

$$x(\delta^{in}(V - v)) - x(\delta^{out}(V - v)) \leq d(v).$$

These force the difference between $d^{in}(v)$ and $d^{out}(v)$ to be fixed, and so the resulting orientation must have $d^{in}(v) = d_D^{in}(v) - d(v)$, where $d_D^{in}(v)$ is the indegree in the initial orientation. These extra constraints are only defined on singletons and complement of singletons, and one can verify that the resulting function is still crossing submodular no matter what $d(v)$ is. We note that the degree-constrained orientation problem (even without connectivity requirement) already captures many interesting combinatorial problems such as bipartite matching, score sequences of tournament and basketball league winner problems.

7.5 Minimum bounded degree submodular flows

In this section, we consider the minimum bounded degree submodular flow problem, which is a generalization of the submodular flow problem, we just addressed earlier. In this problem, we are given a directed graph $D = (V, A)$, a crossing submodular set function $f : 2^V \to \mathbb{Z} \cup \{+\infty\}$, a node set $W \subseteq V$, and a function $g : W \to \mathbb{Z}_+$. A *degree-constrained 0–1 submodular flow* is a vector $x \in \{0, 1\}^{|A|}$ with the following properties:

$$x(\delta^{in}(S)) - x(\delta^{out}(S)) \leq f(S) \quad \text{for every } S \subseteq V,$$

$$x(\delta(v)) \leq g(v) \quad \text{for every } v \in W,$$

where $\delta(v) = \delta^{in}(v) \cup \delta^{out}(v)$. If $W = \emptyset$, then this is the well-studied submodular flow problem we encountered earlier. (Even though we have a minimization problem rather than the maximization version we introduced earlier, the transformation between the two is direct by negating the weights w.) However, the addition of the degree constraints makes the feasibility problem NP-complete. We show the following by adapting the iterative proof of Theorem 7.1.1.

Theorem 7.5.1 *There exists a polynomial time algorithm for the minimum bounded degree submodular flow problem which returns a 0–1 submodular flow of cost at most* OPT *that violates each degree constraint by at most one, where* OPT *is the cost of an optimal solution which satisfies all the degree constraints.*

7.5.1 Linear Programming Relaxation

The proof of Theorem 7.5.1 is based on the natural linear programming relaxation for the problem which we denote $LP_{bdsmf}(D, f, w, g)$.

minimize $$\sum_{a \in A} w_a x_a$$

subject to
$$x(\delta^{in}(S)) - x(\delta^{out}(S)) \leq f(S) \qquad \forall S \subseteq V$$
$$x(\delta(v)) \leq g(v) \qquad \forall v \in W$$
$$0 \leq x_a \leq 1 \qquad \forall a \in A$$

As before, this linear program can be solved by using an algorithm for minimizing submodular functions as a separation oracle.

7.5.2 Characterization of extreme point solutions

The following characterization of the extreme point solutions follows from Lemma 7.2.3 and the Rank Lemma.

Lemma 7.5.2 *Let x be any extreme point solution to $LP_{bdsmf}(D, f, w, g)$ with $0 < x_a < 1$ for each arc $a \in A(D)$. Then there exist a cross-free family $\mathcal{C}$ and a set $T \subseteq W$ such that*

(i) *$x(\delta^{in}(S)) - x(\delta^{out}(S)) = f(S)$ for each $S \in \mathcal{C}$ and $x(\delta(v)) = g(v)$ for each $v \in T$.*
(ii) *The vectors in $\{\chi(S) : S \in \mathcal{C}\} \cup \{\chi(\delta(v)) : v \in T\}$ are linearly independent.*
(iii) *$|\mathcal{C}| + |T| = |A(D)|$.*

7.5.3 Iterative algorithm

Before we go into the iterative algorithm for the minimum bounded degree submodular flow problem, let us first note that separate indegree and outdegree constraints can be incorporated into the submodular flow problem. This is achieved by a "node-splitting" technique, which will be useful in the iterative algorithm. Suppose we are given an indegree bound B_v^{in} and an outdegree bound B_v^{out} on a vertex v. To incorporate these constraints, we split the vertex v into two new vertices v^{in} and v^{out}, such that an arc uv is replaced by uv^{in} and an arc vu is replaced by $v^{out}u$. See Figure 7.4 for an illustration. The set function f is modified as follows:

$$f'(S) = \begin{cases} B_v^{in} & \text{if } S = \{v_{in}\}, \\ B_v^{out} & \text{if } S = V - \{v_{out}\}, \\ f(S) & \text{if } S \cap \{v^{in}, v^{out}\} = \emptyset, \\ f(S - \{v^{in}, v^{out}\} + v) & \text{if } \{v^{in}, v^{out}\} \subseteq S, \\ \infty & \text{otherwise.} \end{cases}$$

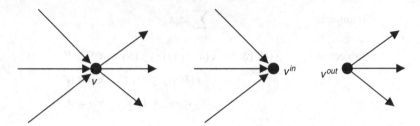

Figure 7.4 The node-splitting operation.

Iterative Minimum Bounded Degree Submodular Flow Algorithm

(i) Initialize $F = \emptyset$ and $f' \leftarrow f$.

(ii) While $A \neq \emptyset$ do

    (a) Compute an optimal extreme point solution x to LP_{bdsmf} (D, f', w, g). Delete all arcs a with $x_a = 0$.

    (b) For each arc $a = uv$ with $x_a = 1$, delete a from D, add a to F, decrease $g(u)$ and $g(v)$ by 1, and update $f'(S) \leftarrow f(S) - d_F^{in}(S) + d_F^{out}(S)$ for each $S \subseteq V$.

    (c) **(Relaxation 1)** For each vertex $v \in W$ with $d(v) \leq g(v)+1$, remove v from W.

    (d) **(Relaxation 2)** For each vertex $v \in W$ with $g(v) = 1$, remove v from W, add an indegree constraint $x(\delta^{in}(v)) \leq 1$ and an outdegree constraint $x(\delta^{out}(v)) \leq 1$.

(iii) Return the solution x.

Figure 7.5 Minimum bounded degree submodular flow algorithm.

It can be verified that f' is a crossing submodular function if f is a crossing submodular function, and thus the new problem is also a submodular flow problem. By construction, v^{in} has no outgoing arcs, and so the submodular flow constraint $x(\delta^{in}(v^{in})) - x(\delta^{out}(v^{in})) \leq f'(v^{in})$ reduces to the indegree constraint $x(\delta^{in}(v^{in})) \leq B_v^{in}$. Similarly, v^{out} has no incoming arcs, and so the submodular flow constraint $x(\delta^{in}(V - v^{out})) - x(\delta^{out}(V - v^{out})) \leq f'(V - v^{out})$ reduces to the outdegree constraint $x(\delta^{out}(v^{out})) \leq B_v^{out}$. Therefore, a feasible submodular flow in this new problem is a feasible submodular flow in the original problem satisfying the indegree and outdegree constraints on v.

With this node-splitting technique, we are ready to describe the iterative algorithm for the minimum bounded degree submodular flow problem (see Figure 7.5).

7.5.4 Correctness and performance guarantee

The iterative algorithm is similar to that for the submodular flow problem, but with two relaxation steps. The relaxation step in (2)c. is the usual step of removing a degree constraint on v when $d(v) \leq g(v) + 1$, and so the degree violation on v is at most one. The relaxation step in (2)d. is a new step, where a degree constraint on v is replaced by an indegree constraint and an outdegree constraint on v, which can be incorporated into the submodular flow problem via the node-splitting technique. Observe that the current solution corresponds to a feasible solution of this relaxation. Since $x(\delta^{in}(v)) \leq 1$ and $x(\delta^{out}(v)) \leq 1$, this means that the degree bound on v is violated by at most 1. Note that using the node-splitting technique the size of the graph is increased by 1 . However, the number of arcs is never increased, and $|W|$ decreases, so the number of steps is polynomial. Hence Theorem 7.2.4 would follow if the algorithm always terminates successfully.

A counting argument is used to prove that the algorithm always terminates. Each arc is assigned two tokens, for a total of $2|A|$ tokens. For each arc a, one token is assigned to each endpoint. We shall show that if none of the steps in the algorithm can be applied, then each set in $\mathcal{C}$ and each degree constraint in T can collect two tokens, and there are some tokens left. This would imply $|A| > |\mathcal{C}| + |T|$, which contradicts that x is an extreme point solution.

By Step (2)d. and Step (2)c. of the algorithm, we may assume that $g(v) \geq 2$ and $d(v) \geq g(v) + 2$ for every $v \in W$. Hence, $d(v) \geq 4$ for $v \in W$, and thus each degree constraint has two extra tokens. The remaining counting argument is very similar to that of Lemma 7.2.6, and so only the difference is highlighted here. The proof is by induction on the height of the subtree defined by the laminar family (constructed from the cross-free family as in Section 7.2.4). If a set S is the smallest set containing a vertex v with degree constraint, then S can collect two tokens from the extra tokens on v. Otherwise, the same argument as in Lemma 7.2.6 will give two tokens to S. This shows that each set in $\mathcal{L}$ and each degree constraint in T can collect two tokens. Finally, the same argument as in the last paragraph of Lemma 7.2.5 will prove that there is some unused token, a contradiction. Therefore, the algorithm always terminates, and this completes the proof of Theorem 7.5.1.

7.5.5 Applications

We close with some applications of the minimum bounded degree submodular flow problem.

Minimum bounded degree directed cut cover

Let $D = (V, A)$ be a directed graph. Recall that a set of vertices X is called a directed cut if $\delta^{out}(X) = \emptyset$, and a subset of arcs F is called a directed cut cover if $|F \cap \delta(X)| \neq \emptyset$ for every directed cut X (recall that $\delta(X) = \delta^{in}(X) \cup \delta^{out}(X) = \delta^{in}(X)$ for such sets X). In the minimum bounded degree directed cut cover problem, we are given a directed graph $D = (V, A)$, a cost function $c : A \to \mathbb{Z}$, and a degree bound $g(v)$ for each $v \in V$. The task is to find a directed cut cover $F \subseteq A$ of minimum cost such that $|F \cap \delta(v)| \leq g(v)$ for every $v \in V$. As seen in Section 7.4, the directed cut cover problem can be reduced to the submodular flow problem. Thus, Theorem 7.5.1 implies the following result.

Corollary 7.5.3 *There exists a polynomial time algorithm for the minimum bounded degree directed cut cover problem, which returns a directed cut cover F of cost at most* OPT *and $|F \cap \delta(v)| \leq g(v) + 1$ for each vertex $v \in V$, where* OPT *is the cost of an optimal solution that satisfies all the degree constraints.*

Minimum bounded degree graph orientation

In the minimum bounded degree graph orientation problem, we are given a directed graph $D = (V, A)$, a cost function $c : A \to \mathbb{Z}$, and a degree bound $g(v)$ for every $v \in V$. The task is to find an arc set of minimum cost whose reversal makes the digraph strongly k-arc-connected, with the additional constraint that the number of arcs reversed at each node v is at most $g(v)$. As seen in Section 7.4, graph orientation problems (with crossing supermodular requirements) can be reduced to the submodular flow problem. Thus, Theorem 7.5.1 implies the following result.

Corollary 7.5.4 *There exists a polynomial time algorithm for the minimum bounded degree graph orientation problem, which finds an arc set of cost at most* OPT *whose reversal makes the digraph strongly k-arc-connected and such that the number of arcs reversed at each node v is at most $g(v) + 1$, where* OPT *is the cost of an optimal solution that satisfies all degree constraints.*

7.6 Notes

The polyhedral result on submodular flows is due to Edmonds and Giles [39], generalizing the result by Lucchesi and Younger [95] on directed cut cover and the polymatroid intersection theorem by Edmonds [37]. This paper by Edmonds and Giles also introduced the notion of totally dual integrality and demonstrated the power of the uncrossing technique, which was developed earlier by Lucchesi and Younger [95] and Lovász [93].

The starting point of graph orientation problems is the result by Robbins [114] showing that a graph has a strongly connected orientation if and only if it is 2-edge-connected. This result is extended by Nash-Williams [104] to obtain Theorem 7.4.7 and a further generalization on local edge-connectivities. The reduction of graph orientation problems to the submodular flows problem is due to Frank (see [44] for a survey). The result on degree constrained submodular flow problem is from Kíraly et al. [80]. Gabow [55] also solves a degree constrained orientation problem using iterative rounding.

Exercises

7.1 Fill in the details of the proof of Lemma 7.2.2.

7.2 Prove Claim 7.3.1.

7.3 (a) Generalize the proof of the integrality of the LP formulation for the submodular flow problem when box constraints are present.

   (b) Generalize the proof of the integrality of the dual of submodular flow when the primal has box constraints. (*Hint*: Observe that upper and lower bound introduce extra variables on arcs. Argue separately with tight arc constraints for which these variables are zero and nonzero.)

7.4 Prove Theorem 7.4.5.

7.5 Prove the discrete separation theorem (Theorem 7.4.6) using a construction similar to that for the polymatroid intersection Theorem 7.4.5.

7.6 Verify that the degree-constrained graph-orientation problem introduced in Section 7.4.3 by verifying that the extra degree constraints introduced there still result in a submodular function in the right-hand side of the constraints.

7.7 Dilworth's theorem states that in any partially ordered set, the size of the maximum antichain is equal to the minimum number of chains needed to cover the whole set. Show that Dilworth's theorem is a special case of the submodular flow problem.

7.8 (Frank and Tardos [46]) We outline the reduction of the minimum cost rooted k-connected subgraph problem (in Chapter 6) to the submodular flow problem. The proof is divided into two main steps.

   (a) Let $G = (A, B; E)$ be a simple bipartite graph. Let p be an intersecting supermodular function and c be a nonnegative cost function on the edges. Call a subset $R \subseteq E$ *supporting* if $\Gamma_R(X) \geq p(X)$ for every $X \subseteq A$, where $\Gamma_R(X) := \{y \in B \mid yx \in R \text{ for some } x \in A\}$. Prove that the minimum-cost supporting set of a bipartite graph can be found in polynomial time via a reduction to the submodular flow problem.

(b) Let $D = (V, E)$ be a directed graph. For sets $X \subseteq V$ and $F \subseteq E$ denote $O_F(X) := \{u \in V - X :$ there is a $uv \in F$ with $v \in X\}$. Let p be an intersecting supermodular function and c be a non-negative cost function on the edges. We call a subset $F \subseteq E$ of edges *out-supporting* if $|O_F(X)| \geq p(X)$ for every $X \subseteq V$. Use (a) to prove that the minimum-cost out-supporting set of a digraph can be found in polynomial time.

(c) Conclude from (b) that the minimum cost rooted k-connected subgraph problem can be solved optimally in polynomial time.

7.9 Show that the minimum bounded degree submodular flow problem can be solved in polynomial time if there are only degree constraints on the in-degree and the out-degree of nodes. In particular, show that the method outlined in Section 7.5.3 works by showing that the modified function f' is indeed submodular.

7.10 What do the results in this chapter (mainly Theorem 7.5.1) imply for the feedback arc set problem in directed planar graphs?

8

Network matrices

In this chapter, we consider a simple model, based on a directed tree representation of the variables and constraints, called network matrices. We show how this model as well as its dual have integral optima when used as constraint matrices with integral right-hand sides. Finally, we show the applications of these models, especially in proving the integrality of the dual of the matroid intersection problem in Chapter 5, as well as the dual of the submodular flow problem in Chapter 7.

While our treatment of network matrices is based on its relations to uncrossed structures and their representations, they play a crucial role in the characterization of totally unimodular matrices, which are all constraint matrices that yield integral polytopes when used as constraint matrices with integral right-hand sides [121]. Note that total unimodularity of network matrices automatically implies integrality of the dual program when the right-hand sides of the dual are integral.

The integrality of the dual of the matroid intersection and submodular flow polyhedra can be alternately derived by showing the Total Dual Integrality of these systems [121]. Although our proof of these facts uses iterative rounding directly on the dual, there is a close connection between these two lines of proof since both use the underlying structure on span of the constraints defining the extreme points of the corresponding linear program.

8.1 The model and main results

Let $T = (V, E(T))$ be a directed tree (where all the arcs do not necessarily point toward a root – hence it is a weakly directed spanning tree, or a spanning tree on V in the undirected sense), and let $D = (V, E(D))$ be a directed graph on the same vertex set V.

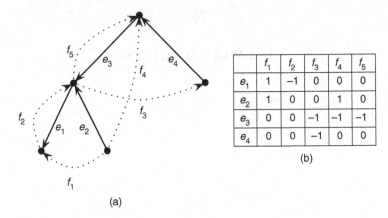

(a)

	f_1	f_2	f_3	f_4	f_5
e_1	1	−1	0	0	0
e_2	1	0	0	1	0
e_3	0	0	−1	−1	−1
e_4	0	0	−1	0	0

(b)

Figure 8.1 (a) Tree T is shown in bold edges and graph D in dotted edges. (b) The corresponding network matrix.

Define N, an $|E(T)| \times |E(D)|$ matrix in the following way for arcs $e \in E(T)$ and $f \in E(D)$. Let P be the path from tail of f to the head of f in T. See Figure 8.1 for an example.

$$\left(N_{ef} = \begin{cases} 0 & \text{if } e \text{ does not occur on } P \\ +1 & \text{if } e \text{ occurs in the forward direction on } P \\ -1 & \text{if } e \text{ occurs in the reverse direction on } P \end{cases} \right)$$

Such $\{0, +1, -1\}$ matrices arising from a given directed tree T and a given directed graph D on the same set of vertices are called *network matrices*.

A well-known result in combinatorial optimization is the integrality of linear programs with network constraint matrices.

Theorem 8.1.1 *Let N be a network matrix and b be an integral vector. Then the extreme point solutions of the linear program $\{\max c^T x : Nx \leq b\}$ are integral.*

This follows from the result that network matrices are actually a subclass of a broader class of constraint matrices that have integral extreme point solutions, called *totally unimodular* matrices. The latter are matrices that have all square subdeterminants equal to 0, +1, or −1, and permit several equivalent rich characterizations – for more on them, see the books by Schrijver [120, 121].

In this chapter, we use an iterative method to prove both Theorems 8.1.1 and its dual version 8.1.2, and discuss some applications of these theorems.

Theorem 8.1.2 *Let N be a network matrix and c be an integral vector. Then the extreme point solutions of the linear program $\{\min b^T y : y^T N \geq c^T\}$ are integral.*

8.2 Primal integrality

Following our framework we start with the natural linear programming relaxation for the problem.

8.2.1 Linear programming relaxation

For a tree arc $e \in E(T)$, denote $I(e)$ as the set of arcs in $E(D)$ whose tail-head paths in T contain e and are oriented in the same direction as e, and $O(e)$ as the set of arcs whose tail-head paths in T also contain e but are oriented in the opposite direction as e. We denote the following linear program by $LP_{net}(T, D)$.

$$\text{maximize} \quad \sum_{f \in E(D)} c_f \cdot x_f$$

$$\text{subject to} \quad \sum_{f \in I(e)} x_f - \sum_{f \in O(e)} x_f \leq b_e \qquad \forall e \in E(T)$$

$$x_f \geq 0 \qquad \forall f \in E(D)$$

8.2.2 Characterization of extreme point solutions

For an arc $e \in E(T)$, the corresponding inequality $\sum_{f \in I(e)} x_f - \sum_{f \in O(e)} x_f \leq b_e$ defines a characteristic vector $\chi(e) \in \mathbb{R}^{|E(D)|}$: The vector has a 1 corresponding to each arc $f \in I(e)$, a -1 corresponding to each arc $f \in O(e)$, and 0 otherwise. The following lemma follows directly from the Rank Lemma.

Lemma 8.2.1 *Let x be any extreme point solution to $LP_{net}(T, D)$ with nonzero x_f for each arc $f \in E(D)$. Then there exists a subset $R \subseteq E(T)$ such that*

(i) $\sum_{f \in I(e)} x_f - \sum_{f \in O(e)} x_f = b_e$ *for each $e \in R$.*
(ii) *The vectors in $\{\chi(e) : e \in R\}$ are linearly independent.*
(iii) $|R| = |E(D)|$.

8.2.3 Iterative algorithm

To devise an iterative algorithm, we look for a variable set to an integral value, and then modify the network representation appropriately by deleting this element and updating the constraint right-hand sides appropriately. The algorithm is shown in Figure 8.2.

Iterative Algorithm for Network Constrained Matrix Linear Programs

(i) While $E(D) \neq \emptyset$ do
    (a) Find an optimal extreme point solution x to $LP_{net}(T, D)$.
    (b) Fix an arc $f = uv \in E(D)$ with $x_f = a_f$ for an integer a_f. For every constraint $e \in E(T)$, update $b_e \leftarrow b_e + \text{sign}(f, e) \cdot a_f$ where $\text{sign}(f, e)$ is -1 if $f \in I(e)$, $+1$ if $f \in O(e)$, and 0 otherwise. Delete the arc f from D, and its corresponding column from the constraint matrix.
(ii) Return the integral solution x.

Figure 8.2 Algorithm for network constrained matrix problems.

8.2.4 Correctness and optimality

A simple verification shows that while fixing the variables in the iterative algorithm, the new constraint matrix is a network matrix as well. Indeed, for an arc f set to an integer value, along with the appropriate changes in the right-hand side to keep the residual program feasible, the network representation of the remaining variables is induced by the original one with the arc f removed from the directed graph D, while the tree T remains unchanged. Thus, assuming the algorithm terminates successfully, a standard inductive argument shows that the returned solution has optimal (maximum) cost.

Theorem 8.2.2 *The iterative algorithm for network constrained matrix linear programs in Figure 8.2 returns an optimal integral solution in polynomial time.*

The following lemma shows that the algorithm will terminate and completes the proof of Theorem 8.2.2.

Lemma 8.2.3 *For any extreme point solution x to $LP_{net}(T, D)$, there is an arc $f \in E(D)$ with integer value (i.e., $x_f = a_f$ for an integer a_f).*

The proof follows closely the proof of the similar lemma (Lemma 7.2.5) for the submodular flow problem. Suppose for contradiction that for each arc $f \in D$, we have that x_f is not integral. From Lemma 8.2.1, we start with a maximal set of tight constraints that are linearly independent at the extreme point solution x and denote the corresponding subset of arcs by R. Note that every arc in D has $x_f > 0$ since there are no integer valued variables. We will show a contradiction to $|R| = |E(D)|$ as stated in Lemma 8.2.1.

First, for ease of description, consider contracting the arcs in $E(T) \setminus R$ to get the reduced tree T'. Let V' denote the vertices in the contracted graph. We update the arcs in $E(D)$ by contracting the vertices accordingly, and call the resulting directed graph D'. Observe that this contraction does not affect any constraint for an arc in $R = E(T')$. We again use a counting argument to derive a contradiction: For each arc in $E(D')$ corresponding to a nonzero variable in x, one token is assigned to its head and one token is assigned to its tail. So the total number of tokens assigned is exactly $2|E(D')|$. These tokens will be redistributed such that each arc $e \in E(T')$ is assigned two tokens, and there are still some excess tokens left. We use a simple token assignment scheme: Every arc in $E(T')$ gets the tokens collected by its lower endpoint in the rooted tree. We then show that the root of the tree also has some tokens. Thus, we have $|E(D)| \geq |E(D')| > |E(T')| = |R|$, giving the desired contradiction. The following lemma shows that the redistribution works.

Lemma 8.2.4 *For the tree T' with root r, the tokens assigned to vertices in the tree can be distributed such that every arc in the subtree gets at least two tokens and the root gets at least two tokens.*

Proof First consider a leaf arc in the tree corresponding to a tight constraint. The nonzero variables contributing to this arc must have an endpoint at the lower end of this leaf arc. Since the right hand side of this arc's constraint is integral and no nonzero variable is integral, there must be at least two nonzero variables corresponding to arcs participating in this constraint, and hence at least two arcs from D' incident on the lower endpoint of this leaf arc as required.

Next, consider an internal arc $e = (u, v) \in T'$ oriented towards the root with lower endpoint u (if it is oriented the other way, the argument is symmetric by switching the signs appropriately). Let the arcs below e incident on u in T' be $e_1, e_2 \ldots e_k$. Consider the tight constraints corresponding to e and subtract from it, those corresponding to $e_1, \ldots, e_k$:

$$\left(\sum_{f \in I(e)} x_f - \sum_{f \in O(e)} x_f \right) - \sum_{i=1}^{k} \text{dir}(e_i, e) \cdot \left(\sum_{f \in I(e_i)} x_f - \sum_{f \in O(e_i)} x_f \right)$$

$$= b_e - \sum_{i=1}^{k} \text{dir}(e_i, e) \cdot b_{e_i}$$

where we define $\text{dir}(e_i, e)$ to be $+1$ if both are oriented in the same direction (along the path to the root) and -1 otherwise. Note that in the preceding sum we are only including the nonzero $a \in D'$. If any arc a originates in a vertex below u in one of the subtrees and ends in another vertex below u in a different subtree, its two contributions in the left-hand side get canceled out. Also, if an arc $a \in D'$ has one endpoint in a vertex below u and the other above u, then, again, its two terms get canceled out in the left-hand side. Thus, the only arcs whose contributions survive in the left-hand side in the preceding equation are those that have one endpoint in u, which are precisely those that give their tokens to u.

Now the left-hand side of the preceding equation cannot be zero since in that case, we have linear dependence between the tight constraints for arcs $e, e_1, \ldots, e_k$, contradicting Lemma 8.2.1. Thus, the left-hand side has a nonzero variable. But the right-hand side is an integer, and all the variables x_a in the left-hand side are nonintegral. Therefore, there must be at least two variables in the left-hand side, thus giving two tokens to the endpoint u as required.

To get extra tokens at the root of T', note that we can always root the tree T' at a leaf, and the argument we provided previously for a leaf applies to the root as well, giving it at least two extra tokens, and hence the desired contradiction.   □

This completes the proof of Lemma 8.2.3.

8.3 Dual integrality

We now look at linear programs that are dual to network constrained problems, and argue their integrality as well. Note that the constraint matrices of these dual linear programs are transposes of network matrices.

8.3.1 Linear programming relaxation

We start with the given linear programming relaxation for the problem. As before, for a tree arc $e \in E(T)$, denote $I(e)$ as the set of arcs in D whose tail-head paths in T contain e and are oriented in the same direction as e, and $O(e)$ as the set of arcs whose tail-head paths in T also contain e but are oriented in the opposite direction as e. Here c_f is integral for each $f \in E(D)$.

$$\text{minimize} \quad \sum_{e \in E(T)} b_e \cdot y_e$$

$$\text{subject to} \quad \sum_{e:f \in I(e)} y_e - \sum_{e:f \in O(e)} y_e \geq c_f \qquad \forall f \in E(D)$$

$$y_e \geq 0 \qquad \forall e \in E(T)$$

This is the dual of $LP_{net}(T, D)$ in the previous section, and we denote it by $LP_{dnet}(T, D)$. We proceed as in the previous section to prove the integrality of $LP_{dnet}(T, D)$, and hence Theorem 8.1.2.

8.3.2 Characterization of extreme point solutions

For an arc $f \in E(D)$, the corresponding inequality $\sum_{e: f \in I(e)} y_e - \sum_{e: f \in O(e)} y_e \geq c_f$ defines a characteristic vector $\chi(f) \in \mathbb{R}^{|E(T)|}$: The vector has a 1 corresponding to each arc e with $f \in I(e)$, a -1 corresponding to each arc e with $f \in O(e)$, and 0 otherwise. Lemma 8.3.1 follows directly from the Rank Lemma.

Lemma 8.3.1 *Let y be any extreme point solution to $LP_{dnet}(T, D)$ with non-integral y_e for each arc $e \in E(T)$. Then there exists a subset $D' \subseteq E(D)$ such that*

(i) $\sum_{e: f \in I(e)} y_e - \sum_{e: f \in O(e)} y_e = c_f$ *for each $f \in D'$.*
(ii) *The vectors in $\{\chi(f) : f \in D'\}$ are linearly independent.*
(iii) $|D'| = |E(T)|$.

8.3.3 Iterative algorithm

To devise an iterative algorithm, as before, we look for a variable set to an integral value, and then modify the network representation appropriately by deleting this element and updating the constraint right hand sides appropriately.

8.3.4 Correctness and optimality

A simple verification shows that the update steps in the algorithm in Figure 8.3 lead to a constraint matrix which is again a transpose of a network matrix, while the directed tree T and the directed graph D are modified by contracting the vertices $\{u, v\}$ corresponding to the arc $e = \{uv\}$ fixed. Thus, assuming the algorithm terminates successfully, it is straightforward to verify that the returned solution has optimal (minimum) cost.

Theorem 8.3.2 *The iterative algorithm for duals of network constrained matrix linear programs in Figure 8.3 returns an optimal integral solution in polynomial time.*

The following lemma shows that the algorithm will terminate.

Lemma 8.3.3 *For any extreme point solution y to $LP_{dnet}(T, D)$, there is an arc $e \in E(T)$ with integer value (i.e., $y_e = a_e$ for an integer a_e).*

Iterative Algorithm for Duals of Network Constrained Matrix LP

(i) While $E(T) \neq \emptyset$ do
  (a) Find an optimal extreme point solution y to $LP_{dnet}(T, D)$.
  (b) Fix an arc $e = uv \in E(T)$ with $y_e = a_e$ for an integer a_e. For every constraint $f \in E(D)$, update $c_f \leftarrow c_f + \text{sign}(e, f) \cdot a_f$ where $\text{sign}(e, f)$ is -1 if $f \in I(e)$, $+1$ if $f \in O(e)$, and 0 otherwise. Contract the arc e from T, and delete the corresponding column from the constraint matrix.
(ii) Return the integral solution y.

Figure 8.3 Algorithm for duals of network constrained matrix problems.

Suppose for contradiction, y_e is not an integer for any arc $e \in E(T)$. From Lemma 8.3.1, we start with a maximal set of tight constraints that are linearly independent at the extreme point solution y, and denote the corresponding subset of arcs by D'. Observe that $y_e > 0$ for each $e \in T$ since no variable is integral. We will show a contradiction to $|D'| = |E(T)|$ as stated in Lemma 8.3.1.

We use a counting argument to derive a contradiction: The arcs in D' corresponding to tight constraints in y also form a graph over the vertices in $V(T)$. First, we argue that the graph formed by D' is acyclic. Since $|E(T)| = |D'|$ and T is a tree, this implies that D' also forms a tree. Then we use the path in D' between the endpoints of an arc $e \in E(T)$ to show that the variable y_e must be set to an integer value, giving us the lemma.

In detail, first suppose for a contradiction that there is a cycle C (in the undirected sense) among the arcs in D'. Fix an orientation of the cycle, and let the arcs encountered in this order be $f_1, f_2, \ldots, f_k$ (not necessarily all oriented in the same direction as the cycle C). Consider the weighted sum of constraints corresponding to $f_1, \ldots, f_k$.

$$\sum_{i=1}^{k} \text{sign}(f_i) \left(\sum_{e: f_i \in I(e)} y_e - \sum_{e: f_i \in O(e)} y_e \right),$$

where $\text{sign}(f_i)$ is $+1$ if it is oriented in the same direction as C and -1 otherwise. Switching the order of summation, this is the same as

$$\sum_{e \in E(T)} y_e \cdot \left(\sum_{f_i \in I(e)} \text{sign}(f_i) - \sum_{f_i \in O(e)} \text{sign}(f_i) \right).$$

It is now easy to verify that since the arcs f_i form a cycle, the terms for every tree arc e cancel out in the above summation to reduce it to zero, thus showing that a cycle of tight constraints in D' are linearly dependent, contradicting Lemma 8.3.1. Thus, there are no cycles in D', and hence D' is also a tree.

Finally, consider an arc $e \in E(T)$ going from a leaf $u \in T$ to its parent v (the case when it is pointed to the leaf can be argued symmetrically). Since D' is a tree, there is an (undirected) path from u to v in D', say, $f_1, f_2, \ldots, f_p$. Again, consider the sum of tight inequalities

$$\sum_{i=1}^{p} \text{sign}(f_i) \left(\sum_{e:f_i \in I(e)} y_e - \sum_{e:f_i \in O(e)} y_e \right) = \sum_{i=1}^{p} c_{f_i}$$

where $\text{sign}(f_i)$ is $+1$ if it is oriented in the same direction as the path from u to v and -1 otherwise. Switching the summation to be over the arcs $e \in E(T)$, we can now see that this sum simplifies to either plus or minus the single term y_e. On the other side, the right-hand sides of the constraints corresponding to the arcs $f_1, \ldots, f_p$ are all integers, and so we finally get that y_e equals either plus or minus this sum which is an integer, as claimed.

This completes the proof of Lemma 8.2.3.

8.4 Applications

Traditional applications of the integrality of network matrices range from the integrality of vertex cover and maximum matching problems in bipartite graphs to its generalization to the max-flow min-cut theorem in digraphs. In this section, we use the framework of network matrices to show integrality of the dual LPs for various problems we encountered earlier, such as the maximum matroid basis problem and the maximum matroid intersection problem in Chapter 5, as well as the submodular flow problem in Chapter 7.

8.4.1 Matroid

In this section, we show the integrality of the dual linear program for the maximum weight basis problem as discussed in Section 5.4.1 and prove Theorem 5.4.2 which we state again.

Theorem 8.4.1 *The linear programming formulation* $LP_{dmat}(M)$ *is integral.*

Proof Let y be an optimal solution to $LP_{dmat}(M)$. Claim 5.4.1 implies that we can assume that the support of y is a chain $\mathcal{C}$. Moreover, the following restricted linear program, denoted by $LP_{rdmat}(M)$, has the same objective value as $LP_{dmat}(M)$.

$$\text{minimize} \qquad \sum_{T \in \mathcal{C}} r(T)y(T)$$

$$\text{subject to} \qquad \sum_{T \in \mathcal{C}: e \in T} y(T) \geq w_e \qquad \forall e \in S$$

$$y(T) \geq 0 \qquad \forall T \in \mathcal{C}$$

In the following lemma, we show the constraint matrix of $LP_{dmat}(M)$ is the transpose of a network matrix when $\mathcal{C}$ is a chain.

Lemma 8.4.2 *Given a set S, let $\mathcal{C}$ be a chain over the subsets of S. Then the $|S| \times |\mathcal{C}|$ matrix N, with the entry (e, R) for $e \in S$ and $R \in \mathcal{C}$ is 1 if and only if $e \in R$, is the transpose of a network matrix.*

Proof Construct a directed tree T with a root vertex r and one vertex for each set in $\mathcal{C}$. There is an arc from $R \in \mathcal{C}$ to $R' \in \mathcal{C}$ if and only if R' is the smallest set containing R. Moreover there is an arc from the set R to root r where R is the largest set in $\mathcal{C}$. Thus T is a directed path towards r.

The graph D is defined over the same vertex set. For each element e in S which is contained in some set of $\mathcal{C}$, there is an arc from the vertex corresponding to the smallest set containing e to the root r. See Figure 8.4. It is easy to check that the network matrix corresponding to (T, D) is exactly the transpose of the matrix N. $\qquad\square$

Theorem 5.4.2 now follows from Theorem 8.1.2. $\qquad\square$

8.4.2 Matroid intersection

In this section, we show the integrality of the dual linear program for the maximum weight common independent set problem as discussed in Section 5.4.2 and prove Theorem 5.4.4, which we state again.

Theorem 8.4.3 *The linear programming formulation $LP_{dint}(M_1, M_2)$ is integral.*

Proof Let y be an optimal solution to $LP_{dint}(M_1, M_2)$. Claim 5.4.1 implies that we can assume that the set $\mathcal{C}_1 = \{T \subseteq S : y_1(T) > 0\}$ and the set $\mathcal{C}_2 = \{T \subseteq S : y_2(T) > 0\}$ are chains over the ground set S. Moreover, the following restricted linear program, denoted by $LP_{rdint}(M_1, M_2)$, has the same objective value as

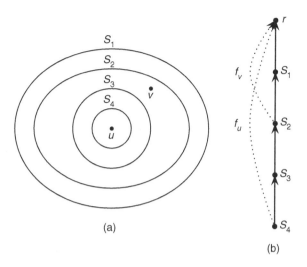

Figure 8.4 (a) The chain $\mathcal{C} = \{S_1, S_2, S_3, S_4\}$ is shown where $u \in S_4$ and $v \in S_2$. (b) The corresponding tree has a vertex r and one vertex for every set S_i. Each element in S corresponds to a nontree arc from the smallest set containing it to r. Hence f_u is from S_4 to r and f_v is from S_2 to r.

$LP_{dint}(M_1, M_2)$.

minimize $\displaystyle\sum_{T \in \mathcal{C}_1} r_1(T) y_1(T) + \sum_{T \in \mathcal{C}_2} r_2(T) y_2(T)$

subject to $\displaystyle\sum_{T \in \mathcal{C}_1 : e \in T} y_1(T) + \sum_{T \in \mathcal{C}_2 : e \in T} y_2(T) \geq w_e \qquad \forall e \in S$

$$y_i(T) \geq 0 \qquad \forall T \in \mathcal{C}_i, \ 1 \leq i \leq 2$$

In the following lemma, we show the constraint matrix of $LP_{rdint}(M)$ is the transpose of a network matrix when $\mathcal{C}_1$ and $\mathcal{C}_2$ are chains.

Lemma 8.4.4 *Given a set S, let $\mathcal{C}_1$ and $\mathcal{C}_2$ be chains over the subsets of S. Consider the $|S| \times (|\mathcal{C}|_1 + |\mathcal{C}_2|)$ matrix N, where the entry (e, R) for $e \in S$ and $R \in \mathcal{C}_1 \cup \mathcal{C}_2$ is 1 if and only if $e \in R$. Then N is the transpose of a network matrix.*

Proof Construct a directed tree T with a vertex r along with one vertex for each set in $\mathcal{C}_1$ or $\mathcal{C}_2$. For each set R in $\mathcal{C}_1$, there is an arc with its tail in R and its head in the smallest set containing R in $\mathcal{C}_1$. If R is the largest set in $\mathcal{C}_1$ then the head of the arc is the root r. For each set R in $\mathcal{C}_2$, there is an arc with its tail in R and its head in the largest set contained in R. For the largest set in $\mathcal{C}_2$ the tail

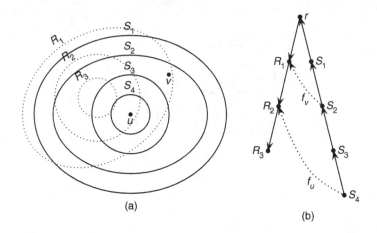

Figure 8.5. (a) The chains $\mathcal{C}_1 = \{S_1, S_2, S_3, S_4\}$ and $\mathcal{C}_2 = \{R_1, R_2, R_3\}$ are shown where $u \in S_4 \cap R_2$ and $v \in S_2 \cap R_1$. (b) The corresponding tree has a vertex r and one vertex for every set in $\mathcal{C}_1 \cup \mathcal{C}_2$. Each element in S corresponds to a non-tree arc from the smallest set containing it in $\mathcal{C}_1$ to the smallest containing it in $\mathcal{C}_2$. Hence f_u is from S_4 to R_2 and f_v is from S_2 to R_1.

of the arc is the root r. Thus, the tree T is a directed path toward the smallest set in $\mathcal{C}_2$.

We now define the graph D with the same vertex set as T. For each element of S which is contained in some set of $\mathcal{C}_1$ or $\mathcal{C}_2$, there is an arc from the smallest set in $\mathcal{C}_1$ containing e to the smallest set in $\mathcal{C}_2$ containing e. If no set in $\mathcal{C}_1$ or $\mathcal{C}_2$ contains e, then the head or the tail is changed to r accordingly. See Figure 8.5.

Again it is straightforward to check that the network matrix corresponding to (T, D) is the transpose of the matrix N.   □

Theorem 5.4.4 now follows from Theorem 8.1.2.   □

8.4.3 Submodular flows

In this section, we show that the dual linear program of the submodular flow problem is integral by reducing the constraint matrix to a network matrix as discussed in Section 7.3 and prove Theorem 7.3.2, which we state again.

Theorem 8.4.5 *The linear program $LP_{dsmf}(D, f, w)$ is integral for any vector* $w \in \mathcal{Z}^m$.

Proof Let y be an optimal solution to $LP_{dsmf}(D, f, w)$. Claim 7.3.1 implies that we can assume that the support of y is a cross-free family $\mathcal{C}$. Moreover, the following restricted linear program, denoted by $LP_{rdsmf}(D, f, w)$, has the same objective value as $LP_{dsmf}(D, f, w)$.

maximize
$$\sum_{S \in \mathcal{C}} f(S) y(S)$$

subject to
$$\sum_{S \in \mathcal{C}: a \in \delta^{in}(S)} y(S) - \sum_{S \in \mathcal{C}: a \in \delta^{out}(S)} y(S) \le w_a \qquad \forall a \in A$$

$$y(S) \ge 0 \qquad \forall S \in \mathcal{C}$$

We leave it as an exercise to verify that the the constraint matrix of $LP_{rdsmf}(D, f, w)$ is the transpose of a network matrix when $\mathcal{C}$ is a cross-free family. (This also follows directly from Corollary 13.21a of Schrijver [121].) □

8.5 Notes

A matrix A is called totally unimodular if every square submatrix has determinant in $\{0, +1, -1\}$. It is easy to see that if the constraint matrix of a linear program is totally unimodular and the right-hand side of the constraints is integral, then the linear program is integral. Total unimodularity is a very strong tool for proving integrality of linear programs for many optimization problems. The fact that network matrices are totally unimodular was proved by Tutte [129]. Total Dual Integrality, introduced by Edmonds and Giles [39], is a weaker condition than total unimodularity but is also very powerful tool in establishing integrality of linear programs for optimization problems. Indeed, almost all integrality results discussed in this book have been proven to be integral showing that the given linear programming description is also totally dual integral (see also [121]).

Exercises

8.1 Perhaps the most famous application of the fact that network matrix constraints result in integer solutions for LPs is to show the max-flow min-cut theorem: Given a directed graph with nonnegative capacities on the arcs, and a source node s and a sink node t, the maximum flow problem asks for the maximum set of disjoint paths from s to t obeying the capacities on the edges (i.e., the maximum number of paths using an arc is at most its capacity).

Formulate a LP relaxation for the maximum flow problem with the property that its constraint matrix is a network matrix. (*Hint:* Write one constraint per node except for t denoting flow conservation at all nodes except s, and observe that the constraint matrix is the node-arc incidence matrix of the digraph minus one row; show that such matrices have a network representation.)

8.2 One can formulate a linear program for the max-flow problem by first converting it into a circulation problem: namely, adding an extra arc from t to s and now insisting that the flow is conserved at all nodes (in-flow equals out-flow everywhere). To enforce a certain flow, we can add lower and upper bound constraints on the flow through all the arcs in the digraph. Formalize this equivalence, and show that this extended formulation also continues to have integral extreme points by casting it as a network matrix constrained problem.

8.3 Show using the integrality of the duals of network constrained matrices and strong LP duality, that the maximum $s - t$ flow in a digraph is the capacity of a minumum $s - t$ cut.

8.4 Prove Theorem 8.4.5. (*Hint*: Represent the cross-free family as a tree as in the proof of Theorem 7.2.4.)

9

Matchings

Given a weighted undirected graph, the maximum matching problem is to find a matching with maximum total weight. In his seminal paper, Edmonds [35] described an integral polytope for the matching problem, and the famous *Blossom* Algorithm for solving the problem in polynomial time.

In this chapter, we will show the integrality of the formulation given by Edmonds [35] using the iterative method. The argument will involve applying uncrossing in an involved manner and hence we provide a detailed proof. Then, using the local ratio method, we will show how to extend the iterative method to obtain approximation algorithms for the hypergraph matching problem, a generalization of the matching problem to hypergraphs.

9.1 Graph matching

Matchings in bipartite graphs are considerably simpler than matchings in general graphs; indeed, the linear programming relaxation considered in Chapter 3 for the bipartite matching problem is not integral when applied to general graphs. See Figure 9.1 for a simple example.

9.1.1 Linear programming relaxation

Given an undirected graph $G = (V, E)$ with a weight function $w : E \to \mathcal{R}$ on the edges, the linear programming relaxation for the maximum matching problem due to Edmonds is given by the following $LP_M(G)$. Recall that $E(S)$ denotes the set of edges with both endpoints in $S \subseteq V$ and $x(F)$ is a shorthand for $\sum_{e \in F} x_e$ for $F \subseteq E$.

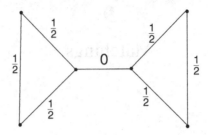

Figure 9.1 In this example, if the weight of the cut edge is small, then the fractional solution is an optimal solution to the linear program with only degree constraints.

$$
\begin{aligned}
\text{maximize} \quad & \sum_{e \in E} w_e x_e \\
\text{subject to} \quad & x(\delta(v)) \leq 1 && \forall v \in V \\
& x(E(S)) \leq \frac{|S| - 1}{2} && \forall S \subset V, \ |S| \ \text{odd} \\
& x_e \geq 0 && \forall e \in E
\end{aligned}
$$

Although there are exponentially many inequalities in $LP_M(G)$, there is an efficient separation oracle for this linear program, obtained by Padberg and Rao using Gomory-Hu trees. We refer the reader to the exercises for a description of the separation algorithm. In this section we prove the following main theorem.

Theorem 9.1.1 *Every extreme point solution to the linear program $LP_M(G)$ is integral.*

9.1.2 Characterization of extreme point solutions

We prove the following crucial lemma characterizing extreme point solutions to $LP_M(G)$. Again the uncrossing technique and the Rank Lemma form the basis of the argument, but there are also some parity arguments involved since the constraints are only defined on odd-sets. For a subset of arcs $F \subseteq E$, it defines a characteristic vector $\chi(F) \in \mathbb{R}^{|E|}$ with a 1 corresponding to each edge in F and 0 otherwise.

Lemma 9.1.2 *Let x be an extreme point solution to $LP_M(G)$ with $0 < x_e < 1$ for each edge $e \in E(G)$. Then there exists a laminar family $\mathcal{L}$ of odd-sets and a set of vertices $T \subseteq V$ such that*

(i) *$x(E(S)) = (|S| - 1)/2$ for each $S \in \mathcal{L}$ and $x(\delta(v)) = 1$ for each $v \in T$.*
(ii) *The vectors in $\{\chi(E(S)) : S \in \mathcal{L}\} \cup \{\chi(\delta(v)) : v \in T\}$ are linearly independent.*

(iii) $E(S)$ *is connected for each set* $S \in \mathcal{L}$.
(iv) $|E| = |\mathcal{L}| + |T|$.

To prove Lemma 9.1.2, we first prove the following claim about *tight odd-sets*, which are the sets S with $|S|$ odd and $x(E(S)) = (|S| - 1)/2$.

Lemma 9.1.3 *If* A, B *are tight odd-sets and* $A \cap B \neq \emptyset$, *then one of the following is true:*

(i) $A \cap B$ *and* $A \cup B$ *are tight odd-sets and* $\chi(E(A)) + \chi(E(B)) = \chi(E(A \cap B)) + \chi(E(A \cup B))$.
(ii) $A \setminus B$ *and* $B \setminus A$ *are tight odd-sets, the degree constraints in* $A \cap B$ *are tight, and* $\chi(E(A)) + \chi(E(B)) = \chi(E(A \setminus B)) + \chi(E(B \setminus A)) + \sum_{v \in A \cap B} \chi(\delta(v))$.

Proof First consider the case that $|A \cap B|$ is odd. Since $|A| + |B| = |A \cap B| + |A \cup B|$, this implies that $|A \cup B|$ is also odd. Hence, we have

$$\frac{|A| - 1}{2} + \frac{|B| - 1}{2} = x(E(A)) + x(E(B))$$
$$\leq x(E(A \cap B)) + x(E(A \cup B))$$
$$\leq \frac{|A \cap B| - 1}{2} + \frac{|A \cup B| - 1}{2}$$
$$= \frac{|A| - 1}{2} + \frac{|B| - 1}{2}$$

where the first inequality follows from supermodularity of the function $|E(S)|$ (Proposition 2.3.6), and the second inequality follows from the constraints of $LP_M(G)$. Hence both inequalities are satisfied at equality. The second inequality thus implies that $A \cap B$ and $A \cup B$ are tight odd-sets, while the first inequality implies that there are no edges between $A \setminus B$ and $B \setminus A$ and thus $\chi(E(A)) + \chi(E(B)) = \chi(E(A \cap B)) + \chi(E(A \cup B))$.

Next we consider the case when $|A \cap B|$ is even, in which case $|A \setminus B|$ is odd. Since $|A| + |B| = |A \setminus B| + |B \setminus A| + 2|A \cap B|$, it follows that $|B \setminus A|$ is also odd, and hence:

$$\frac{|A| - 1}{2} + \frac{|B| - 1}{2} = x(E(A)) + x(E(B))$$
$$\leq x(E(A \setminus B)) + x(E(B \setminus A)) + \sum_{v \in A \cap B} x(\delta(v))$$

$$\le \frac{|A \setminus B| - 1}{2} + \frac{|B \setminus A| - 1}{2} + |A \cap B|$$

$$= \frac{|A| - 1}{2} + \frac{|B| - 1}{2}$$

where the first inequality can be verified by counting the contribution of each edge, and the second inequality follows from the odd-set constraints of $A \setminus B$ and $B \setminus A$ and the degree constraints in $A \cap B$. Therefore, both inequalities must hold as equalities. The second inequality thus implies that $A \setminus B$ and $B \setminus A$ are both tight odd-sets, and also all the degree constraints in $A \cap B$ are tight. The first inequality implies that there are no edges with one endpoint in $A \cap B$ and another endpoint in $V - (A \cup B)$, and therefore $\chi(E(A)) + \chi(E(B)) = \chi(E(A \setminus B)) + \chi(E(B \setminus A)) + \sum_{v \in A \cap B} \chi(\delta(v))$.   □

The next claim shows that a tight odd-set that is not connected can be "replaced" by a connected tight odd-set and some tight degree constraints.

Claim 9.1.4 *If S is a tight odd-set for which $E(S)$ is not connected, then there exists a tight odd-set $R \subset S$ such that R is a connected component in S, and $2\chi(E(S)) = 2\chi(E(R)) + \sum_{v \in S \setminus R} \chi(\delta(v))$ and $x(\delta(v)) = 1$ for each $v \in S \setminus R$.*

Proof Since $|S|$ is odd, there exists a connected component R of $E(S)$ with $|R|$ odd, and

$$|S| - 1 = 2x(E(S))$$

$$= 2x(E(R)) + 2x(E(S - R))$$

$$= 2x(E(R)) + \sum_{v \in S - R} x(\delta(v)) - x(\delta(S - R))$$

$$\le |R| - 1 + |S - R| - x(\delta(S - R))$$

$$= |S| - 1 - x(\delta(S - R))$$

where the second equality follows because R is a connected component, the third equality follows from the fact that $\sum_{v \in S \setminus R} x(\delta(v)) = 2(x(E(S - R))) + x(\delta(S - R))$, and the inequality follows because of the odd-set constraint of R and the degree constraints for vertices in $S - R$. Hence, the inequality must hold as an equality, which implies that R is a tight odd-set that is connected, and $x(\delta(v)) = 1$ for each $v \in S \setminus R$. Furthermore, we must have $x(\delta(S - R)) = 0$, which implies that $\delta(S - R) = \emptyset$ and thus $2\chi(E(S)) = 2\chi(E(R)) + \sum_{v \in S \setminus R} \chi(\delta(v))$.   □

With the uncrossing operations developed in Lemma 9.1.3 and Claim 9.1.4, we are now ready to prove Lemma 9.1.2.

Proof of 9.1.2 The proof structure is similar to that of Lemma 4.1.5, but the details are more subtle. Let $\mathcal{F} = \{S \mid x(E(S)) = (|S| - 1)/2\}$ be the set of tight odd-sets and $T = \{\{v\} \mid x(\delta(v)) = 1\}$ be the set of tight vertices for an extreme point solution x to $LP_M(G)$. Denote by span$(\mathcal{F} \cup T)$ the vector space generated by the characteristic vectors in $\{\chi(E(S)) \mid S \in \mathcal{F}\} \cup \{\chi(\delta(v)) \mid v \in T\}$. Let $\mathcal{L}$ be a maximal laminar family of $\mathcal{F}$ with the additional property that each set $S \in \mathcal{L}$ is connected. Using Lemma 9.1.3 and Claim 9.1.4, we will prove that span$(\mathcal{L} \cup T) = $ span$(\mathcal{F} \cup T)$, and then the lemma follows directly from the Rank Lemma.

Suppose, by way of contradiction, that span$(\mathcal{L} \cup T) \subset $ span$(\mathcal{F} \cup T)$. Recall that two sets A and B intersect if $A \cap B, A - B, B - A$ are all nonempty. As in Lemma 4.1.5, we define intersect$(A, \mathcal{L}) = |\{B \in \mathcal{L} \mid A \text{ and } B \text{ are intersecting}\}|$ (i.e., the number of sets in $\mathcal{L}$ that intersect A). Since span$(\mathcal{L} \cup T) \subset $ span$(\mathcal{F} \cup T)$, there exists a set $A \in \mathcal{F}$ with $\chi(E(A)) \notin $ span$(\mathcal{L} \cup T)$. Choose such a set A with minimum intersect$(A, \mathcal{L})$ and then minimum $|A|$. We will show that $\chi(E(A)) \in $ span$(\mathcal{L} \cup T)$, leading to a contradiction.

First suppose that intersect$(A, \mathcal{L}) = 0$, then A must be disconnected; otherwise, $\mathcal{L} \cup A$ is also a laminar family with each set in $\mathcal{L} \cup A$ connected, contradicting the maximality of $\mathcal{L}$. By Claim 9.1.4, there is a tight odd-set B which is a connected component in A, and

$$2\chi(E(A)) = 2\chi(E(B)) + \sum_{v \in A \setminus B} \chi(\delta(v)) \tag{9.1}$$

where every vertex in $A \setminus B$ is in T. By Claim 9.1.5 we have intersect$(B, \mathcal{L}) \leq $ intersect$(A, \mathcal{L}) = 0$. Since $|B| < |A|$, by the choice of A, $\chi(E(B)) \in $ span $(\mathcal{L} \cup T)$, and hence by (9.1) it follows that $\chi(E(A)) \in $ span$(\mathcal{L} \cup T)$, a contradiction.

Therefore intersect$(A, \mathcal{L}) \geq 1$, and let $B \in \mathcal{L}$ be a set that intersects A. Since A, B are tight odd sets, by Lemma 9.1.3, either $A \cap B$ and $A \cup B$ are both tight odd-sets, or $A \setminus B$ and $B \setminus A$ are both tight odd-sets. First, consider the case when $A \cap B$ and $A \cup B$ are tight odd-sets. By Claim 9.1.6, both intersect$(A \cap B, \mathcal{L})$ and intersect$(A \cup B, \mathcal{L})$ are smaller than intersect$(A, \mathcal{L})$. Since A and B are both connected, $A \cup B$ is also connected, and thus $\chi(E(A \cup B)) \in $ span$(\mathcal{L} \cup T)$ by the choice of A. If $A \cap B$ is also connected, then we have $\chi(E(A \cap B)) \in $ span$(\mathcal{L} \cup T)$ by the choice of A. Otherwise, if $A \cap B$ is not connected, then by Claim 9.1.4 there is a tight odd-set R which is a connected component in $A \cap B$ such that

$$2\chi(E(A \cap B)) = 2\chi(E(R)) + \sum_{v \in (A \cap B) \setminus R} \chi(\delta(v)) \tag{9.2}$$

where every vertex in $(A \cap B) \setminus R$ is in T. By Claim 9.1.5 and Claim 9.1.6, we have intersect$(R, \mathcal{L}) \leq$ intersect$(A \cap B, \mathcal{L}) <$ intersect$(A, \mathcal{L})$, and thus $\chi(E(R)) \in \text{span}(\mathcal{L} \cup T)$ by the choice of A, and hence $\chi(E(A \cap B)) \in \text{span}(\mathcal{L} \cup T)$ by (9.2). Therefore, in either case, we have $\chi(E(A \cap B)) \in \text{span}(\mathcal{L} \cup T)$. Since $\chi(E(A)) + \chi(E(B)) = \chi(E(A \cap B)) + \chi(E(A \cup B))$ by Lemma 9.1.3 and $\chi(E(B)), \chi(E(A \cap B)), \chi(E(A \cup B))$ are all in span$(\mathcal{L} \cup T)$, this implies that $\chi(E(A)) \in \text{span}(\mathcal{L} \cup T)$ as well, a contradiction.

Finally we consider the case when $A \setminus B$ and $B \setminus A$ are tight odd-sets. By Lemma 9.1.3, we have

$$\chi(E(A)) + \chi(E(B)) = \chi(E(A \setminus B)) + \chi(E(B \setminus A)) + \sum_{v \in A \cap B} \chi(\delta(v)) \quad (9.3)$$

where each vertex in $A \cap B$ is in T. By Claim 9.1.6 both intersect$(A \setminus B, \mathcal{L})$ and intersect$(B \setminus A, \mathcal{L})$ are smaller than intersect$(A, \mathcal{L})$. If $A \setminus B$ is connected, then $\chi(E(A \setminus B)) \in \text{span}(\mathcal{L} \cup T)$ by the choice of A. Otherwise, if $A \setminus B$ is not connected, we can use a similar argument (using Claim 9.1.4) as in the previous paragraph to show that $\chi(E(A \setminus B)) \in \text{span}(\mathcal{L} \cup T)$. Similarly we have $\chi(E(B \setminus A)) \in \text{span}(\mathcal{L} \cup T)$. Since $\chi(E(B)), \chi(E(A \setminus B)), \chi(E(B \setminus A))$ are all in span$(\mathcal{L} \cup T)$, by (9.3) we also have $\chi(E(A)) \in \text{span}(\mathcal{L} \cup T)$, a contradiction.

To finish the proof of Lemma 9.1.2 it remains to prove the following two claims, whose proofs are deferred to the exercises.

Claim 9.1.5 *If A is not connected and R is a connected component in A, then we have $intersect(R, \mathcal{L}) \leq intersect(A, \mathcal{L})$.*

Claim 9.1.6 *If $A \notin \mathcal{L}$ and $B \in \mathcal{L}$ are intersecting, then all the four numbers $intersect(A \cap B, \mathcal{L})$, $intersect(A \cup B, \mathcal{L})$, $intersect(A \setminus B, \mathcal{L})$ and $intersect(B \setminus A, \mathcal{L})$ are strictly smaller than $intersect(A, \mathcal{L})$.* ∎

9.1.3 Iterative algorithm

Figure 9.2 shows a simple iterative procedure which returns a matching of optimal cost and also shows that $LP_M(G)$ is integral.

9.1.4 Correctness and optimality

Assuming that we can always find an edge e with $x_e = 1$ in Step (ii)b. of the algorithm, the returned solution is a maximum matching by using the by-now standard inductive argument. It remains to show that the algorithm always finds an edge e with $x_e = 1$ in Step (ii)b.

Iterative Matching Algorithm

(i) Initialization $F \leftarrow \emptyset$.

(ii) While $V(G) \neq \emptyset$ do

    (a) Find an optimal extreme point solution x to $LP_M(G)$ and remove every edge e with $x_e = 0$ from G.

    (b) If there is an edge $e = \{u, v\}$ with $x_e = 1$, then update $F \leftarrow F \cup \{e\}$, $G \leftarrow G \setminus \{u, v\}$.

(iii) Return F.

Figure 9.2 General matching algorithm.

Lemma 9.1.7 *Given any extreme point x to $LP_M(G)$ there must exist an edge e with $x_e = 0$ or $x_e = 1$.*

Proof Suppose for contradiction that $0 < x_e < 1$ for each edge $e \in E$. Let $\mathcal{L}$ be a laminar family of tight odd-sets and T be a set of tight vertices satisfying the properties given by Lemma 9.1.2. Let $\mathcal{L}' = \mathcal{L} \cup T$ be the extended laminar family. We show a contradiction to the fact that $|E| = |\mathcal{L}| + |T| = |\mathcal{L}'|$ by a token counting argument. Initially, each edge is given one token, for a total of $|E|$ tokens. Each edge will give its token to the smallest set in $\mathcal{L}'$ that contains both of its endpoints. Then we will redistribute the tokens inductively so that each member in $\mathcal{L}'$ receives one token and there are some tokens left. This will imply that $|E| > |\mathcal{L}'|$ giving us the desired contradiction.

Recall that a laminar family naturally defines a forest L as follows: Each node of L corresponds to a set in $\mathcal{L}'$, and there is an edge from set S to set R if S is the smallest set containing R, in which case we say S is the parent of R and R is a child of S. In this problem, the number of tokens a set $S \in \mathcal{L}'$ received is equal to the number of edges induced in S but not induced in the children of S. Henceforth, when we consider $S \in \mathcal{L}'$, it is more convenient to consider the graph G_S formed by contracting the children of S in $G[S]$ into singletons. See Figure 9.1.4. For a vertex $v \in G_S$, we let $R_v \in \mathcal{L}'$ be the corresponding child of S in $G[S]$. The following claim shows that G_S and $G[S]$ have similar properties.

Claim 9.1.8 *For $S \in \mathcal{L}'$, $|G_S|$ is odd and $x(E(G_S)) = \frac{|G_S| - 1}{2}$.*

Proof Let the children of S be $R_1, R_2, \ldots, R_k$. Since each R_i is of odd cardinality, contracting it into a singleton does not change the parity of the size, and hence $|G_S|$ is odd since $|S|$ is odd. Also, since each R_i is a tight odd-set, we have

$$x(E(G_S)) = x(E(S)) - \sum_{i=1}^{k} x(E(R_i)) = \frac{|S|-1}{2} - \sum_{i=1}^{k} \frac{|R_i|-1}{2} = \frac{|G_S|-1}{2}.$$

□

We say a set $S \in \mathcal{L}'$ is *degree-tight* if $x(\delta(S)) = 1$, and the characteristic vector $\chi(\delta(S))$ can be written as a linear combination of the characteristic vectors in the subtree of $\mathcal{L}$ rooted at S. Note that the tight vertices in T are the singleton degree-tight sets. The following claim gives a partial characterization when a set $S \in \mathcal{L}' - T$ is degree-tight.

Claim 9.1.9 *A set $S \in \mathcal{L}' - T$ is degree-tight if every vertex v in G_S is degree-tight.*

Proof Since $S \in \mathcal{L}'$, by Claim 9.1.8, we have $2x(E(G_S)) = |G_S| - 1$. Therefore, $x(\delta(S)) = x(\delta(G_S)) = \sum_{v \in G_S} x(\delta(v)) - 2x(E(G_S)) = |G_S| - (|G_S| - 1) = 1$. Note that

$$\chi(\delta(S)) = \sum_{v \in G_S} \chi(\delta(v)) - 2\chi(E(G_S)). \tag{9.4}$$

As each v is degree-tight, each $\chi(\delta(v))$ can be written as a linear combination of the characteristic vectors in the subtree of L rooted at R_v. Note also that $\chi(E(G_S)) = \chi(E(S)) - \sum_{v \in G_S} \chi(E(R_v))$. Therefore, by (9.4), $\chi(\delta(S))$ can be written as a linear combination of the characteristic vectors in the subtree of L rooted at S, and hence S is a degree-tight set. □

The token is redistributed inductively by the following lemma, in which degree-tight sets play a special role.

Lemma 9.1.10 *For any rooted subtree of L with root S, the tokens assigned to edges induced in S can be distributed such that every node in the subtree gets at least one token. Furthermore, the root S gets at least one token unless S is degree-tight.*

Proof We prove the lemma by induction. Let the degree-tight children of S be $R_1, R_2, \ldots, R_k$. Note that if a child R of S is not degree-tight, then R has already received one token from the edges induced in R by the induction hypothesis. Let $m := |E(G_S)|$ be the number of edges in G_S. Since each edge in G_S gives one token to S, S has m tokens. If $m \geq k+1$, then the tokens received by S can be redistributed so that each R_i receives one token and S receives one token, as desired.

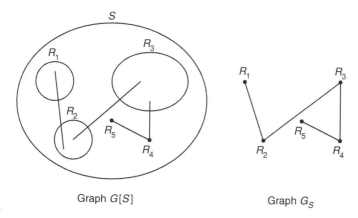

Figure 9.3 In this example, the nodes R_2 and R_4 are in G_1 and R_1, R_3 and R_5 are in G_2.

Hence, we assume that $m \leq k$. Since $G[S]$ is connected by Lemma 9.1.2, G_S is also connected, and thus $m \geq |G_S| - 1$. Suppose $m = |G_S|$. Then $k \geq m = |G_S|$, and so every vertex in G_S is degree-tight, and hence S is a degree-tight set by Claim 9.1.9. Therefore, by redistributing the $m = k$ tokens of S to give one token to each R_i, the lemma follows.

Henceforth, we assume that $m = |G_S| - 1$. Since G_S is connected, it implies that G_S is a tree, and thus is a bipartite graph. Let G_1 and G_2 be the bipartition of G_S. See Figure 9.1.4. Since $|G_S|$ is odd, we can assume $|G_1| < |G_2|$, which implies that $|G_1| \leq \frac{|G_S|-1}{2}$.

Since G_S is bipartite, we have $E(G_S) \subseteq \bigcup_{v \in G_1} \delta(v)$, and thus

$$\frac{|G_S| - 1}{2} = x(E(G_S)) \leq \sum_{v \in G_1} x(\delta(v)) \leq |G_1| \leq \frac{|G_S| - 1}{2} \qquad (9.5)$$

where the second inequality of (9.5) follows from the degree constraints of vertices in G_1. Thus, equalities hold as equalities. The second inequality of (9.5) implies that $x(\delta(v)) = 1$ for each $v \in G_1$, and it follows that

$$x(\delta(S)) = \sum_{v \in G_S} x(\delta(v)) - 2x(E(G(S))) = |G_S| - (|G_S - 1) = 1. \qquad (9.6)$$

The first inequality of (9.5) implies that $\chi(E(G_S)) = \sum_{v \in G_1} \chi(\delta(v))$, and so

$$\chi(E(S)) = \chi(E(G_S)) + \sum_{v \in G_S} \chi(E(R_v)) = \sum_{v \in G_1} \chi(\delta(v)) + \sum_{v \in G_S} \chi(E(R_v)).$$
$$\qquad (9.7)$$

Recall that we assume that $k \geq m = |G_S| - 1$. Suppose $k = |G_S|$. Then each vertex v in G_1 is degree-tight, and therefore each $\chi(\delta(v))$ can be written as a linear combination of the characteristic vectors in the subtree of L rooted at R_v. It follows from (9.7) that $\chi(E(S))$ can be written as a linear combination of the characteristic vectors in the subtree of L rooted at S (but not including S itself), contradicting the linear independence of the characteristic vectors in $\mathcal{L}'$ as described in Lemma 9.1.2.

Therefore, since we assume $k \geq m$, the only case left is $k = |G_S| - 1$, in which case exactly one vertex w in S is not degree-tight. If $w \in G_2$, then every vertex v in G_1 is degree-tight, and we would have the same contradiction as in the previous paragraph. Therefore, we assume $w \in G_1$, and thus every vertex in G_2 is degree-tight. Since $\chi(E(G_S)) = \sum_{v \in G_1} \chi(\delta(v))$ (see the sentence preceding (9.7)), we have

$$\chi(\delta(S)) = \sum_{v \in G_1 \cup G_2} \chi(\delta(v)) - 2\chi(E(G_S)) = \sum_{v \in G_2} \chi(\delta(v)) - \chi(E(G_S)).$$

As each vertex v in G_2 is degree-tight, $\chi(\delta(v))$ can be written as a linear combination of the characteristic vectors in the subtree of L rooted in R_v. Note also that $\chi(E(G_S)) = \chi(E(S)) - \sum_{v \in G_S} \chi(E(R_v))$, and thus $\chi(\delta(S))$ can be written as a linear combination of the characteristic vectors in the subtree of L rooted at S. This and (9.6) imply that S is a degree-tight set. Therefore, by redistributing the $m = k = |G_S| - 1$ tokens of S to give one token to each R_i, the lemma is satisfied. $\qquad\square$

To complete the proof of Lemma 9.1.7, we consider the graph G_V formed by contracting the roots of $\mathcal{L}'$ in G into singletons. Let the degree-tight vertices of G_V be $v_1, \ldots, v_l$, and let R_{v_i} be the corresponding odd-set of v_i in G. By Lemma 9.1.10, $v_1, \ldots, v_l$ are the only vertices in G_V requiring a token. Each edge in G_V has an unassigned token; we let $m := |E(G_V)|$. To prove Lemma 9.1.7, it suffices to show that $m > l$. Since each v_i is degree-tight, and there is no edge e with $0 < x_e < 1$, each v_i is of degree at least two in G_V. Hence,

$$2m = \sum_{v \in G_V} |\delta(v)| \geq \sum_{i=1}^{l} |\delta(v_i)| \geq 2l.$$

Suppose for contradiction that $m = l$. Then the inequalities must hold as equalities. The second inequality implies that G_V is a disjoint union of cycles, while the first inequality implies that every vertex in the cycles is a degree-tight vertex. Consider a cycle C in G_V. Since every vertex in C is degree-tight, we have $2x(E(C)) = \sum_{v \in C} x(\delta(v)) = |C|$. Therefore, C cannot be an odd cycle;

otherwise, $\bigcup_{v \in C} R_v$ is an odd set violating the corresponding odd set constraint in $LP_M(G)$. So C is an even cycle, and let C_1, C_2 be the bipartition of C. Then

$$\sum_{v \in C_1} \chi(\delta(v)) = \sum_{v \in C_2} \chi(\delta(v)). \tag{9.8}$$

As each vertex $v \in C$ is degree-tight, $\chi(\delta(v))$ can be written as a linear combination of the characteristic vectors in the subtree of L rooted in R_v. Hence, (9.8) implies a linear dependence among the constraints in $\mathcal{L}'$, contradicting Lemma 9.1.2. Therefore, $m > l$, and this implies that $|E| > |\mathcal{L}'|$, completing the proof. $\qquad\square$

9.2 Hypergraph matching

A hypergraph $H = (V, E)$ consists of a set V of vertices and a set E of hyperedges, where each hyperedge $e \in E$ is a subset of vertices. A subset $M \subseteq E(H)$ of hyperedges is a *matching* if every pair of hyperedges in M has an empty intersection. Given a hypergraph, a weight w_e on each hyperedge e, the hypergraph matching problem is to find a matching with maximum total weight. The graph matching problem is the special case when every hyperedge has exactly two vertices. A hypergraph is called k-*uniform* if every hyperedge has exactly k vertices. A hypergraph H is called k-*partite* if H is k-uniform and the set of vertices can be partitioned into k disjoint sets $V_1, V_2, \ldots, V_k$ so that each hyperedge intersects every set of the partition in exactly one vertex. Note that a bipartite graph is a 2-partite hypergraph. The main result of this section is the following theorem.

Theorem 9.2.1 *For the hypergraph matching problem, there is a polynomial time $(k - 1 + \frac{1}{k})$-approximation algorithm for k-uniform hypergraphs, and a $(k - 1)$-approximation algorithm for k-partite hypergraphs.*

We prove Theorem 9.2.1 for 3-partite hypergraphs. This is also known as the 3-dimensional matching problem, one of the classical NP-complete problem. The generalizations to k-uniform and k-partite hypergraphs are deferred to the exercises.

9.2.1 Linear programming relaxation

We use the standard linear programming relaxation for the hypergraph matching problem. In the following, $\delta(v)$ denotes the set of hyperedges that contains v.

$$\text{maximize} \qquad \sum_{e \in E} w_e x_e$$

$$\text{subject to} \qquad \sum_{e \in \delta(v)} x_e \leq 1 \qquad \qquad \forall v \in V$$

$$x_e \geq 0 \qquad \qquad \forall e \in E$$

For the analysis of the iterative algorithm, we consider a slightly more general linear program, denoted by $LP_M(H, \mathcal{B})$, where $\mathcal{B}$ denotes the vector of all degree bounds $0 \leq B_v \leq 1$ for each vertex $v \in V$. Initially $B_v = 1$ for each $v \in V$.

$$\text{maximize} \qquad \sum_{e \in E} w_e x_e$$

$$\text{subject to} \qquad \sum_{e \in \delta(v)} x_e \leq B_v \qquad \qquad \forall v \in V$$

$$x_e \geq 0 \qquad \qquad \forall e \in E$$

9.2.2 Characterization of extreme point solutions

Lemma 9.2.2 follows by a direct application of the Rank Lemma 1.2.3.

Lemma 9.2.2 *Given any extreme point solution x to $LP_M(H, \mathcal{B})$ with $x_e > 0$ for each $e \in E$, there exists $W \subseteq V$ such that*

(i) $x(\delta(v)) = B_v > 0$ *for each $v \in W$.*
(ii) *The vectors in $\{\chi(\delta(v)) : v \in W\}$ are linearly independent.*
(iii) $|W| = |E|$.

9.2.3 Iterative algorithm and local ratio method

The algorithm consists of two phases. In the first phase, we use an iterative algorithm to provide a "good" ordering of the hyperedges. In the second phase, we apply the local ratio method to this good ordering to obtain a matching with cost at most twice the optimum. The algorithm is presented in Figure 9.4. In the following, let $N[e]$ be the set of hyperedges that intersect the hyperedge e. Note that $e \in N[e]$.

We remark that if the problem is unweighted, then there is a direct iterative rounding algorithm (see exercises). Also, after we have the ordering, there is an alternative (but inefficient) rounding method based on a greedy coloring procedure. See the exercises at the end of this chapter for more details about these two remarks.

Iterative 3-Dimensional Matching Algorithm

(i) Find an optimal extreme point solution x to $LP_M(H,\mathcal{B})$ with $B_v = 1$ for all v. Initialize $F \leftarrow \emptyset$.

(ii) For i from 1 to $|E(H)|$ do

    (a) Find a hyperedge e with $x(N[e]) \leq 2$.

    (b) Set $f_i \leftarrow e$ and $F \leftarrow F \cup \{f_i\}$.

    (c) Remove e from H.

    (d) Decrease B_v by x_e for all $v \in e$.

(iii) $M \leftarrow$ local-ratio(F,w), where w is the weight vector of the hyperedges.

(iv) Return M.

Figure 9.4 Three-dimensional matching algorithm.

Local-Ratio(F,w)

(i) Remove from F all hyperedges with nonpositive weights.

(ii) If $F = \emptyset$, then return $\emptyset$.

(iii) Choose from F the hyperedge e with the smallest index. Decompose the weight vector $w = w_1 + w_2$ where

$$w_1(e') = \begin{cases} w(e) & \text{if } e' \in N[e], \\ 0 & \text{otherwise.} \end{cases}$$

(iv) $M' \leftarrow$ Local-Ratio(F, w_2).

(v) If $M' \cup \{e\}$ is a matching, return $M' \cup \{e\}$; else return M'.

Figure 9.5 The local ratio routine.

The local-ratio routine described later provides an efficient procedure to obtain a 2-approximate solution for the 3-dimensional matching problem.

To prove the correctness of the algorithm, we show that the iterative algorithm always succeeds in finding an ordering with a "good" property. Then, using the property of the ordering, we prove that the local ratio method in Figure 9.5 will return a matching with cost at least half the optimum. The good property of the ordering is defined in the following theorem.

Theorem 9.2.3 *After Step (ii) of the iterative algorithm in Figure 9.4, there is an ordering of the hyperedges with $x(N[e_i] \cap \{e_i, e_{i+1}, \ldots, e_m\}) \leq 2$ for all*

$1 \leq i \leq m$, where m is the number of hyperedges in x with positive fractional value.

The proof of Theorem 9.2.3 consists of two steps. First, in Lemma 9.2.4, we prove that there is a hyperedge e with $x(N[e]) \leq 2$ in an extreme point solution to $LP_M(H,\mathcal{B})$. Since the initial solution x is an extreme point solution, this implies that the first iteration of Step (ii) of the iterative algorithm will succeed. Then we prove in Lemma 9.2.5 that the remaining solution (after removing e and updating B_v) is still an extreme point solution to $LP_M(H,\mathcal{B})$. Therefore, by applying Lemma 9.2.4 inductively, the iterative algorithm will succeed in finding an ordering of hyperedges $\{e_1,\ldots,e_m\}$ with $x(N[e_i] \cap \{e_i,e_{i+1},\ldots,e_m\}) \leq 2$ for all $1 \leq i \leq m$. Now we prove Lemma 9.2.4.

Lemma 9.2.4 *Suppose x is an extreme point solution to $LP_M(H,\mathcal{B})$. If $x_e > 0$ for all $e \in E$, then there is a hyperedge e with $x(N[e]) \leq 2$.*

Proof Let W be the set of tight vertices as described in Lemma 9.2.2. To show that there is a hyperedge with the required property, we first prove that in any extreme point solution to $LP_M(H,\mathcal{B})$ there is a vertex in W of degree at most two. Suppose for contradiction that every vertex in W is of degree at least three. This implies that

$$|W| = |E| = \frac{\sum_{v \in V} |\delta(v)|}{3} \geq \frac{\sum_{v \in W} |\delta(v)|}{3} \geq |W|$$

where the first equality follows from Lemma 9.2.2, the second equality follows because every hyperedge contains exactly three vertices. Hence the inequalities must hold as equalities. In particular the first inequality implies that every hyperedge is contained in W. Let V_1, V_2, V_3 be the tripartition of V, and $W_i = W \cap V_i$ for $1 \leq i \leq 3$. Since each hyperedge intersects W_i exactly once, we have

$$\sum_{v \in W_1} \chi(\delta(v)) = \sum_{v \in W_2} \chi(\delta(v)).$$

This implies that the characteristic vectors in W are not linearly independent, contradicting Lemma 9.2.2. Therefore, there is a vertex $u \in W$ of degree at most two. Let $e = \{u,v,w\}$ be the hyperedge in $\delta(u)$ with larger weight. Since u is of degree at most two, this implies that $2x_e \geq x(\delta(u))$. Therefore,

$$x(N[e]) \leq x(\delta(u)) + x(\delta(v)) + x(\delta(w)) - 2x_e \leq x(\delta(v)) + x(\delta(w))$$
$$\leq B_v + B_w \leq 2$$

$\square$

The following lemma allows Lemma 9.2.4 to be applied inductively to complete the proof of Theorem 9.2.3.

Lemma 9.2.5 *In any iteration of Step (ii) of the algorithm in Figure 9.4, the restriction of the fractional solution is an extreme point solution to* $LP_M(H, \mathcal{B})$.

Proof Suppose the graph in the current iteration is $H = (V, E)$. Let x_E be the restriction of the initial extreme point solution x to E. We prove by induction on the number of iterations that x_E is an extreme point solution to $LP_M(H, \mathcal{B})$. This holds in the first iteration by Step (i) of the algorithm. Let $e = \{v_1, v_2, v_3\}$ be the hyperedge found in Step (ii)(a) of the algorithm. Let $E' = E - e$ and $H' = (V, E')$. Let $\mathcal{B}'$ be the updated degree bound vector. We prove that $x_{E'}$ is an extreme point solution to $LP_M(H', \mathcal{B}')$. Since the degree bounds of v_1, v_2, v_3 are decreased by exactly x_e, it follows that $x_{E'}$ is still a feasible solution. Suppose to the contrary that $x_{E'}$ is not an extreme point solution to $LP_M(H', \mathcal{B}')$. This means that $x_{E'}$ can be written as a convex combination of two different feasible solutions y_1 and y_2 to $LP_M(H', \mathcal{B}')$. Extending y_1 and y_2 by setting the fractional value on e to be x_e, this implies that x_E can be written as a convex combination of two different feasible solutions to $LP_M(H, \mathcal{B})$, contradicting that x_E is an extreme point solution. Hence $x_{E'}$ is an extreme point solution to $LP_M(H', \mathcal{B}')$.
$\square$

Now we use the local-ratio method to obtain an efficient approximation algorithm for the 3-dimensional matching problem. We need the following basic result of the local-ratio method.

Theorem 9.2.6 (Local-Ratio Theorem [11]) *Let* $\mathcal{C}$ *be a set of vectors in* $\mathbb{R}^n$. *Let* $w, w_1, w_2 \in \mathbb{R}^n$ *be such that* $w = w_1 + w_2$. *Suppose* $x \in \mathcal{C}$ *is r-approximate with respect to* w_1 *and r-approximate with respect to* w_2. *Then* x *is r-approximate with respect to* w.

Using the ordering in Theorem 9.2.3, we prove the performance guarantee of the approximation algorithm. Note that by construction the local ratio routine returns a matching. It remains to prove that the cost of the returned matching is at least half the optimum.

Theorem 9.2.7 *Let* x *be an optimal extreme point solution to* $LP_M(H, \mathcal{B})$. *The matching* M *returned by the algorithm in Figure 9.5 satisfies* $w(M) \geq \frac{1}{2} \cdot w \cdot x$.

Proof The proof is by induction on the number of hyperedges having positive weights. The theorem holds in the base case when there are no hyperedges with positive weights. Let e be the hyperedge e chosen in Step 9.2.3 of the algorithm. Since e has the smallest index in the ordering, by Theorem 9.2.3, we have $x(N[e]) \leq 2$. Let w, w_1, w_2 be the weight vectors computed in Step (iii) of the algorithm. Let y' and y be the characteristic vectors for M' and M obtained in Step (iv) and Step (v) respectively. Since $w(e) > 0$ and $w_2(e) = 0$, w_2 has fewer hyperedges with positive weights than w. By the induction hypothesis, $w_2 \cdot y' \geq \frac{1}{2} \cdot w_2 \cdot x$. Since $w_2(e) = 0$, this implies that $w_2 \cdot y \geq \frac{1}{2} \cdot w_2 \cdot x$. By Step (v) of the algorithm, at least one hyperedge in $N[e]$ is in M. Since $x(N[e]) \leq 2$ and $w_1(e') = w(e)$ for all $e' \in N[e]$, it follows that $w_1 \cdot y \geq \frac{1}{2} \cdot w_1 \cdot x$. Therefore, by Theorem 9.2.6, we have $w \cdot y \geq \frac{1}{2} \cdot w \cdot x$. This shows that M is a 2-approximate solution to the 3-dimensional matching problem. $\square$

9.2.4 Partial Latin square

As an application, we show that the partial Latin square problem can be directly reduced to the 3-dimensional matching problem. A partial Latin square of order n is an n-by-n array whose cells are empty or contain one color from $\{1, \ldots, n\}$, with the restriction that each color appears at most once in each row and at most once in each column. For a partial Latin square L, the number of nonempty cells in L is denoted by $|L|$, and the color of a nonempty cell in row i and column j is denoted by $L(i, j)$. For two partial Latin squares L and L', we say $L \preceq L'$ if $L(i, j) = L'(i, j)$ for each nonempty cell in L. Given a partial Latin square L, the partial Latin square extension problem is to find a partial Latin square L' with $L \preceq L'$ and $|L'| - |L|$ maximized.

We show an approximation ratio preserving reduction from the partial Latin square extension problem to the 3-dimensional matching problem. Given a partial Latin square L of order n, we construct a tripartite hypergraph $H = (V, E)$ with $3n^2$ vertices. Let V_{xy}, V_{xz}, V_{yz} be the tripartition of V. In V_{xy} there is one vertex $x_i y_j$ corresponding to each pair of row i and column j for all $1 \leq i, j \leq n$. Similarly, in V_{xz} there is one vertex $x_i z_k$ corresponding to each pair of row i and color k for all $1 \leq i, k \leq n$, and in V_{yz} there is one vertex $y_j z_k$ corresponding to each pair of column j and color k for all $1 \leq j, k \leq n$. There is a hyperedge $e = \{x_i y_j, x_i z_k, y_j z_k\}$ in H if the cell in row i and column j is empty and the color k does not appear in row i or column j. There is a one-to-one correspondence between matchings of size m in H and valid extensions of m cells for L. Indeed, if $e = \{x_i y_j, x_i z_k, y_j z_k\}$ is in the matching, then we fill the cell in row i and column j by color k, and vice versa.

9.3 Notes

The work of Edmonds [35] first showed the polyhedral characterization for the general matching problem. It forms the first class of polytopes whose characterization does not simply follow just from total unimodularity, and its description was a "break-through in polyhedral combinatorics" [121]. Cunningham and Marsh [32] showed that Edmonds' description is actually totally dual integral. In the same paper [35], Edmonds also presented the famous *Blossom* algorithm for solving the maximum matching problem in polynomial time.

Most existing algorithms for the 3-dimensional matching problem are based on local search [5, 14, 31, 72]. Hurkens and Schrijver [72] gave a $(\frac{k}{2} + \epsilon)$-approximation algorithm for the unweighted problem, and Berman [14] gave a $(\frac{k+1}{2} + \epsilon)$-approximation algorithm for the weighted problem. The result presented in this chapter is by Chan and Lau [26], giving an algorithmic proof for the results by Füredi [51] and Füredi, Kahn, and Seymour [52]. There is a local search 1.5-approximation algorithm for the partial Latin square extension problem [69]; the reduction in Section 9.2.4 shows that the result in [69] can be derived from the result in [72].

Exercises

9.1 Verify Claim 9.1.5 and Claim 9.1.6.

9.2 Adapt the arguments in this chapter to show an integral formulation for the maximum weight k-matching problem of choosing a set of k independent edges of maximum weight in a given undirected graph. In particular, argue that it suffices to add one equality constraint insisting that the sum of chosen edges is k to our formulation for maximum matchings to achieve this.

9.3 In an instance of the T-join problem, we are given a graph $G = (V, E)$ with weight function $w : E \to \mathcal{R}^+$ and a set T of even cardinality, the task is to find a subgraph H such that the degree of v in $H, d_H(v)$ is even if $v \notin T$ and odd if $v \in T$.

(a) Show that if $T = V$, then the optimal T-join is the minimum weight perfect matching.

(b) Generalize the linear programming formulation for the perfect matching problem to obtain a formulation for the T-join.

(c) Generalize the argument for the perfect matching problem to obtain integrality of the linear programming formulation for the T-join problem.

9.4 (Padberg and Rao [109]) A Gomory-Hu (cut-equivalent) tree for graph $G = (V, E)$ with weight function w on edges is a tree T with vertex set V and a new weight function w' on edges of T. The edges of T can be distinct from the edges of G (i.e., T need not be a subgraph of G). The tree satisfies the following properties.

(i) For every pair of vertices u, v, the weight of minimum (u, v)-cut in G (w.r.t. w) is equal to the weight of the minimum (u, v)-cut in T (w.r.t. w').

(ii) For each edge $e \in E(T)$, $w'(e)$ is the weight of the cut $\delta_G(S)$ where the removal of e from T results in components S and $V \setminus S$.

Given a weighted undirected graph, a Gomory-Hu tree for it can be constructed in polynomial time (see e.g., [30] for details). Use this fact to prove the following.

(a) Show that the minimum weight odd cut (which has an odd number of vertices on either side) can be obtained using the Gomory-Hu tree.

(b) Obtain an efficient separation oracle for the perfect matching problem in general graphs.

(c) Can you use the ideas in (a) and (b) to also supply an efficient separation oracle for $LP_M(G)$ for the maximum matching problem in general graphs?

9.5 Let $\mathcal{T} = \{S \subseteq V : |S| \text{ is odd and } x^*(\delta(S)) = 1\}$ where x^* is an extreme point of $LP_M(G)$. Solving the linear program using the ellipsoid method enables us to get a set family $\mathcal{F} \subseteq \mathcal{T}$ such that constraints for sets in $\mathcal{F}$ are independent and span all the tight constraints in $\mathcal{T}$. But $\mathcal{F}$ need not be laminar. Give a polynomial time algorithm that, given $\mathcal{F}$, returns a laminar family $\mathcal{L} \subseteq \mathcal{T}$ such that constraints for sets in $\mathcal{L}$ are independent and span all the tight constraints in $\mathcal{T}$.

9.6 Modify Lemma 9.2.4 to prove that there is an edge e with $x(N[e]) \le k - 1 + \frac{1}{k}$ for k-uniform hypergraphs, and an edge e with $x(N[e]) \le k - 1$ for k-partite hypergraphs. Use this to generalize the 3-dimensional matching result to prove Theorem 9.2.1.

9.7 Show that the algorithm in Figure 9.4 can be modified to give a direct iterative rounding 2-approximation algorithm (without using the local-ratio routine) for the unweighted problem.

9.8 This exercise is to develop an alternative proof that the integrality gap of the 3-dimensional matching problem is at most 2. Given a hypergraph H with fractional value x_e on each edge, a *fractional* hyperedge coloring is a set of weighted matchings $\{M_1, \ldots, M_l\}$ of H so that $\sum_{i:e \in M_i} w(M_i) = x_e$. A fractional hyperedge coloring is called a fractional hyperedge k-coloring if the total weight on the matchings is equal to k. Use a greedy coloring algorithm on the ordering in Theorem 9.2.3 to obtain a fractional hyperedge 2-coloring of the hypergraph. Conclude that the integrality gap of the 3-dimensional matching problem is at most 2.

9.9 Consider the following *colorful* graph matching problem. Given a undirected graph in which each edge e has weight w_e and a color $c(e)$, the colorful graph matching problem is to find a maximum weighted matching in which each color appears at most once. Extend the argument in this chapter to obtain a 2-approximation algorithm for this problem.

9.10 A projective plane is a hypergraph that satisfies the following properties:

(a) Given any two vertices, there is a unique hyperedge that contains both of them.

(b) Given any two hyperedges, there is exactly one vertex contained in both of them.

(c) There are four vertices such that no hyperedge contains more than two of them.

It is known that an r-uniform projective plane exists if $r-1$ is a prime power (see e.g., [96]). A truncated r-uniform projective plane is obtained by removing a vertex and all of its incident hyperedges from a r-uniform projective plane. Prove that a k-uniform projective plane has integrality gap $k-1+\frac{1}{k}$, and a truncated k-uniform projective plane has integrality $k-1$ for the linear programming relaxation for the hypergraph matching problem.

9.11 Can you demonstrate any application of the *weighted* hypergraph matching problem to the partial Latin square extension problem?

10

Network design

In this chapter, we study the survivable network design problem. Given an undirected graph $G = (V, E)$ and a connectivity requirement r_{uv} for each pair of vertices u, v, a *Steiner network* is a subgraph of G in which there are at least r_{uv} edge-disjoint paths between u and v for every pair of vertices u, v. The survivable network design problem is to find a Steiner network with minimum total cost. In the first part of this chapter, we will present the 2-approximation algorithm given by Jain [75] for this problem. We will present his original proof, which introduced the iterative rounding method to the design of approximation algorithms.

Interestingly, we will see a close connection of the survivable network design problem to the traveling salesman problem. Indeed the linear program, the characterization results, and presence of edges with large fractional value are identical for both problems. In the (symmetric) TSP, we are given an undirected graph $G = (V, E)$ and cost function $c : E \to \mathbb{R}_+$, and the task is to find a minimum-cost Hamiltonian cycle. In the second part of this chapter, we will present an alternate proof of Jain's result, which also proves a structural result about extreme point solutions to the traveling salesman problem.

In the final part of this chapter, we consider the minimum bounded degree Steiner network problem, where we are also given a degree upper bound B_v for each vertex $v \in V$, and the task is to find a minimum-cost Steiner network satisfying all the degree bounds. Using the idea of iterative relaxation, we show how to extend Jain's technique to this more general problem. We will first present a constant factor bicriteria approximation algorithm, and then show how to improve it to obtain additive approximation guarantee on the degree violation.

10.1 Survivable network design problem

The survivable network design problem generalizes the minimum Steiner tree problem, the minimum Steiner forest problem, and the minimum

164

k-edge-connected subgraph problem. Hence, the results in this chapter also apply to these problems.

10.1.1 Linear programming relaxation

To formulate the problem as a linear program, we represent the connectivity requirements by a skew supermodular function. As stated in Definition 2.3.10, a function $f : 2^V \to \mathbb{Z}$ is called skew supermodular if at least one of the following two conditions holds for any two subsets $S, T \subseteq V$.

$$f(S) + f(T) \leq f(S \cup T) + f(S \cap T),$$

or

$$f(S) + f(T) \leq f(S \backslash T) + f(T \backslash S).$$

It can be verified that the function f defined by $f(S) = \max_{u \in S, v \notin S} \{r_{uv}\}$ for each subset $S \subseteq V$ is a skew supermodular function (see Exercise 2.2.10). Thus, one can write the following linear programming relaxation for the survivable network design problem, denoted by LP_{sndp}, with the function f being skew supermodular.

$$
\begin{aligned}
\text{minimize} \quad & \sum_{e \in E} c_e x_e \\
\text{subject to} \quad & x(\delta(S)) \geq f(S) && \forall S \subseteq V \\
& 0 \leq x_e \leq 1 && \forall e \in E
\end{aligned}
$$

It is not known whether there is a polynomial time separation oracle for a general skew supermodular function f. This linear program for the minimum Steiner network problem, however, can be solved in polynomial time by using a maximum flow algorithm as a separation oracle.

10.1.2 Characterization of extreme point solutions

For a subset $S \subseteq V$, the corresponding constraint $x(\delta(S)) \geq f(S)$ defines a characteristic vector $\chi(\delta(S))$ in $\mathbb{R}^{|E|}$: The vector has a 1 corresponding to each edge $e \in \delta(S)$, and a 0 otherwise. By the strong submodularity of the cut function of undirected graphs (see Section 2.3.1), we have

$$x(\delta(X)) + x(\delta(Y)) \geq x(\delta(X \cap Y)) + x(\delta(X \cup Y)) \text{ and}$$
$$x(\delta(X)) + x(\delta(Y)) \geq x(\delta(X - Y)) + x(\delta(Y - X))$$

for any two subsets X and Y. When f is skew supermodular, it follows from standard uncrossing arguments, as in spanning trees (Chapter 4) and maximum matchings (Chapter 9), that an extreme point solution to LP_{sndp} is characterized by a laminar family of tight constraints. Lemma 10.1.1 follows from these uncrossing arguments and the Rank Lemma.

Lemma 10.1.1 *Let the requirement function f of LP_{sndp} be skew supermodular, and let x be an extreme point solution to LP_{sndp} with $0 < x_e < 1$ for every edge $e \in E$. Then, there exists a laminar family $\mathcal{L}$ such that*

(i) *$x(\delta(S)) = f(S)$ for each $S \in \mathcal{L}$.*
(ii) *The vectors in $\{\chi(\delta(S)) : S \in \mathcal{L}\}$ are linearly independent.*
(iii) *$|E| = |\mathcal{L}|$.*

10.1.3 Iterative algorithm

Figure 10.1 describes Jain's iterative rounding algorithm.

10.1.4 Correctness and performance guarantee

Jain developed a token counting argument and proved an important theorem about the extreme point solutions to LP_{sndp}.

Theorem 10.1.2 *Suppose f is an integral skew supermodular function and x is an extreme point solution to LP_{sndp}. Then there exists an edge $e \in E$ with $x_e \geq \frac{1}{2}$.*

Assuming Theorem 10.1.2, the iterative algorithm will terminate, and it can be shown by an inductive argument that the returned solution is a 2-approximate

---

Iterative Minimum Steiner Network Algorithm

(i) Initialization $F \leftarrow \emptyset$, $f' \leftarrow f$;
(ii) While $f' \not\equiv 0$ do
    (a) Find an optimal extreme point solution x to LP_{sndp} with cut requirement f' and remove every edge e with $x_e = 0$.
    (b) If there exists an edge e with $x_e \geq 1/2$, then add e to F and delete e from the graph.
    (c) For every $S \subseteq V$: update $f'(S) \leftarrow \max\{f(S) - d_F(S), 0\}$.
(iii) Return $H = (V, F)$.

Figure 10.1 Minimum Steiner network algorithm.

solution (see Theorem 6.3.2 for a similar proof). We prove Theorem 10.1.2 by a counting argument, following the original proof of Jain, which will be useful later for the minimum bounded degree Steiner network problem.

Suppose for a contradiction that every edge e has $0 < x_e < \frac{1}{2}$. By Lemma 10.2.1, there is a laminar family $\mathcal{L}$ of tight constraints that defines x. We assign two tokens to each edge, one to each endpoint, for a total of $2|E|$ tokens. Then we will redistribute the tokens so that each member in $\mathcal{L}$ receives at least two tokens and there are some tokens left. This would imply that $|E| > |L|$, contradicting Lemma 10.2.1.

Let S be a subset of vertices. Define its corequirement $\operatorname{coreq}(S) := \sum_{e \in \delta(S)} (\frac{1}{2} - x_e)$. We call a set $S \in \mathcal{L}$ *special* if $coreq(S) = \frac{1}{2}$. Given a laminar family, it can be represented as a forest of trees if its sets are ordered by inclusion. Recall that in this forest, a set $R \in \mathcal{L}$ is a child of $S \in \mathcal{L}$ if S is the smallest set in $\mathcal{L}$ that contains R. We say an endpoint v is *owned* by S if S is the smallest set in $\mathcal{L}$ that contains v. The following lemma is useful to establish that a certain set is special. A proof can be found in Vazirani's book [132], and it is omitted here.

Lemma 10.1.3 *Suppose S has α children and owns β endpoints where $\alpha + \beta = 3$. If all children of S are special, then S is special.*

The redistribution of tokens is by an inductive argument based on the following lemma, which would yield the contradiction that $|E| > |L|$.

Lemma 10.1.4 *For any rooted subtree of the forest $\mathcal{L}$ with root S, the tokens assigned to vertices in S can be redistributed such that every member in the subtree gets at least two tokens, and the root S gets at least three tokens. Furthermore, S gets exactly three tokens only if S is special; otherwise, S gets at least four tokens.*

Proof The proof is by induction. For the base case, consider a leaf node S in the laminar family. Since $f(S) \geq 1$ and $x_e < \frac{1}{2}$ for all e, this implies that $d(S) \geq 3$ and thus S can collect three tokens. Furthermore, S collects exactly three tokens only if $coreq(S) = d(S)/2 - x(\delta(S)) = 1/2$. In this case, $f(S) = 1$ and $d(S) = 3$, and thus S is special. This verifies the base case.

For the induction step, consider a nonleaf node S. For a child R of S, we say R has one excess token if R has three tokens, and R has at least two excess tokens if R has at least four tokens. By the induction hypothesis, each child has at least one excess token and has exactly one excess token only if it is special. We will divide the cases by the number of children of S.

(i) S has at least four children: Then S can collect four tokens by taking one excess token from each child.

(ii) S has three children: If any child of S has two excess tokens or if S owns any endpoint, then S can collect four tokens. Otherwise, all three children of S are special and S does not own any enpdoint, but then S is special by Lemma 10.1.3, and so three tokens are enough for the induction hypothesis.

(iii) S has two children: If both children have two excess tokens, then S can collect four tokens. So assume that one child of S is special, but then it can be shown that S must own at least one endpoint (see the exercises or Lemma 23.20 of [132]). If both children of S are special, then S is special by Lemma 10.1.3, and so three tokens are enough for the induction hypothesis. Otherwise, S can collect four tokens.

(iv) S has one child R: Since $\chi(\delta(S))$ and $\chi(\delta(R))$ are linearly independent, S must owns at least one endpoint. As both $f(S)$ and $f(R)$ are integers and there is no edge of integral value, this actually implies that S cannot own exactly one endpoint, and thus S owns at least two endpoints. If R is not special, then S can collect four tokens; otherwise, S is special by Lemma 10.1.3 and so three tokens are enough for the induction hypothesis.   □

The extra tokens in the roots of the laminar family give us the desired contradiction. This proves Theorem 10.1.2, and thus the 2-approximation algorithm for the survivable network design problem follows.

10.2 Connection to the traveling salesman problem

In this section, we formulate a generalization of the survivable network design problem and the traveling salesman problem. Then we present a proof that any extreme point solution of this generalization has an edge e with $x_e \geq \frac{1}{2}$, and in some cases, $x_e = 1$. This will generalize Jain's result and a result of Boyd and Pulleyblank on the traveling salesman problem. The new proof uses the fractional token technique and does not need the notion of special sets used in the previous section to prove Jain's result.

10.2.1 Linear programming relaxation

The following is a linear programming relaxation that models both the survivable network design problem and the traveling salesman problem, denoted by LP_f, where f is a skew supermodular function. It is similar to the linear programming relaxation for the minimum bounded degree Steiner network problem in the next section.

$$\text{minimize} \qquad \sum_{e \in E} c_e x_e$$

$$\text{subject to} \qquad x(\delta(S)) \geq f(S) \qquad \forall S \subseteq V$$

$$x(\delta(v)) = f(v) \qquad \forall v \in W$$

$$0 \leq x_e \leq 1 \qquad \forall e \in E$$

For the survivable network design problem, we set $f(S) = \max_{u \in S, v \notin S} \{r_{uv}\}$ for each subset $S \subseteq V$, and set $W = \emptyset$. For the traveling salesman problem, we set $f(S) = 2$ for each $S \subset V$, $f(V) = 0$, and $W = V$.

10.2.2 Characterization of extreme point solutions

The following characterization follows from a straightforward application of the uncrossing technique using the fact that f is skew-supermodular, and the same characterization of extreme point solutions as in Lemma 10.1.1 holds for LP_f to give the following lemma.

Lemma 10.2.1 *Let the requirement function f of LP_f be skew supermodular, and let x be an extreme point solution to LP_f with $0 < x_e < 1$ for every edge $e \in E$. Then, there exists a laminar family $\mathcal{L}$ such that*

(i) $x(\delta(S)) = f(S)$ for each $S \in \mathcal{L}$.
(ii) *The vectors in $\{\chi(\delta(S)) : S \in \mathcal{L}\}$ are linearly independent.*
(iii) $|E| = |\mathcal{L}|$.

10.2.3 Existence of edges with large fractional value

Boyd and Pulleyblank [19] proved that there is an edge e with $x_e = 1$ in any extreme point solution to the traveling salesman problem. The following theorem provides a common generalization to their result and Jain's result (Theorem 10.1.2).

Theorem 10.2.2 *Let f be an integral skew supermodular function, and x be an extreme point solution to LP_f with $x_e > 0$ for all e. Then there exists an $e \in E$ with $x_e \geq \frac{1}{2}$. Moreover, if $f(S)$ is an even integer for each subset $S \subseteq V$, then there exists an edge e with $x_e = 1$.*

Proof [First part]: We first prove that $x_e \geq \frac{1}{2}$ for some edge $e \in E$ in any extreme point solution x to LP_f. Suppose for a contradiction that $0 < x_e < \frac{1}{2}$

for each $e \in E$. Then we will show that $|E| > |\mathcal{L}|$, contradicting Lemma 10.2.1. The proof is by a fractional token counting argument. We give one token to each edge in E, and then we will reassign the tokens such that we can collect one token for each member in $\mathcal{L}$ and still have extra tokens left, giving us the contradiction that $|E| > |\mathcal{L}|$. Each edge $e = uv$ is given one token, which is reassigned as follows.

(i) **(Rule 1)** Let $S \in \mathcal{L}$ be the smallest set containing u and $R \in \mathcal{L}$ be the smallest set containing v. Then e gives x_e tokens each to S and R.

(ii) **(Rule 2)** Let T be the smallest set containing both u and v. Then e gives $1 - 2x_e$ tokens to T.

We now show that each set S in $\mathcal{L}$ receives at least one token. Let S be any set with children $R_1, \ldots, R_k$ where $k \geq 0$ (if S does not have any children, then $k = 0$). We have the following equalities.

$$x(\delta(S)) = f(S),$$

$$x(\delta(R_i)) = f(R_i) \quad \forall\, 1 \leq i \leq k.$$

Subtracting, we obtain

$$x(\delta(S)) - \sum_{i=1}^{k} x(\delta(R_i)) = f(S) - \sum_{i=1}^{k} f(R_i). \tag{10.1}$$

We divide the edges involved in the left-hand side of (10.1) into three types, where

$$A = \{e : |e \cap (\cup_i R_i)| = 0, |e \cap S| = 1\},$$

$$B = \{e : |e \cap (\cup_i R_i)| = 1, |e \cap S| = 2\},$$

$$C = \{e : |e \cap (\cup_i R_i)| = 2, |e \cap S| = 2\}.$$

Then (10.1) can be rewritten as

$$x(A) - x(B) - 2x(C) = f(S) - \sum_{i=1}^{k} f(R_i). \tag{10.2}$$

Observe that $A \cup B \cup C \neq \emptyset$; otherwise, the characteristic vectors $\chi(\delta(S))$, $\chi(\delta(R_1)), \ldots, \chi(\delta(R_k))$ are linearly dependent. For each edge $e \in A$, S receives x_e tokens from e by Rule 1. For each edge $e \in B$, S receives $1 - x_e$ tokens from e by Rule 1 and Rule 2. For each edge $e \in C$, S receives $1 - 2x_e$ tokens from e by Rule 2. Hence, the total tokens received by S is exactly

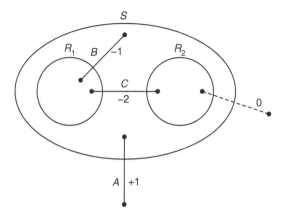

Figure 10.2 Example for expression $x(\delta(S)) - \sum_{i=1}^{k} x(\delta(R_i))$ with $k = 2$ children. The dashed edges cancel out in the expression. Edge-sets A, B, C shown with their respective coefficients.

$$\sum_{e \in A} x_e + \sum_{e \in B}(1 - x_e) + \sum_{e \in C}(1 - 2x_e)$$
$$= x(A) + |B| - x(B) + |C| - 2x(C)$$
$$= |B| + |C| + f(S) - \sum_{i=1}^{k} f(R_i)$$

where the last equality follows from (10.2). Since f is integral and the preceding expression is nonzero (since $A \cup B \cup C \neq \emptyset$), the right-hand side is at least one, and thus every set $S \in \mathcal{L}$ receives at least one token in the reassignment.

It remains to show that there are some unassigned tokens, which would imply the contradiction that $|E| > |\mathcal{L}|$. Let R be any maximal set in $\mathcal{L}$. Consider any edge $e \in \delta(R)$. The fraction of the token by Rule 2 for edge e is unassigned, as there is no set $T \in \mathcal{L}$ with $|T \cap e| = 2$, which gives us the desired contradiction. This proves the first part of the theorem.

[Second part]: The proof of the second part is almost identical to the proof of the first part, except that we use scaled token assignment rules. Each edge $e = uv$ is given one token which it reassigns as follows.

(i) **(Rule 1′)** Let S be the smallest set containing u and R be the smallest set containing v in $\mathcal{L}$. Then e gives $x_e/2$ tokens each to S and R.
(ii) **(Rule 2′)** Let T be the smallest set containing both u and v. Then e gives $1 - x_e$ tokens to T.

We now show that each set in $\mathcal{L}$ receives at least one token. Let S be any set with children $R_1, \ldots, R_k$ where $k \geq 0$. We have the following equalities.

$$x(\delta(S)) = f(S),$$

$$x(\delta(R_i)) = f(R) \quad \forall\, 1 \leq i \leq k.$$

Dividing by two and subtracting, we obtain

$$\frac{x(\delta(S)) - \sum_i x(\delta(R_i))}{2} = \frac{f(S) - \sum_i f(R_i)}{2}.$$

The edges involved in the left-hand side are divided into types A, B, C exactly as in the first part. Then the preceding equation becomes

$$\frac{x(A) - x(B)}{2} - x(C) = \frac{f(S) - \sum_i f(R_i)}{2}.$$

Observe that $A \cup B \cup C \neq \emptyset$; otherwise, there is a linear dependence among the constraints for S and its children. Also, S receives $\frac{x_e}{2}$ tokens for each edge $e \in A$ by Rule $1'$, $1 - \frac{x_e}{2}$ tokens for each edge $e \in B$ by Rule $1'$ and Rule $2'$, and $1 - x_e$ tokens for each edge $e \in C$ by Rule $2'$. Hence, the total tokens received by S is exactly

$$\sum_{e \in A} \frac{x_e}{2} + \sum_{e \in B} \left(1 - \frac{x_e}{2}\right) + \sum_{e \in C} (1 - x_e)$$

$$= \frac{x(A)}{2} + |B| - \frac{x(B)}{2} + |C| - x(C)$$

$$= |B| + |C| + \frac{f(S) - \sum_i f(R_i)}{2}.$$

Since $A \cup B \cup C \neq \emptyset$ and f is an even-valued function, this is a positive integer. Thus, every set $S \in \mathcal{L}$ receives at least one token in the reassignment.

Now, we show that there are some unassigned tokens showing the strict inequality $|\mathcal{L}| < |E|$. Let R be any maximal set $\mathcal{L}$. Then, consider any edge $e \in \delta(R)$. Then, (add) the fraction of the (end addition) token by Rule $2'$ for edge e is unassigned as there is no set $T \in \mathcal{L}$ with $|T \cap e| = 2$. This gives us the desired contradiction. $\qquad \square$

10.3 Minimum bounded degree Steiner networks

In the minimum bounded degree Steiner network problem, given an undirected graph $G = (V, E)$ with edge costs, connectivity requirements r_{uv} for each pair

$u, v \in V$, and degree bounds b_v for each vertex $v \in V$, the task is to find a subgraph H of G of minimum cost such that there are r_{uv} edge disjoint paths between u and v for each $u, v \in V$, and degree of vertex v in H is at most B_v. In general, the minimum bounded degree Steiner network problem does not admit any polynomial factor approximation algorithm, since the minimum cost Hamiltonian cycle problem is a special case. Instead, we will present *bicriteria* approximation algorithms, that both violate the degree bounds as well as deliver a suboptimal cost solution. In this section, we will first present a $(2, 2B_v + 3)$-approximation algorithm for the minimum bounded degree Steiner network problem, where B_v denotes the degree upper bound on node v. By this, we mean that the algorithm outputs a Steiner network whose cost is at most twice that of the objective value of the linear programming relaxation, and whose degree at any node v is at most $2B_v + 3$. In the next section, we will present an algorithm with only an additive violation on the degree bounds.

10.3.1 Linear programming relaxation

The linear programming formulation for the minimum bounded degree Steiner network problem, denoted by LP_{bdsn}, is a straightforward generalization of LP_{sndp} for the survivable network design problem, with $f(S) = \max_{u \in S, v \notin S} \{r_{uv}\}$ for each subset $S \subseteq V$. Notice that the degree constraints are only present on a subset $W \subseteq V$ of vertices.

$$
\begin{aligned}
\text{minimize} \quad & \sum_{e \in E} c_e x_e \\
\text{subject to} \quad & x(\delta(S)) \geq f(S) && \forall S \subseteq V \\
& x(\delta(v)) \leq B_v && \forall v \in W \\
& 0 \leq x_e \leq 1 && \forall e \in E
\end{aligned}
$$

10.3.2 Characterization of extreme point solutions

As the degree constraints are defined only on single vertices, the same uncrossing technique (as in Lemma 10.2.1) can be applied to show that an optimal extreme point solution is characterized by a laminar family of tight constraints.

Lemma 10.3.1 *Let the requirement function of LP_{bdsn} be skew supermodular, and let x be an extreme point solution to LP_{bdsn} with $0 < x_e < 1$ for every edge $e \in E$. Then, there exists a laminar family $\mathcal{L}$ of tight sets such that $\mathcal{L}$ partitions into a set of singletons $\mathcal{L}'$ for the degree constraints, and the remaining sets $\mathcal{L}'' = \mathcal{L} - \mathcal{L}'$ for the connectivity constraints, such that*

Iterative Minimum Bounded Degree Steiner Network Algorithm

(i) Initialization $F \leftarrow \emptyset$, $f' \leftarrow f$.

(ii) While $f' \not\equiv 0$ do

    (a) Find an optimal extreme point solution x with cut requirement f' and remove every edge e with $x_e = 0$.

    (b) **(Relaxation):** If there exists a vertex $v \in W$ with degree at most 4, then remove v from W.

    (c) **(Rounding):** If there exists an edge $e = (u, v)$ with $x_e \geq 1/2$, then add e to F and delete e from the graph and decrease B_u and B_v by $1/2$.

    (d) For every $S \subseteq V$: update $f'(S) \leftarrow \max\{f(S) - d_F(S), 0\}$.

(iii) Return $H = (V, F)$.

Figure 10.3 Minimum bounded degree Steiner network algorithm.

(i) $x(\delta(v)) = B_v > 0$ *for all* $\{v\} \in \mathcal{L}'$ *and* $x(\delta(S)) = f(S) \geq 1$ *for all* $S \in \mathcal{L}''$.

(ii) *The vectors in* $\{\chi(\delta(S)) : S \in \mathcal{L}\}$ *are linearly independent.*

(iii) $|E| = |\mathcal{L}|$.

10.3.3 Iterative algorithm

The iterative algorithm in Figure 10.3 is similar to that for the minimum Steiner network problem, with a new relaxation step where we remove degree constraints of vertices with low degree.

10.3.4 Correctness and performance guarantee

The performance guarantee follows by an inductive argument as in Lemma 6.3.2, assuming the algorithm terminates. We will prove the following lemma showing that the algorithm will terminate.

Lemma 10.3.2 *Let x be an extreme point solution to LP_{bdsn} with $x_e > 0$ for every edge e, and W be the set of vertices with degree constraints. Then either one of the following holds:*

(i) *There exists an edge e with $x_e \geq \frac{1}{2}$.*

(ii) *There exists a vertex $v \in W$ with degree $d(v) \leq 4$.*

In the following we use a token counting argument to prove Lemma 10.3.2. The counting argument is similar to that of Theorem 10.1.2. Each edge is assigned two tokens, for a total of $2|E|$ tokens. For each edge e, one token is assigned to each endpoint. We shall show that if none of the steps in the algorithm can be applied, then each set in $\mathcal{L}''$ and each degree constraint in $\mathcal{L}'$ can collect two tokens, and there are some tokens left. This would imply $|E| > |\mathcal{L}|$, contradicting that x is an extreme point solution.

We prove the same statement as in Lemma 10.1.4 to get the contradiction. The counting argument is similar, and we only highlight the differences here. By Step 2(b), we may assume that $d(v) \geq 5$ for each $v \in W$, and hence each degree constraint has three extra tokens. The case when the node $S \in \mathcal{L}$ does not own a vertex in W is exactly the same as in Lemma 10.1.4. Henceforth, we consider a node $S \in \mathcal{L}$ that owns a vertex $v \in W$. If S has another child R, then S can collect three tokens from v and at least one token from R, as desired. Otherwise, by linear independence of $\chi(\delta(S))$ and $\chi(\delta(v))$, S owns at least one endpoint and thus S can collect three tokens from v and at least one more token from the endpoints it owns as required. This completes the proof of Lemma 10.3.2.

10.4 An additive approximation algorithm

In this section, we show how to achieve additive guarantee on the degree bounds that depend only on the maximum connectivity requirement, denoted by $r_{max} = \max_{u,v}\{r_{uv}\}$.

Theorem 10.4.1 *There is a polynomial time $(2, B_v + 6r_{max} + 3)$-approximation algorithm for the minimum bounded degree Steiner network problem, which returns a solution with cost at most twice the optimum, while the degree of each vertex v is at most $B_v + 6r_{max} + 3$.*

For minimum bounded degree Steiner trees, since the maximum connectivity requirement is one, this algorithm will output a solution that violates the degree bounds only by an additive constant, and of cost within twice the optimal.

10.4.1 Iterative algorithm

The iterative algorithm in Figure 10.4 uses the same linear programming relaxation LP_{bdsn} as in the previous section. The difference is that we only pick an edge e with $x_e \geq \frac{1}{2}$ when both endpoints have "low" degrees.

10.4.2 Correctness and performance guarantee

First, we show that the degree of any vertex v in the returned solution H is at most $B_v + 6r_{max} + 3$, assuming that the algorithm terminates. We define the set W_h of vertices (defined in Step (ii)a. of the algorithm) with fractional degree

Additive Approximation for Minimum Bounded Degree Steiner Network

(i) Initialization $F \leftarrow \emptyset$, $f' \leftarrow f$.

(ii) While $f' \not\equiv 0$ do

    (a) Find an optimal extreme point solution x to LP_{bdsn} satisfying f' and remove every edge e with $x_e = 0$. Set $W_h = \{v \in W \mid \sum_{e \in \delta(v)} x_e \geq 6r_{max}\}$ and $B_v = \sum_{e \in \delta(v)} x_e$ for $v \in W$.

    (b) If there exists an edge $e = (u,v)$ with $x_e = 1$, then add e to F and remove e from G and decrease B_u and B_v by 1.

    (c) **(Relaxation):** If there exists a vertex $v \in W$ with degree at most 4, then remove v from W.

    (d) **(Rounding):** If there exists an edge $e = (u,v)$ with $x_e \geq \frac{1}{2}$ and $u,v \notin W_h$, then add e to F and remove e from G and decrease B_u and B_v by x_e.

    (e) For every $S \subseteq V$: $f'(S) \leftarrow \max\{f(S) - d_F(S), 0\}$.

(iii) Return $H = (V, F)$.

Figure 10.4 Additive approximation for minimum bounded degree Steiner network.

at least $6r_{max}$ as *high* degree vertices. Observe that the fractional degree of each vertex is nonincreasing during the algorithm, since we reset the degree upper bound in Step (ii)a. in each iteration. Consider an edge e with v as an endpoint. When $v \in W_h$, e is picked only if $x_e = 1$ in Step (ii)b. of the algorithm. Hence, while $v \in W_h$, at most $B_v - 6r_{max}$ edges incident at v are added to H. While $v \in W \setminus W_h$, e is picked only if $x_e \geq \frac{1}{2}$ in Step (ii)d. of the algorithm. Hence, while $v \in W \setminus W_h$, strictly less than $12r_{max}$ edges incident at v are added to H. Finally, by Step (ii)(c) of the algorithm, a degree constraint is removed only if v is incident to at most four edges, where possibly all of them are added to H. Therefore, the degree of v in H is strictly less than $(B_v - 6f_{max}) + 12f_{max} + 4 = B_v + 6f_{max} + 4$. As B_v is an integer, the degree of v in H is at most $B_v + 6f_{max} + 3$. Moreover, since we always included edges with value at least half in F in each iteration, by induction, the cost of the final solution is at most twice the optimal objective value of LP_{bdsn}. This proves Theorem 10.4.1, assuming that the algorithm terminates.

The following lemma proves that the algorithm will always terminate. With the same characterization as in Lemma 10.3.1, we use a more careful counting argument to prove stronger properties of the extreme point solutions to LP_{bdsn} than those in Lemma 10.3.2.

Lemma 10.4.2 *Let x be an extreme point solution to LP_{bdsn} with $x_e > 0$ for all e, and W be the set of vertices with degree constraints, and $W_h = \{v \in W \mid \sum_{e \in \delta(v)} x_e \geq 6r_{max}\}$. Then at least one of the following holds:*

(i) *There exists an edge e with $x_e = 1$.*
(ii) *There exists an edge $e = \{u, v\}$ with $x_e \geq 1/2$ and $u, v \notin W_h$.*
(iii) *There exists a vertex $v \in W$ with degree at most 4.*

We will prove Lemma 10.4.2 by a token counting argument as in Lemma 10.3.2. Suppose for contradiction that none of the conditions in Lemma 10.4.2 holds. Then each edge e has $x_e < 1$, and each edge e with $\frac{1}{2} \leq x_e < 1$ (we call such an edge a *heavy edge*) must have at least one endpoint in W_h, and each vertex in W must have degree at least five. We give two tokens to each edge for a total of $2|E|$ tokens. Then, the tokens will be reassigned so that each member of $\mathcal{L}''$ gets at least two tokens, each vertex in $\mathcal{L}'$ gets at least two tokens, and there are still some excess tokens left. This will imply that $|E| > |\mathcal{L}|$, contradicting Lemma 10.3.1.

The main difference from Lemma 10.3.2 is the existence of heavy edges (with an endpoint in W_h), which our algorithm is not allowed to pick. Since there exist heavy edges, a set $S \in \mathcal{L}$ may only have two edges in $\delta(S)$, and hence S may not be able to collect three tokens as in Lemma 10.1.4. To get around this, we use a different token assignment scheme and revise the definition of corequirement, so that a similar induction hypothesis would work.

Token assignment scheme If $e = uv$ is a heavy edge with $u \in W_h$ and $v \notin W$, then v gets two tokens from e and u gets zero tokens. For every other edge e, one token is assigned to each endpoint of e.

Co-requirement We revise the definition of co-requirement for the presence of heavy edges:

$$\text{coreq}(S) = \sum_{e \in \delta(S),\, x_e < 1/2} (1/2 - x_e) + \sum_{e \in \delta(S),\, x_e \geq 1/2} (1 - x_e)$$

It is useful to note that this definition reduces to the original definition of corequirement, if every edge e with $x_e \geq \frac{1}{2}$ is thought of as two parallel edges, each aiming to achieve a value of $\frac{1}{2}$ and each has fractional value $\frac{x_e}{2}$: Summing $\frac{1}{2} - \frac{x_e}{2}$ over both edges gives $1 - x_e$. We say a set is *special* if $\text{coreq}(S) = \frac{1}{2}$ as in the proof of Jain's theorem.

After this initial assignment, each vertex in $V \setminus W_h$ receives at least as many tokens as their degree. Moreover, each vertex in $W \setminus W_h$ receive at least five tokens, as their degree is at least five. Note that a vertex $v \in W_h$ might not have any tokens if all the edges incident at it are heavy edges. However, by exploiting the fact that $f(S) \leq r_{max}$, we will show that vertices in W_h can *get back* enough tokens. We prove the following lemma which shows that the tokens can be reassigned in a similar way as in Lemma 10.1.4.

Lemma 10.4.3 *For any subtree of $\mathcal{L}$ rooted at S, we can reassign tokens such that each node in the subtree gets at least two tokens and the root S gets at least three tokens. Moreover, the root S gets exactly three tokens only if S is special; otherwise it gets at least four tokens.*

The following is a key claim showing if S owns a vertex in W_h, then there are enough tokens for S and the vertices in W_h that it owns.

Claim 10.4.4 *Suppose S owns $w \geq 1$ vertices in W_h. Then the number of excess tokens from the children of S, plus the number of tokens owned by S, plus the number of tokens left with vertices in $W_h \cap S$ is at least $2w + 4$.*

Proof Suppose S has c children. As each child has at least one excess token by the induction hypothesis, if $c \geq 6w$, then we have $6w$ tokens which is at least $2w + 4$. Henceforth, we assume that $c < 6w$. Let $B := \sum_{v \in W_h} x(\delta(v))$, where the sum is over all vertices $v \in W_h$ owned by S. Note that $B \geq 6wr_{max}$ by the definition of W_h. For a child R of S, as $x(\delta(R)) = f(R) \leq r_{max}$, at most r_{max} units of B are contributed by the edges in $\delta(R)$. Similarly, at most r_{max} units of B are contributed by the edges in $\delta(S)$. Hence, at least $r_{max}(6w - c - 1)$ units of B are from the edges with both endpoints owned by S. Since there is no edge e with $x_e = 1$, there are at least $r_{max}(6w - c - 1) + 1$ such edges. Let $e = uv$ be such an edge with $v \in W_h$ owned by S. If $u \in W$, then both u and v get one token from e in the initial assignment. If $u \notin W$, then u gets two tokens from e in the initial assignment, but these two tokens are owned by S. Hence, the number of tokens owned by S plus the number of tokens left with vertices in W_h owned by S is at least $r_{max}(6w - c - 1) + 1$. Furthermore, S can also collect one excess token from each child. So, the total number of tokens that S can collect is at least $r_{max}(6w - c - 1) + c + 1$, which is a decreasing function of c. As $c < 6w$, the number of tokens is minimized at $c = 6w - 1$, which is at least $2w + 4$, proving the claim. $\square$

We now proceed by induction on the height of the subtree to prove Lemma 10.4.3.

Base case S is a leaf node. Claim 10.4.4 implies that S can collect enough tokens if it owns vertices in W_h. Hence, assume $S \cap W_h = \emptyset$. First, consider the case when $S \cap W \neq \emptyset$. Any vertex $v \in W \setminus W_h$ has at least five tokens, and thus has three excess tokens. If S owns two such vertices or S owns another endpoint, then S gets at least four tokens as required. Otherwise, we have $\chi(\delta(v)) = \chi(\delta(S))$, contradicting Lemma 10.3.1.

Henceforth, we consider the case when $S \cap W = \emptyset$. Then S can get at least $|\delta(S)| = d(S)$ tokens from the vertices owned by S. Note that $d(S) \geq 2$, as $x(\delta(S))$ is an integer, and there is no edge e with $x_e = 1$. If $d(S) \geq 4$, then S gets at least four tokens. If $d(S) = 3$ and $d(S)$ contains a heavy edge, then S can get four tokens from the vertices it owns. If it does not contain a heavy edge, then S receives three tokens and $\mathrm{coreq}(S) = \frac{1}{2}$, for which three tokens are enough. If $d(S) = 2$, then at least one edge is a heavy edge. If both edges are heavy, then S can get four tokens; otherwise, if only one edge is heavy then $\mathrm{coreq}(S) = \frac{1}{2}$ and so three tokens are enough.

Induction step If S owns any vertex in W_h, then we are done by Claim 10.4.4. Thus, we can assume that S does not own any vertex in W_h. By the induction hypothesis, any child of S has at least one excess token. So, if S owns a vertex in $W \setminus W_h$, then S can collect at least four tokens. Hence, we can assume that S does not own any vertex in W, and the proof of these cases are almost identical to that in Lemma 10.1.4 with the definition of corequirement revised; the details are omitted.

10.4.3 Steiner forests

In the special cases of Steiner trees and Steiner forests, the connectivity requirement function is a $\{0, 1\}$-function, and hence $r_{\max} = 1$. Theorem 10.4.1 thus implies that there is a $(2, B_v + 9)$-approximation algorithm for this problem, but it is possible to obtain a better bound.

Theorem 10.4.5 *There is a polynomial time $(2, B_v + 3)$-approximation algorithm for the minimum bounded degree Steiner network problem when $r_{max} = 1$.*

The iterative algorithm is similar where the improvement comes from the following fact [89, 124]: There is a heavy edge between two vertices without degree constraints. The proof is by a more involved counting argument that uses a different induction hypothesis.

10.5 Notes

The algorithm for the survivable network design problem is due to Jain [75], who introduced the iterative rounding method in the design of approximation

algorithms. Subsequently, the iterative rounding method has been applied to
other network design problems, including directed network design [54, 79,
97], element-connectivity network design and vertex-connectivity network
design [28, 43]. The existence of a 1-edge in the traveling salesman problem
is due to Boyd and Pulleyblank [19], and the proof presented in this chapter is
from the work of Nagarajan, Ravi, and Singh [103]. The algorithm for the minimum bounded degree Steiner network problem is by Lau et al. [88], who first
used the iterative relaxation idea in degree-bounded network design problems.
The subsequent work with additive violation on the degree bounds is by Lau
and Singh [89]. Louis and Vishnoi [92] improved the bicriteria bound to obtain
a $(2, 2B + 2)$-approximation. The weighted degree constrained network design
problem were considered by Fukunaga and Nagamochi [49] and Nutov [108].

Exercises

10.1 Prove Lemma 10.1.3.

10.2 Show the following statement in the proof of Lemma 10.1.4: If set S has
two children, one of which has a corequirement of $1/2$, then it must own
at least one endpoint.

10.3 Give a 2-approximation algorithm for the traveling salesman problem,
using the fact there is always an edge e with $x_e = 1$ in the linear
programming relaxation LP_f.

10.4 Show that the result of Boyd and Pulleyblank on the existence of a 1-edge
in the subtour relaxation for the TSP can be derived as a corollary of the
result of Jain on the existence of a $\frac{1}{2}$-edge for the SNDP. In particular
show that an extreme point for the former scaled down by a factor of two
is feasible and is an extreme point for the spanning tree case of SNDP to
derive the result.

10.5 Consider the subtour elimination LP for asymmetric TSP [70]. Find the
largest value ρ such that there is always some arc variable with $x_a \geq \rho$.

10.6 Design a bicriteria approximation algorithm for the minimum bounded
degree strongly k-arc-connected subgraph problem in directed graphs.

 (a) Write a "cut-cover" linear programming relaxation for the problem.
     Show that the connectivity requirement function for this problem is
     a crossing supermodular function.

 (b) Use the uncrossing technique to show that an extreme point solution
     is defined by a cross-free family of tight constraints.

 (c) (Gabow [54]) Prove that there is an arc with value at least $\frac{1}{3}$ in any
     extreme point solution when there are no degree constraints in the
     problem.

(d) Apply the iterative relaxation step to obtain a bicriteria approximation algorithm for the problem.

10.7 Let P be the Petersen graph, and let w_1, w_2, w_3 be the neighbors of a vertex v in P. Take three copies of $P - v$ and three new vertices v_1, v_2, v_3, and attach them as follows: For $1 \leq j \leq 3$, add edges from v_j to each w_j in the three copies of $P - v$. Prove that the resulting graph is a 3-regular 3-edge-connected graph with no Hamiltonian cycle. By setting $B_v = 1$ for each vertex and connectivity requirement $r_{uv} = 1$ for each pair of vertices, show that this is an integrality gap example in which there is a feasible solution to LP_{bdsn} but there is no Steiner network with degree at most $2B_v$ (or $B_v + 1$) for each vertex.

10.8 Show that the following example gives an integrality gap of at least an additive $n/4$ for the degree violation for LP_{bdsn}. The input is a complete bipartite graph $B = (X, Y, E)$, where $X = \{x_1, x_2\}$ and $Y = \{y_1, \ldots, y_n\}$. We set the connectivity requirements between y_i and y_j to be 1 for all i, j, between x_1 and x_2 to be $\frac{n}{2}$, and 0 otherwise.

10.9 Can you use the fractional token technique in Section 10.2 to obtain the results for the minimum bounded degree Steiner network problem presented in this chapter?

11

Constrained optimization problems

In previous chapters, we have used the iterative relaxation method to obtain approximation algorithms for degree bounded network design problems. In this chapter, we illustrate that similar techniques can be applied to other constrained optimization problems. In the first part, we study the partial vertex cover problem and show an iterative 2-approximation algorithm for the problem. In the second part, we study the multicriteria spanning tree problem and present a polynomial time approximation scheme for the problem.

11.1 Vertex cover

We first give a simple iterative 2-approximation algorithm for the vertex cover problem, and then show that it can be extended to the partial vertex cover problem.

Given a graph $G = (V, E)$ and a nonnegative cost function c on vertices, the goal in the vertex cover problem is to find a set of vertices with minimum cost that covers every edge (i.e., for every edge at least one endpoint is in the vertex cover). In Chapter 3, we showed that the vertex cover problem in bipartite graphs is polynomial time solvable and gave an iterative algorithm for finding the minimum cost vertex cover. In general graphs, the vertex cover problem is NP-hard. Nemhauser and Trotter [105] gave a 2-approximation for the problem. Indeed, they prove a stronger property of *half-integrality* of the natural linear programming relaxation. We prove this result and its extensions to the partial vertex cover problem in the next section.

11.1.1 Linear programming relaxation

The linear programming relaxation, denoted by LP_{vc}, is the same as in Section 3.4 for the vertex cover problem in bipartite graphs.

182

$$\text{minimize} \quad \sum_{v \in V} c_v x_v$$

$$\text{subject to} \quad x_u + x_v \geq 1 \qquad \forall e = \{u, v\} \in E$$

$$x_v \geq 0 \qquad \forall v \in V$$

We shall prove the following theorem of Nemhauser and Trotter using the simple characterization of the extreme point solutions to the linear program.

Theorem 11.1.1 *Let* x *be an extreme optimal solution to* LP_{vc}. *Then* $x_v \in \{0, \frac{1}{2}, 1\}$ *for each* $v \in V$.

Theorem 11.1.1 implies Theorem 11.1.2 as a corollary.

Theorem 11.1.2 *There exists a 2-approximation algorithm for the vertex cover problem.*

Proof Let x be the optimal extreme point solution to LP_{vc}. Construct a vertex cover by picking each vertex v such that $x_v = \frac{1}{2}$ or $x_v = 1$. Theorem 11.1.1 implies that it is a feasible vertex cover, and it costs at most twice that of the fractional solution x. □

11.1.2 Characterization of extreme point solutions

We use the same characterization as in Lemma 3.4.3 for the vertex cover problem in bipartite graphs. For a set $W \subseteq V$, let $\chi(W)$ denote the vector in $\mathbb{R}^{|V|}$: The vector has a 1 corresponding to each vertex $v \in W$, and 0 otherwise. This vector is called the characteristic vector of W.

Lemma 11.1.3 *Given any extreme point* x *to* LP_{vc} *with* $x_v > 0$ *for each* $v \in V$, *there exists* $F \subseteq E$ *such that*

(i) $x_u + x_v = 1$ *for each* $e = \{u, v\} \in F$.
(ii) *The vectors in* $\{\chi(\{u, v\}) : \{u, v\} \in F\}$ *are linearly independent.*
(iii) $|V| = |F|$.

11.1.3 Iterative algorithm

We now give a simple iterative rounding algorithm for obtaining a 2-approximation algorithm for the vertex cover problem in Figure 11.1.

11.1.4 Correctness and performance guarantee

We now present the proof of Theorem 11.1.1, which also shows the correctness of the algorithm in Figure 11.1.

Iterative Vertex Cover Algorithm

(i)   Initialization $W \leftarrow \emptyset$.
(ii) Find an optimal extreme point solution x to LP_{vc}.
(iii) While $E \neq \emptyset$ do
    (a) For all vertices $v \in V$ with $x_v = 1$ include $v \in W$ and remove v
        from G.
    (b) For all vertices $v \in V$ with $x_v = 0$, remove v from G.
    (c) For all vertices $v \in V$ with $x_v = \frac{1}{2}$, include $v \in W$ and remove v
        from G.
(iv) Return W.

Figure 11.1 Vertex cover algorithm.

Proof In Step (3)a., we select all vertices with $x_v = 1$ and remove all such vertices. Then any vertex with $x_v = 0$ must now be an isolated vertex and hence can be removed. Thus, we obtain a vertex cover instance on the remaining graph. We assume the remaining graph is connected; otherwise, we apply the same argument to each connected component. From Lemma 11.1.3, there is a subset of edges F with linearly independent tight constraints. As $|F| = |V|$, it follows that F contains a cycle C. We will show that $x_v = \frac{1}{2}$ for each vertex in C. First, notice that C must be an odd cycle; otherwise, the characteristic vectors in $\{\chi(\{u,v\}) : \{u,v\} \in E(C)\}$ are linearly dependent (the sum of the vectors for the "odd" edges is the same as that for the "even" edges in the cycle). As C is an odd cycle, the unique solution to these equations is $x_v = \frac{1}{2}$ for each $v \in C$. Now, observing that $x_v + x_u = 1$ for any $\{u,v\} \in F$ and $x_v = \frac{1}{2}$ imply that $x_u = \frac{1}{2}$, each vertex u reachable from the cycle C in F must also have $x_u = \frac{1}{2}$, proving Theorem 11.1.1. $\square$

11.2 Partial vertex cover

We now show how to extend the 2-approximation algorithm for the vertex cover problem to the more general partial vertex cover problem. Given a graph $G = (V, E)$ and a nonnegative cost function c on vertices and a bound L, the goal in the partial vertex cover problem is to find a set of vertices with minimum cost that covers at least L edges. The problem is NP-hard since it generalizes the vertex cover problem when $L = |E|$. We give a 2-approximation algorithm based on iterative rounding of a natural linear programming relaxation.

Theorem 11.2.1 *There is a 2-approximation algorithm for the partial vertex cover problem.*

11.2.1 Linear programming relaxation

We proceed by first performing a *pruning* step where we guess the *costliest* vertex, say v in the optimal solution. We then obtain the *pruned* graph where we remove all vertices with cost more than v and include v in the solution. Since there are at most $n = |V|$ choices for the costliest vertex, we can consider all these choices and return the cheapest of the solutions returned by the algorithm on each of the pruned graphs.

We now formulate a linear program for the pruned instance. The linear program, denoted by LP_{pvc}, has a variable x_v for each vertex v and a variable y_e for each edge $e \in E$. In an integral solution, y_e is set to one only if one of the endpoints is picked in the partial vertex cover.

$$
\begin{aligned}
\text{minimize} \quad & \sum_{v \in V} c_v x_v \\
\text{subject to} \quad & \sum_{v \in e} x_v \geq y_e && \forall e \in E \\
& \sum_{e \in E} y_e = L \\
& 0 \leq x_v \leq 1 && \forall v \in V \\
& 0 \leq y_e \leq 1 && \forall e \in E
\end{aligned}
$$

As we proceed with the iterative algorithm, we will work with a graph where edges could be of size one only. For example, when we have a variable with $x_v = 0$, we will remove v from all edges containing v. Such edges will contain only one vertex but not two vertices.

11.2.2 Characterization of extreme point solutions

We give a simple characterization of the extreme point solutions based on the Rank Lemma.

Lemma 11.2.2 *Given an extreme point solution x to LP_{pvc} with $0 < x_v < 1$ for all $v \in V$ and $0 < y_e < 1$ for all $e \in E$, there is a subset $F \subseteq E$ of edges such that*

(i) $\sum_{v \in e} x_v = y_e$ *for each $e \in F$.*

Iterative Partial Vertex Cover Algorithm

(i) Initialization $W \leftarrow \emptyset$;

(ii) While $E \neq \emptyset$ do

  (a) Find an optimal extreme point solution (x, y) to LP_{pvc}. If there is an edge $e \in E$ with $y_e = 0$, then remove e from G. If there is a vertex $v \in V$ with $x_v = 0$, then remove v from G and from all the edges containing it (i.e., $e \leftarrow e \setminus \{v\}$ for all $e \in E$).

  (b) If there is a vertex $v \in V$ with $x_v \geq \frac{1}{2}$, then include $v \in W$ and remove v and all the edges incident at v from G. Update $L \leftarrow L - |\{e : e \ni v\}|$.

  (c) If G contains a single vertex v, then include $v \in W$ and remove v and all the edges incident at v from G. Update $L \leftarrow L - |\{e : e \ni v\}|$.

(iii) Return W.

Figure 11.2 Partial vertex cover algorithm.

(ii) *The constraints in $\{\sum_{v \in e} x_v = y_e : e \in F\} \cup \{\sum_{e \in E} y_v = L\}$ are linearly independent.*

(iii) $|F| + 1 = |V| + |E|$.

11.2.3 Iterative algorithm

The following is the iterative algorithm for the partial vertex cover problem is in Figure 11.2.

11.2.4 Correctness and performance guarantee

We now show that the algorithm in Figure 11.2 is a 2-approximation algorithm for the pruned instances, proving Theorem 11.2.1 for the correct guess of the costliest vertex in the optimal solution. The following lemma shows that the algorithm will terminate.

Lemma 11.2.3 *Let G be a graph with $|V(G)| \geq 2$. Then at least one of the following must hold.*

(i) *There exists a vertex v with $x_v \in \{0, 1\}$.*

(ii) *There exists an edge e with $y_e = 0$.*

(iii) *There exists an edge e with $y_e = 1$, and therefore $x_v \geq \frac{1}{2}$ for some $v \in e$.*

Proof Suppose for contradiction that none of these conditions holds. Then we have $0 < x_v < 1$ for all vertices and $0 < y_e < 1$ for all edges. From Lemma 11.2.2, there exists a subset of edges F such that $|F| + 1 = |E| + |V|$. Since $|F| \leq |E|$, this implies that $|V| \leq 1$, a contradiction. $\square$

Now, we prove that the iterative algorithm is a 2-approximation algorithm for the correct guess of the costliest vertex.

Proof of Theorem 11.2.1 Whenever we pick a vertex with $x_v \geq \frac{1}{2}$, a simple inductive argument shows that we pay a cost of at most twice the optimal fractional solution. Moreover whenever $y_e = 1$, we must have $x_v \geq \frac{1}{2}$ for some $v \in e$ as $|e| \leq 2$ for each edge e. For the last vertex picked in Step (2)c., the cost of this vertex is at most the cost of the costliest vertex. Since the LP value of the costliest vertex was set to 1 in the preprocessing step, the cost of the last vertex picked is also charged to the LP solution. ∎

11.3 Multicriteria spanning trees

In the multicriteria spanning tree problem, we are given a graph $G = (V, E)$ and nonnegative cost functions $c_0, c_1, \ldots, c_k$ on the edges and bounds $L_1, L_2, \ldots, L_k$ for each cost function c_i for $1 \leq i \leq k$. The goal is to find a minimum c_0-cost tree that has c_i-cost at most L_i.

Ravi and Goemans [113] gave an algorithm for two cost functions c_0 and c_1, which, given a positive ϵ, returns a tree T with optimal c_0-cost and $c_1(T) \leq (1+\epsilon)L_1$. The running time of the algorithm is polynomial for any fixed ϵ. We present the following generalization of their result.

Theorem 11.3.1 *Given a graph $G = (V, E)$ and nonnegative cost functions $c_0, c_1, \ldots, c_k$ on the edges and bounds $L_1, L_2, \ldots, L_k$ for each of the cost functions except c_0, and given any fixed $\epsilon > 0$, there exists an algorithm which returns a tree of optimal c_0-cost and has c_i-cost at most $(1+\epsilon)L_i$. The running time of the algorithm is polynomial for fixed k and ϵ.*

11.3.1 Linear programming relaxation

We formulate the following linear programming relaxation, denoted by LP_{mcst}, which is a straightforward extension of the linear program for minimum spanning tree problem considered in Section 4.1.

$$\text{minimize} \quad \sum_{e \in E} c_0(e) x_e$$

$$\text{subject to} \quad x(E(V)) = |V| - 1$$

$$x(E(S)) \leq |S| - 1 \qquad \forall S \subset V$$

$$\sum_{e \in E} c_i(e) x_e \leq L_i \qquad \forall 1 \leq i \leq k$$

$$x_e \geq 0 \qquad \forall e \in E$$

11.3.2 Characterization of extreme point solutions

We now give a characterization of the extreme point solutions to LP_{mcst}. This follows directly from the Rank Lemma and the characterization of extreme point solutions of the spanning tree linear program considered in Section 4.1.

Lemma 11.3.2 *Let x be an extreme point solution to LP_{mcst} with $x_e > 0$ for each edge e. Then there exists a set $J \subseteq \{1, \ldots, k\}$ and a laminar family $\mathcal{L}$ such that*

(i) $\sum_{e \in E} c_i(e) x_e = L_i$ *for each $i \in J$ and $x(E(S)) = |S| - 1$ for each $S \in \mathcal{L}$.*
(ii) *The vectors in $\{\chi(E(S)) : S \in \mathcal{L}\}$ are linearly independent.*
(iii) $|\mathcal{L}| + |J| = |E|$.

11.3.3 Iterative algorithm

The first step in the algorithm is a pruning step. Observe that no feasible solution can include an edge whose c_i-cost is more than L_i. We extend this step further and *guess* all the edges in the optimal solution whose c_i-cost is least $\frac{\epsilon}{k} L_i$. For any i, there can be at most $\frac{k}{\epsilon}$ such edges in the optimal solution. Thus, the number of possibilities is at most $m^{\frac{k}{\epsilon}}$ where m denotes the number of edges. There are k cost functions to try, and so the total possibilities is at most $m^{\frac{k^2}{\epsilon}}$. After guessing these edges correctly, we throw away all other edges that have c_i-cost at least $\frac{\epsilon}{k} L_i$ and contract the guessed edges in the input graph. Clearly, the rest of the edges in the optimal solution form a spanning tree in the contracted graph, for the correct choice of the guessed edges.

Now we have an instance where $c_i(e) \le \frac{\epsilon}{k} L_i$ for each e and i. We update the bound L_i by subtracting the c_i-costs of the guessed edges, and let L_i' denote the residual bounds. We solve the linear program LP_{mcst} with the updated bounds L_i'. Step *(iii)* of the algorithm in Figure 11.3 can be interpreted as removing all the k constraints bounding the length under the cost functions $c_1, \ldots, c_k$. Removing these constraints gives us the linear program for the spanning tree problem, which is integral and its optimal solution is a minimum c_0-cost spanning tree.

11.3.4 Correctness and performance guarantee

To prove Theorem 11.3.1, first we claim that the support of LP_{mcst} on a graph with n vertices has at most $n + k - 1$ edges. In fact, from Lemma 11.3.2, we have $|E| = |\mathcal{L}| + |J|$. But $|\mathcal{L}| \le n - 1$, since $\mathcal{L}$ is a laminar family without singletons (see Proposition 4.1.7) and $|J| \le k$, proving the claim. By the results in Chapter 4, the c_0-cost of the tree T returned by the algorithm is at most the c_0-cost of the LP solution and hence is optimal for the correct guess of *costly*

Algorithm for Multicriteria Spanning Tree

(i) Guess all the edges in the optimal solution with $c_i(e) \geq \frac{\epsilon}{k} L_i$ for some $i \in [k]$. Include these edges in the solution and contract them. Delete all other edges from G with $c_i(e) \geq \frac{\epsilon}{k} L_i$. Update L_i for all $i \in [k]$.

(ii) Find an optimal extreme point solution x to LP_{mcst} and remove every edge e with $x_e = 0$.

(iii) Pick any minimum c_0-cost tree in the support graph.

Figure 11.3 Multicriteria spanning tree algorithm.

edges. Now we show that the c_i-cost of the tree returned by the algorithm is at most $L'_i + \epsilon L_i$. Note that any tree must contain $n - 1$ edges out of the $n + k - 1$ edges in the support graph. Hence, the maximum c_i-cost tree has cost at most $k \cdot \frac{\epsilon}{k} L_i = \epsilon L_i$ more than that of the minimum c_i-cost tree in this support graph. In turn, the minimum c_i-cost tree has cost at most the c_i-cost of the optimal fractional solution, which is at most L'_i by feasibility. Altogether, the maximum c_i-cost of the solution returned is no more than $L'_i + \epsilon L_i$. Adding the cost of the edges guessed in the first step we obtain that the tree returned by the algorithm has c_i-cost at most $(L'_i + \epsilon L_i) + (L_i - L'_i) = (1 + \epsilon) L_i$, proving Theorem 11.3.1.

11.4 Notes

The paper by Bshouty and Burroughs [21] was the first to give a 2-approximation algorithm for the partial vertex cover problem using LP-rounding. Subsequently, other combinatorial 2-approximation algorithms based on the local-ratio method [9] and the primal-dual algorithm [62] were proposed.

Ravi and Goemans [113] presented a polynomial time approximation scheme (PTAS) for the bicriteria spanning tree problem via the Lagrangian relaxation method. The result presented in this chapter for the multicriteria spanning problem is from the work of Grandoni, Ravi, and Singh [64].

Exercises

11.1 Weighted Partial Vertex Cover: In an instance of the weighted vertex cover problem, we are given a graph $G = (V, E)$ with nonnegative cost function c on vertices and a nonnegative weight function w on edges and a weight target B. The goal is to find a vertex set $V' \subseteq V$ of minimum cost such that the edges covered by V' weigh at least B.

(a) Write a linear programming formulation for the partial vertex cover problem.

(b) Extend the proof of Theorem 11.2.1 to obtain a 2-approximation for this problem.

11.2 Partial Set Cover: In an instance of the set cover problem, we are given a ground set V, a collection of subsets $S = \{S_1, S_2, \ldots, S_m\}$ of V with a nonnegative cost function c on the subsets, a nonnegative weight function w on the elements of V, and a weight target B. The goal is to find non-negative a subset $S' \subseteq S$ of minimum cost such that the elements covered by S' weigh at least B.

(a) Write a linear programming formulation for the partial set cover problem.

(b) Extend the proof of the weighted partial vertex cover problem to obtain an f-approximation algorithm for the problem, where f denotes the maximum number of subsets in S containing a particular element in V.

11.3 Prize Collecting Vertex Cover: In an instance of the prize collecting vertex cover problem, we are given a graph $G = (V, E)$ with nonnegative cost function c on vertices and a nonnegative penalty function w on edges. The cost of any solution defined by $V' \subset V$ is the cost of vertices in V' plus the penalty of the edges not covered by V'. The task is to find a subset $V' \subset V$ of minimum total cost.

(a) Write a linear programming formulation for the prize collecting vertex cover problem.

(b) Give a simple iterative procedure to achieve a 2-approximation for the problem.

(c) Show that an approximation factor of 2 needs to be paid only for the vertex cost and not for the edge penalties (i.e., the total cost of your approximate solution is at most the penalty cost for the edges paid by the LP solution plus twice the LP cost for the vertices).

11.4 Multicriteria Matroid Basis: In this problem, we are given a matroid $M = (V, \mathcal{I})$, nonnegative cost functions $c_i : V \to \mathbb{R}$ for $0 \le i \le k$, bounds L_i for each $1 \le i \le k$, and the task is to the find the minimum c_0-cost basis of M such that its c_i-cost is at most L_i.

(a) Write a linear programming relaxation for the multicriteria matroid basis problem.

(b) Extend the proof of Theorem 11.3.1 to give a polynomial time approximation scheme for the problem, with running time polynomial for fixed ϵ and k.

12

Cut Problems

In this chapter, we present 2-approximation algorithms for three "cut" problems: the triangle cover problem, the feedback vertex set problem on bipartite tournaments, and the node multiway cut problem. All the algorithms are based on iterative rounding but require an additional step: As usual the algorithms will pick variables with large fractional values and compute a new optimal fractional solution iteratively, but unlike previous problems we do not show that an optimal extreme point solution must have a variable with large fractional value. Instead, when every variable in an optimal fractional solution has a small fractional value, we will use the complementary slackness conditions to show that there are some special structures that can be exploited to finish rounding the fractional solution. These algorithms do not use the properties of extreme point solutions, but we will need the complementary slackness conditions stated in Section 2.1.4. The results in this chapter illustrate an interesting variant and the flexibility of the iterative rounding method.

12.1 Triangle cover

Given an undirected graph with weights on the edges, the triangle cover problem is to find a subset of edges F with minimum total weight that intersects all the triangles (3-cycles) of the graph (i.e., $G - F$ is triangle-free).

12.1.1 Linear programming relaxation

The following is a simple linear programming formulation for the triangle cover problem, denoted by $LP_{tri}(G)$, in which x_e is a variable for edge e and w_e is the weight of edge e.

$$\text{minimize} \qquad \sum_{e \in E} w_e x_e$$

$$\text{subject to} \qquad \sum_{e \in T} x_e \geq 1 \qquad \forall \text{ triangle } T$$

$$x_e \geq 0 \qquad \forall e \in E$$

12.1.2 Iterative algorithm

The algorithm will first iteratively pick edges with large fractional value. When there is no edge with $x_e \geq \frac{1}{2}$ and the graph is still not triangle-free, the algorithm will compute a bipartite subgraph H with at least half the total weight of the edges, and add all the edges not in H to the solution.

12.1.3 Correctness and performance guarantee

The algorithm in Figure 12.1 can be implemented in polynomial time: There is a simple linear time algorithm to find a bipartite subgraph with at least half the total weight in Step (4). In particular, consider the following greedy algorithm: Process the nodes in an arbitrary order, and put them in one of two sides of the bipartition, greedily putting a node on the side so that at least half the weight of the edges from it to the existing nodes crosses the bipartition. In the end, at least half the total weight of all the edges cross the bipartition, which is a 2-approximation to the maximum-weight cut.

To prove the approximation guarantee of the algorithm, the key step is to prove that Step (iv) gives a 2-approximate solution in the remaining graph, for which we will need the complementary slackness conditions.

Iterative Triangle Cover Algorithm

 (i) Initialization $F \leftarrow \emptyset$.
 (ii) Compute an optimal fractional solution x to $LP_{tri}(G)$.
 (iii) While there is an edge e with $x_e \geq \frac{1}{2}$ do
    (a) For an edge e with $x_e \geq \frac{1}{2}$, update $F \leftarrow F \cup \{e\}$ and $G \leftarrow G - e$.
    (b) Compute an optimal fractional solution x to $LP_{tri}(G)$.
 (iv) If G is not triangle-free, then find a bipartite subgraph H with at least half the total weight, and update $F \leftarrow F \cup (E(G) - E(H))$.
 (v) Return F.

Figure 12.1 Triangle cover algorithm.

Theorem 12.1.1 *The algorithm in Figure 12.1 is a 2-approximation algorithm for the triangle cover problem.*

Proof The main difference from previous iterative algorithms is in the last step, where we add all the edges not in H to F. Notice that in this last step the algorithm does not consider the fractional values of the remaining edges, but only consider their weights. Suppose we could prove that

$$\sum_{e \in E(G) - E(H)} w_e \leq 2 \sum_{e \in E(G)} w_e x_e \qquad (12.1)$$

where the right-hand side is twice the objective value in the remaining fractional solution after the while loop. Then we know that $E(G) - E(H)$ is a 2-approximate solution for the triangle cover problem in the remaining graph, as the objective value is a lower bound on the optimal value. Since we only pick edges with fractional value at least $\frac{1}{2}$ in the loop, by a standard inductive argument as in previous chapters, we could show that the iterative algorithm in Figure 12.1 is an overall 2-approximation algorithm for the triangle cover problem.

We now use the complementary slackness conditions to prove (12.1). The following is the dual program of $LP_{tri}(G)$, in which there is one variable for each triangle T in G.

maximize $\qquad \sum_{T} y_T$

subject to $\qquad \sum_{T : e \in T} y_T \leq w_e \qquad \forall e \in E$

$$y_T \geq 0 \qquad \forall \text{ triangle } T \in G$$

We can assume without loss of generality that every edge e in G belongs to some triangle; otherwise, we could delete e from G without changing any minimal solution to the triangle cover problem. Also, there is no edge with fractional value at least $\frac{1}{2}$ in Step (4) of the algorithm because of the termination condition of the while loop. Since every edge e is in some triangle T, this implies that $x_e > 0$ for every edge e in Step (4); otherwise, some other edge in T must have a fractional value of at least $\frac{1}{2}$ in order to satisfy the constraint for T in $LP_{tri}(G)$. As x is an optimal solution for $LP_{tri}(G)$, by the primal complementary slackness conditions (see Section 2.1.4.1), in any dual optimal solution y we must have

$$\sum_{T : e \in T} y_T = w_e$$

for every edge e in G. Hence, the objective value of any dual optimal solution y is

$$\sum_T y_T = \frac{1}{3} \sum_{e \in E} \sum_{T:e \in T} y_T = \frac{1}{3} \sum_{e \in E} w_e$$

where the first equality follows because every triangle is counted exactly thrice on the right-hand side, and the second equality follows from the primal complementary slackness conditions. By the LP duality theorem (Theorem 2.1.9), the objective value of the primal program is equal to that of the dual program. Therefore, in Step (iv) of the algorithm, the objective value for the primal solution is

$$\sum_{e \in E} w_e x_e = \sum_T y_T = \frac{1}{3} \sum_{e \in E} w_e.$$

As H computed in Step (4) satisfies the property that $\sum_{e \in E(H)} w_e \geq \frac{1}{2} \sum_{e \in E(G)} w_e$, we have

$$\sum_{e \in E(G) - E(H)} w_e \leq \frac{1}{2} \sum_{e \in E(G)} w_e = \frac{3}{2} \sum_{e \in E(G)} w_e x_e.$$

This implies (12.1), completing the proof of the theorem.   □

A similar result holds for the directed triangle cover problem (see the exercises).

12.2 Feedback vertex set on bipartite tournaments

Given a directed graph D with nonnegative weights on the vertices, the feedback vertex set problem is to find a subset of vertices S with minimum total weight that intersects all the directed cycles (i.e., $D - S$ has no directed cycles). There is no known constant factor approximation algorithm for this problem. In this section, we present a 2-approximation algorithm for the feedback set problem on a special class of directed graphs called bipartite tournaments. A bipartite tournament is obtained from an undirected complete bipartite graph by assigning exactly one direction to each edge (i.e., for each edge uv, exactly one of the arcs in $\{uv, vu\}$ is present in the bipartite tournament). The feedback vertex set problem is easier in bipartite tournaments because of the following property.

Proposition 12.2.1 *A bipartite tournament has no directed cycle if and only if it has no directed cycle of length four.*

Proof Suppose there is a directed cycle of length $2k$ for $k \geq 3$, say $x_1, y_1, x_2, y_2, \ldots, x_{2k}, y_{2k}$. Consider the orientation of the arc between x_1 and

y_2. If it is oriented from y_2 to x_1, we have found a directed 4-cycle; else, we can shortcut the cycle to a $2(k-1)$ cycle and proceed by induction on k to complete the proof. □

12.2.1 Linear programming relaxation

By Proposition 12.2.1, the problem of intersecting all directed cycles in a bipartite tournament is equivalent to the problem of intersecting all directed four-cycles. Thus, we can write the following simple linear programming formulation for the feedback vertex set problem on bipartite tournaments, denoted by $LP_{4cyc}(D)$, in which x_v is the variable for vertex v and w_v is the weight of vertex v.

minimize $\quad\displaystyle\sum_{v\in V} w_v x_v$

subject to $\quad\displaystyle\sum_{v\in C} x_v \geq 1 \qquad \forall$ directed cycle C of length 4

$$x_v \geq 0 \qquad \forall v \in V$$

12.2.2 Iterative algorithm

The algorithm in Figure 12.2 will first iteratively pick vertices with large fractional value. When there is no vertex with $x_v \geq \frac{1}{2}$, the algorithm will then add all the vertices with positive fractional value on one side of the bipartite graph to the solution.

12.2.3 Correctness and performance guarantee

First, we prove that the solution returned by the algorithm is indeed a feedback vertex set. Every directed cycle C of length 4 has exactly two vertices in X and two vertices in Y, where X and Y are the bipartition of D. Let the vertices in C be $\{x_1, y_1, x_2, y_2\}$ where $\{x_1, x_2\} \subseteq X$ and $\{y_1, y_2\} \subseteq Y$. After the loop, the fractional value of each vertex is smaller than $\frac{1}{2}$. So if C is still present after the loop, then at least one of x_1 or x_2 must have positive fractional value to satisfy the constraint for C in $LP_{4cyc}(D)$. Hence X^+ (as defined in Step (4)) intersects all directed cycles of length 4 in the remaining graph. Therefore, $S \cup X^+$ is a feedback vertex set in the original graph. To prove the performance guarantee, we will prove that X^+ is a 2-approximate solution in the remaining graph, for which we need the complementary slackness conditions.

Theorem 12.2.2 *The algorithm in Figure 12.2 is a 2-approximation algorithm for the feedback vertex set problem on bipartite tournaments.*

Iterative Feedback Vertex Set Algorithm on Bipartite Tournaments

(i) Initialization $S \leftarrow \emptyset$.

(ii) Compute an optimal fractional solution to $LP_{4cyc}(D)$.

(iii) While there is a vertex v with $x_v \geq \frac{1}{2}$ do

    (a) For a vertex v with $x_v \geq \frac{1}{2}$, update $S \leftarrow S \cup \{v\}$ and $D \leftarrow D - v$.

    (b) Compute an optimal fractional solution x to $LP_{4cyc}(D)$.

(iv) Let the bipartition of D be X and Y, and let X^+ be the set of vertices in X with positive fractional value.

(v) Return $S \cup X^+$.

Figure 12.2   Feedback vertex set algorithm on bipartite tournaments.

Proof The main difference from standard iterative algorithms is in Step (4), where we add all the vertices in X^+ to the solution regardless of their fractional values. Suppose we could prove that

$$\sum_{v \in X^+} w_v \leq 2 \sum_{v \in V} w_v x_v \qquad (12.2)$$

where the right-hand side is twice the objective value in the remaining fractional solution after the while loop. Then we know that X^+ is a 2-approximate solution for the feedback vertex set problem in the remaining graph. As we only pick vertices with fractional value at least $\frac{1}{2}$ in the loop, by an inductive argument as in previous chapters, we could show that the iterative algorithm in Figure 12.2 is an overall 2-approximation algorithm for the feedback vertex set problem in bipartite tournaments.

We use the complementary slackness conditions to prove (12.2). The following is the dual program of $LP_{4cyc}(D)$, in which there is one variable for each directed cycle C of length 4 in D.

maximize $\displaystyle\sum_C y_C$

subject to $\displaystyle\sum_{C:v \in C} y_C \leq w_v \qquad \forall v \in V$

                    $y_C \geq 0 \qquad \forall$ directed cycle C of length 4

As x is an optimal solution, by the primal complementary slackness conditions, in any optimal dual solution y, we must have

$$\sum_{C:v \in C} y_C = w_v$$

for each vertex $v \in X^+$. Hence, the objective value of any dual optimal solution y is

$$\sum_C y_C \geq \frac{1}{2} \sum_{v \in X^+} \sum_{C:v \in C} y_C = \frac{1}{2} \sum_{v \in X^+} w_v$$

where the first inequality follows because each directed 4-cycle intersects X^+ at most twice. By the LP duality theorem, we have

$$\sum_{v \in V} w_v x_v = \sum_C y_C \geq \frac{1}{2} \sum_{v \in X^+} w_v.$$

This proves (12.2), completing the proof of the theorem. $\square$

12.3 Node multiway cut

Given an undirected graph G with nonnegative weights on the vertices and a subset $T \subset V$ of terminal vertices, the node multiway cut problem is to find a subset S of vertices in $V - T$ with minimum total weight that intersects every path with both endpoints in T (i.e., in $G - S$ there is no path between any pair of vertices in T).

12.3.1 Linear programming relaxation

The node multiway cut problem can be formulated by the following linear program, denoted by $LP_{cut}(G)$. In the following, x_v denotes the indicator variable for vertex $v \in V - T$, w_v denotes the weight of the vertex $v \in V - T$, and $\mathcal{P}$ denotes the set of all paths between any two terminal vertices.

$$
\begin{aligned}
\text{minimize} \quad & \sum_{v \in V-T} w_v x_v \\
\text{subject to} \quad & \sum_{v \in P} x_v \geq 1 && \forall P \in \mathcal{P} \\
& x_v \geq 0 && \forall v \in V - T
\end{aligned}
$$

There could be exponentially many constraints in $LP_{cut}(G)$, but this can still be solved by the ellipsoid algorithm in polynomial time, since we can use a shortest path algorithm to construct a separation oracle for this linear program.

12.3.2 Iterative algorithm

The iterative algorithm in Figure 12.3 is similar to the previous algorithms in this chapter. It will first iteratively pick vertices set to integral value. When there is no vertex with $x_v = 1$, the algorithm will then add all the "boundary" vertices of the terminal vertices to the solution.

12.3.3 Correctness and performance guarantee

Let $B := \cup_{u \in T} B_u$ be the set of all boundary vertices of terminal vertices. Since each path between two terminal vertices has total fractional value at least one, it follows that B is a node multiway cut in the remaining graph after the while loop; otherwise, there would be a path between two terminals with total fractional value zero. To prove the approximation guarantee, we show that B is a 2-approximate solution in Step (4), for which we will use (both) the complementary slackness conditions.

Theorem 12.3.1 *The algorithm in Figure 12.3 is a 2-approximation algorithm for the node multiway cut problem.*

Proof As in the previous algorithms in this chapter, the main difference from standard iterative algorithms is in the last step, where we add all the vertices in B to the solution regardless of their fractional values. Note that every vertex in B has positive fractional value. Suppose we could prove that

$$\sum_{v \in B} w_v \leq 2 \sum_{v \in V-T} w_v x_v \qquad (12.3)$$

Iterative Node Multiway Cut Algorithm

(i) Initialization $S \leftarrow \emptyset$.

(ii) Compute an optimal fractional solution x to $LP_{cut}(G)$.

(iii) While there is a vertex v with $x_v = 1$ do
   (a) For a vertex v with $x_v = 1$, update $S \leftarrow S \cup \{v\}$ and $G \leftarrow G - v$.
   (b) Compute an optimal fractional solution x to $LP_{cut}(G)$.

(iv) For each vertex $v \in T$, let Z_v be the set of vertices that can be reached from v by paths of total fractional value zero, and let B_v be the set of vertices that are adjacent to Z_v (i.e., $B_v = \{w \in V - Z_v \mid \exists u \in Z_v$ with $uw \in E\}$).

(v) Return $S \cup \bigcup_{v \in T} B_v$.

Figure 12.3 Node multiway cut algorithm.

which is twice the objective value in the remaining fractional solution after the while loop. Then we know that B is a 2-approximate solution for the node multiway cut problem in the remaining graph. As we only pick vertices with value 1 in the loop, by an inductive argument as in previous chapters, we could show that the iterative algorithm in Figure 12.1 is an overall 2-approximation algorithm for the node multiway cut problem.

We use the complementary slackness conditions to prove (12.3). The following is the dual program of $LP_{cut}(G)$, in which there is one variable for each path P of $\mathcal{P}$.

$$\text{maximize} \quad \sum_P y_P$$

$$\text{subject to} \quad \sum_{P:v \in P} y_P \le w_v \qquad \forall v \in V - T$$

$$y_P \ge 0 \qquad \forall P \in \mathcal{P}$$

As x is an optimal solution, by the primal complementary slackness conditions, in any optimal dual solution y, we must have

$$\sum_{P:v \in P} y_P = w_v$$

for each vertex $v \in B$. By the dual complementary slackness conditions, in any optimal primal solution x, we must have

$$\sum_{v \in P} x_v = 1$$

for each path $P \in \mathcal{P}$ with $y_P > 0$.

We now argue that each path P with $y_P > 0$ contains exactly two vertices in B. Let P be a path with $y_P > 0$ connecting two terminals s and t. Since there is no vertex v with $x_v = 1$, B_s and B_t must be disjoint; otherwise, there would be a path from s to t with total fractional value less than one. Hence, P must contain one vertex in B_s and one vertex in B_t. Suppose to the contrary that P contains another vertex in B_r. If $r \in \{s,t\}$, then we can shortcut the path P to use one fewer vertex in B and obtain a shorter path P' from s to t. However, since every vertex in B has a positive fractional value and $\sum_{v \in P} x_v = 1$ by the dual complementary slackness condition, this implies that $\sum_{v \in P'} x_v < 1$, contradicting the fact that x is a feasible solution to $LP_{cut}(G)$. If $r \notin \{s,t\}$, then we can shortcut the path P to obtain a path P'' from s to r, which is shorter than P since it avoids a vertex in B_t. This implies that $\sum_{v \in P''} x_v < 1$, as every vertex in B has a positive fractional value and $\sum_{v \in P} x_v = 1$. Since P'' is a path connecting two terminals s and r, this contradicts the fact that x is a feasible solution to $LP_{cut}(G)$. Therefore, each path P with $y_P > 0$ contains exactly two vertices in B. Hence, the objective value of any dual optimal solution y is

$$\sum_P y_P = \frac{1}{2} \sum_{v \in B} \sum_{P:v \in P} y_P = \frac{1}{2} \sum_{v \in B} w_v$$

where the first equality holds because each path P with $y_P > 0$ uses exactly two vertices in B, and the second equality follows from the complementary slackness conditions. By the LP duality theorem, we have

$$\sum_{v \in V-T} w_v x_v = \sum_P y_P = \frac{1}{2} \sum_{v \in B} w_v.$$

This proves (12.3), completing the proof of the theorem. $\square$

12.4 Notes

The result for the triangle cover problem is from the work of Krivelevich [85]. The algorithm for the feedback vertex set problem on bipartite tournaments is due to van Zuylen [130], improving a 3.5-approximation algorithm by Cai, Deng and Zang [22] and an iterative rounding 3-approximation algorithm by Sasatte [117]. The result for the node mulitway cut problem is due to Garg, Vazirani, and Yannakakis [58].

Exercises

12.1 Design a $\frac{1}{2}$-approximation algorithm for the maximum weighted bipartite subgraph problem.

12.2 Consider the directed triangle cover problem: Given a directed graph with weights on the arcs, find a subset of arcs with minimum total weight that intersect all the directed triangles. Obtain a 2-approximation algorithm for this problem.

12.3 Consider the following "complement" problem to the triangle cover problem: Given an undirected graph with weights on the edges, find a triangle-free subgraph with maximum total weight. Design a $\frac{3}{2}$-approximation algorithm for this problem. (*Hint*: Use the 2-approximation algorithm for the triangle cover problem and the ideas therein.)

12.4 Generalize the result for the triangle cover problem to obtain a $(k - 1)$-approximation algorithm for the k-cycle cover problem when k is odd. What about the case when k is even?

12.5 Consider the feedback vertex set problem on tournaments. A tournament is obtained from a complete undirected graph by assigning exactly one direction to each edge.

(a) Prove that a tournament has a directed cycle if and only if it has a directed 3-cycle.

(b) Use part (a) to write a linear programming relaxation for the problem.

(c) Obtain a 3-approximation algorithm for the problem using the above linear program.

12.6 Consider the directed 4-cycle cover problem in bipartite directed graph (a directed graph with the underlying undirected graph bipartite): Given a bipartite directed graph with weights on the arcs, find a subset of arcs with minimum total weight to intersect all the directed 4-cycles. Design a 2-approximation algorithm for this problem.

Can you also obtain a 2-approximation algorithm for the node-weighted case where the objective is to find a subset of nodes with minimum total weight to intersect all the directed 4-cycles?

12.7 Consider the feedback *arc* set problem on bipartite tournaments, where the objective is to find a subset of arcs with minimum total weight to intersect all the directed cycles. What is the best performance guarantee you can obtain in polynomial time?

12.8 Work out the details of the separation oracle for solving LP_{cut}.

12.9 Show that there is an approximation-ratio preserving reduction from the minimum vertex cover problem to the node multiway cut problem.

12.10 Prove that $LP_{cut}(G)$ is actually *half-integral*: There is always an optimal solution to $LP_{cut}(G)$ with $x_v \in \{0, \frac{1}{2}, 1\}$ for every vertex $v \in V(G)$.

12.11 Consider the multicut problem on trees: Given a tree T with weights on the edges and a set of l pairs of vertices $\{(s_i, t_i) : 1 \le i \le l\}$, the objective is to find a subset of edges F with minimum total weight that intersect all the s_i-t_i paths (i.e., there is no s_i-t_i path in $T \setminus F$ for $1 \le i \le l$).

(a) Write a linear programming relaxation for this problem.

(b) Assume the tree T is rooted at a specific vertex r. An instance of the problem is called *noncrossing*, if for each pair (s_i, t_i), s_i is a descendant of t_i in the rooted tree (T, r). Prove that the foregoing linear programming relaxation always has integral optimal solutions for noncrossing instances.

(c) Use part (b) to obtain a 2-approximation algorithm for the multicut problem on trees. (*Hint*: Construct a noncrossing instance from a non-noncrossing instance.)

12.12 Can you obtain a 2-approximation algorithm for the multicut problem on trees by an iterative rounding algorithm?

13
Iterative relaxation: Early and recent examples

Even though we mentioned the paper by Jain [75] as the first explicit application of the iterative method to approximation algorithms, several earlier results can be reinterpreted in this light, which is what we set out to do in this chapter. We will first present a result by Beck and Fiala [12] on hypergraph discrepancy, whose proof is closest to other proofs in this book. Then we will present a result by Steinitz [127] on rearrangements of sums in a geometric setting, which is the earliest application that we know of. Then we will present an approximation algorithm by Skutella [123] for the single source unsplittable flow problem. Then we present the additive approximation algorithm for the bin packing problem by Karmarkar and Karp [77], which is still one of the most sophisticated uses of the iterative relaxation method. Finally, we sketch a recent application of the iterative method augmented with randomized rounding to the undirected Steiner tree problem [20] following the simplification due to Chakrabarty et al. [24].

13.1 A discrepancy theorem

In this section, we present the Beck–Fiala theorem from discrepancy theory using an iterative method. Given a hypergraph $G = (V, E)$, a 2-coloring of the hypergraph is defined as an assignment $\psi : V \to \{-1, +1\}$ on the vertices. The discrepancy of a hyperedge e is defined as $disc_\chi(e) = \sum_{v \in e} \psi(v)$, and the discrepancy of the hypergraph G is defined as $disc_\psi(G) = \max_{e \in E(G)} |\{disc_\psi(e)\}|$. Beck and Fiala gave an upper bound on the discrepancy based on the maximum degree of the hypergraph (defined as $\max_v |\{e : v \in e\}|$).

Theorem 13.1.1 *Given a hypergraph $G = (V, E)$ with maximum degree d, there is a coloring ψ with discrepancy $disc_\psi(G) \leq 2d - 1$.*

13.1.1 Linear programming relaxation

Consider the following feasibility linear program LP_{disc} for the hypergraph 2-coloring problem. There is a variable x_v for each vertex $v \in V$, which is either 1 or -1 depending on whether $\psi(v) = 1$ or $\psi(v) = -1$. Initially we set $B_e = 0$ for each hyperedge $e \in E$, as $x_v = 0$ for all v is a feasible solution to this linear program (even though it may not be an extreme point solution).

$$\sum_{v \in e} x_v = B_e \qquad\qquad \forall e \in E,$$
$$-1 \ \leq \ x_v \leq 1 \qquad\qquad \forall v \in V.$$

13.1.2 Characterization of extreme point solutions

For a hyperedge e the corresponding constraint $\sum_{v \in e} x_v = B_e$ defines a characteristic vector $\chi : E \to \mathbb{R}^{|V|}$ with a 1 corresponding to each vertex $v \in e$ and 0 otherwise. The following characterization is a direct application of the Rank Lemma.

Lemma 13.1.2 *Given any extreme point solution to LP_{disc} with $-1 < x_v < 1$ for each $v \in V$, there exists a subset $F \subseteq E$ such that*

(i) *$\sum_{v \in e} x_v = B_e$ for each $e \in F$.*
(ii) *The characteristic vectors for the constraints in F are linearly independent.*
(iii) *$|F| = |V|$.*

13.1.3 Iterative algorithm

The iterative algorithm is similar to that for the minimum bounded degree spanning tree problem. In each iteration, we either fix the variables with value $+1, -1$ or remove the constraint for a "small" hyperedge.

13.1.4 Correctness and performance guarantee

We first show that the discrepancy of ψ is at most $2d - 1$ assuming that the algorithm terminates. Consider any hyperedge e. Note that the updates of B_e over the course of the algorithm ensure that the updated LPs solved in the subsequent iterations continue to remain feasible. We prove by induction that $B_e + disc_\psi(e) = 0$ while the constraint for e is present, where B_e is the current target discrepancy in the linear program and $disc_\psi(e)$ is the current discrepancy in the partial solution constructed so far. This condition holds initially as $B_e = 0$ and $disc_\psi(e) = 0$ since $x_v = 0$ for every vertex v. Whenever we set $\psi(v) = 1$

Iterative Algorithm for Beck–Fiala Theorem

(i) Initialization $\psi(v) \leftarrow 0$ for all $v \in V$.

(ii) While $V(G) \neq \emptyset$ do

   (a) Find an extreme point solution x to LP_{disc}.

   (b) If there is a variable with $x_v = 1$ or $x_v = -1$, then set $\psi(v) = x_v$, set $B_e = B_e - x_v$ for each hyperedge e containing v, and remove v from G.

   (c) If there exists a hyperedge $e \in E$ with $|e| \leq d$, then remove the constraint for e and remove e from G.

(iii) Return ψ.

Figure 13.1 Beck–Fiala discrepancy theorem.

or $\psi(v) = -1$, $disc_\psi(e)$ increases by $\psi(v)$ and B_e decreases by $\psi(v)$ for each hyperedge e that contains v, and hence the equality continues to hold. When the constraint for a hyperedge e is removed, there are at most d vertices left in e. Since each variable v has value $-1 < x_v < 1$, the equality $\sum_{v \in e} x_v = B_e = -disc_\psi(e)$ implies that $|disc_\psi(e)| = |\sum_{v \in e} x_v| < d$. Hence, after the constraint is removed, even if we color the remaining vertices arbitrarily, the maximum discrepancy of this edge is strictly less than $2d$.

To complete the proof of Theorem 13.1.1, we show that the algorithm will terminate by a simple counting argument.

Lemma 13.1.3 *Given any extreme point solution x of $LP_{disc}(G)$, at least one of the following must hold:*

(i) *There exists a vertex v with $x_v \in \{-1, 1\}$.*

(ii) *There exists an edge $e \in E$ with $|e| \leq d$.*

Proof Suppose that neither is true. From Lemma 13.1.2 there is a subset of hyperedges $F \subseteq E$ with $|F| = |V|$. Thus, the number of variables $|V|$ is at most $|E|$. As each hyperedge contains strictly more than d vertices,

$$\sum_{e \in E} |e| > d|E|$$

but as each variable occurs in at most d hyperedges, we have

$$\sum_{e \in E} |e| = \sum_{v \in V} d_E(v) \leq d|V|.$$

Thus we must have $|V| > |E|$ which is a contradiction. $\square$

13.2 Rearrangments of sums

In this section, we will present Steinitz's result on rearrangments of sums in a geometric setting using an iterative method. Let V be a subset of vectors in the unit ball B^d in the d-dimensional Euclidean space. Assume that $\sum_{v \in V} v = 0$. The question is whether there is an ordering $v_1, v_2, \ldots, v_n$ of the elements of V such that all partial sums along this order are bounded by a number that only depends on d. Steinitz [127] answers this question affirmatively.

Theorem 13.2.1 *Given a finite set $V \subseteq B^d$ with $\sum_{v \in V} v = 0$, there is an ordering $v_1, v_2, \ldots, v_n$ of the elements of V such that*

$$\| \sum_{i=1}^{k} v_i \| \leq d \quad \text{for all } 1 \leq k \leq n$$

where $\|v\|$ is the Euclidean norm of v.

13.2.1 Linear programming relaxation

The approach is not to directly formulate the problem as an optimization problem, instead the key idea is to consider an auxiliary linear program. In the following k is a constant whose value will be chosen in the range between n and $d + 1$.

$$\sum_{v \in V} \alpha_v v = 0, \tag{13.1}$$

$$\sum_{v \in V} \alpha_v = k - d, \tag{13.2}$$

$$0 \leq \alpha_v \leq 1 \quad \text{for all } v \in V. \tag{13.3}$$

Note that since each vector $v \in V$ is d-dimensional, the equality constraint (13.1) is actually an abbreviation of d linear equality constraints.

13.2.2 Characterization of extreme point solutions

The following lemma is used to "create" a zero-valued variable in the auxiliary linear program.

Lemma 13.2.2 *When $k = |V| - 1$, given any extreme point solution to the auxiliary linear program, there exists a vector v with $\alpha_v = 0$.*

Proof There are $|V|$ variables in this linear program. By the Rank Lemma, there are $|V|$ constraints satisfied as equalities in an extreme point solution.

Iterative Algorithm for Steinitz Theorem

(i) Initialization $k = |V| - 1$.

(ii) While $|V| > d + 1$ do

    (a) Compute an extreme point solution x to the auxiliary linear program.

    (b) Find a vector u with $\alpha_v = 0$. Set $v_{k+1} := u$. Remove u from the problem. Set $k := k - 1$.

(iii) Order the remaining $d + 1$ vectors arbitrarily to obtain $v_1, v_2, \ldots, v_{d+1}$.

(iv) Return the ordering $\{v_1, v_2, \ldots, v_{|V|}\}$.

Figure 13.2 Steinitz's theorem on rearrangments of sums.

The first two constraints contribute $d + 1$ equalities. If $\alpha_v > 0$ for all $v \in V$, then there are at least $|V| - d - 1 = k - d$ vectors with $\alpha_v = 1$. Hence, to satisfy the equality constraint (13.2) in the auxiliary linear program, the remaining $d + 1$ variables must be zero, a contradiction. $\qquad \square$

13.2.3 Iterative algorithm

The iterative algorithm produces the ordering in reverse order. In each iteration the right-hand side of equality (13.2) of the linear program decreases, and some vector with coefficient zero will be put at the end of the ordering among the current vectors.

13.2.4 Correctness and performance guarantee

First, we prove that the algorithm will succeed in producing an ordering. There are two parts: One is to show that the linear program is always feasible, and the other is to show that there is always a vector with coefficient zero. For the first part, initially when $k = |V| - 1$ the solution $\alpha_v = (|V| - 1 - d)/|V|$ for all v is feasible since $\sum_{v \in V} v = 0$. Now suppose there is a feasible solution in the current iteration. When k is decreased by one, we can obtain a feasible solution by scaling down the current solution by a factor of $\frac{k-1-d}{k-d}$. So by induction there is always a feasible solution to the linear program. The second part follows directly from Lemma 13.2.2.

Finally we prove that the norm of all partial sums is at most d. This is trivial for the first d vectors. Now consider the case when $k \geq d + 1$. In the following let α_v be the coefficient of vector v in the iteration when there are exactly k vectors left; note that we can scale down the solution in the last iteration to obtain a feasible solution for $k = d + 1$.

$$\sum_{i=1}^{k} v_i = \sum_{i=1}^{k} v_i - \sum_{i=1}^{k} \alpha_{v_i} v_i = \sum_{i=1}^{k} (1 - \alpha_{v_i}) v_i$$

where the first equation follows because $\sum_{i=1}^{k} \alpha_{v_i} v_i = 0$ by the equality constraint (13.1) in the linear program. Taking norms and using that $1 - \alpha_{v_i} \geq 0$ and $||v_i|| \leq 1$ gives

$$|| \sum_{i=1}^{k} v_i || = || \sum_{i=1}^{k} (1 - \alpha_{v_i}) v_i || \leq \sum_{i=1}^{k} ||(1 - \alpha_{v_i}) v_i ||$$

$$\leq \sum_{i=1}^{k} (1 - \alpha_{v_i}) = k - (k - d) = d$$

where the second last equation follows from the equality constraint (13.2) of the linear program. This completes the proof of Theorem 13.2.1.

13.3 Minimum cost circulation

In this section, we show the integrality of a linear programming relaxation for the minimum cost circulation problem. This proof will serve as a basis for the iterative algorithm for the minimum cost unsplittable flow problem in the next section.

In an instance of the minimum cost circulation problem, we are given a directed graph $D = (V, A)$ with arc costs $c : A \to R$, capacities $u \to R_+$, and a demand function $b : V \to R$. The task is to find a minimum cost flow $x : A \to R^+$ such that $x(\delta^{out}(v)) - x(\delta^{in}(v)) = b_v$ for each $v \in V$. Recall that $x(F)$ for $F \subseteq A$ is a shorthand for $\sum_{e \in F} x_e$. The vertices with $b_v > 0$ are referred to as *sources*, and vertices with $b_v < 0$ are referred to as *sinks*. Note that for feasibility, we must have $\sum_v b_v = 0$. In the following theorem, we prove that when the demands and the capacities are multiples of some integer d, then there is an optimal flow which is d-integral.

Theorem 13.3.1 *Consider an instance of the minimum cost circulation problem with $d | b_v$ (b_v is divisible by d) for each $v \in V$ and $d | u_a$ for each $a \in A$ for some $d \in Z^+$. Then there must exist a minimum cost solution x such that $d | x_a$ for each arc $a \in A$.*

13.3.1 Linear programming relaxation

The following is a standard linear programming formulation for the minimum cost circulation problem, denoted by LP_{circ}.

minimize $$\sum_{a \in A} c_a x_a$$

subject to
$$x(\delta^{out}(v)) - x(\delta^{in}(v)) = b_v \qquad \forall\, v \in V$$
$$0 \;\leq\; x_a \leq u_a \qquad \forall\, a \in A$$

13.3.2 Characterization of extreme point solutions

For each vertex v, the corresponding constraint $x(\delta^{out}(v)) - x(\delta^{in}(v))$ defines a characteristic vector $\chi(v)$ in $\mathbb{R}^{|A|}$ with a 1 corresponding to each arc in $\delta^{out}(v)$ and a -1 corresponding to each arc in $\delta^{in}(v)$ and 0 otherwise. Lemma 13.3.2 is a direct consequence of the Rank Lemma.

Lemma 13.3.2 *Given any extreme point solution x to LP_{circ} with $0 < x_a < u_a$ for each $a \in A$, there exists a subset $W \subseteq V$ such that*

(i) $x(\delta^{out}(v)) - x(\delta^{in}(v)) = b_v$ *for each $v \in W$.*
(ii) *The vectors in $\{\chi(v) : v \in W\}$ are linearly independent.*
(iii) $|A| = |W|$.

The following corollary states the property that will be used later.

Corollary 13.3.3 *Given any extreme point solution x to LP_{circ} with $0 < x_a < u_a$ for each $a \in A$, we must have $|A| \leq |V| - 1$.*

Proof By Lemma 13.3.2, we have $|A| = |W|$. Note that $\sum_{v \in V} \chi(v) = 0$, since every arc is counted exactly once as a positive term and exactly once as a negative term. As the constraints in W are linearly independent, this implies that $|W| \leq |V| - 1$, and thus the corollary follows. $\qquad\square$

13.3.3 Iterative algorithm

We present in Figure 13.3 the iterative algorithm for the minimum cost circulation problem, which will return an optimal solution x with the property that $d\,|\,x_a$ for each $a \in A$.

13.3.4 Correctness and optimality

Observe that each of the update steps maintains the property that the flow fixed on each arc is a multiple of d, since it is either fixed to u_a or is fixed to $\pm b_v$ for some vertex v. Optimality of the cost follows from a simple inductive argument. To prove Theorem 13.3.1, it remains to prove that the algorithm terminates by showing that one of the choices in the while loop is available in each iteration.

Iterative Minimum Cost Circulation Algorithm

(i) Initialization $\mathcal{F} \leftarrow \emptyset$.
(ii) While $V(G) \neq \emptyset$ do
    (a) Find an optimal extreme point solution x to LP_{circ}.
    (b) Fix every arc a with $x_a = 0$. Add a to $\mathcal{F}$ with this value setting, and delete a from G. Also delete vertices with no arcs incident to them.
    (c) If there exists $(v,w) \in A$ such that $x_{(v,w)} = u_{(v,w)}$, then fix (v,w) with this value setting, add a to $\mathcal{F}$, and delete a from G. Update $b_v \leftarrow b_v - x_{(v,w)}$ and $b_w \leftarrow b_w + x_{(v,w)}$.
    (d) Find a vertex v with at most one arc a incident on it. Fix a with value x_a, and add a to $\mathcal{F}$. Update $G \leftarrow G \setminus \{v\}$. If a is an out-arc (v,w), then update $b_w \leftarrow b_w + x_{(v,w)}$; otherwise, $a = (w,v)$, and update $b_w \leftarrow b_w - x_{(v,w)}$.
(iii) Return $\mathcal{F}$.

Figure 13.3 Minimum cost circulation algorithm.

Lemma 13.3.4 *For any extreme point solution x to LP_{circ} with $0 < x_a < u_a$, there is a vertex v with $d(v) = d^{out}(v) + d^{in}(v) \leq 1$.*

Proof Suppose for contradiction that $d(v) \geq 2$ for each $v \in V$. Thus, we have $|A| = \frac{1}{2}\sum_{v \in V} d(v) \geq |V|$. This contradicts Corollary 13.3.3. $\qquad\square$

Thus, we obtain a d-integral minimum cost flow as an optimal solution proving Theorem 13.3.1.

13.4 Minimum cost unsplittable flow

In this section, we show an application of the iterative relaxation method on the minimum cost single source unsplittable flow problem. In an instance of this problem, we are given a graph $G = (V, A)$ with edge costs $c : A \rightarrow R_+$, edge capacities $u : A \rightarrow R_+$, a source $s \in V$, and a set of sinks $T = \{t_1, \ldots, t_k\}$ with demands $d_1, d_2, \ldots, d_k$. The task is to find a minimum cost *unsplittable flow* from the source to the sinks that satisfies the capacity constraints. A flow is called unsplittable if the total flow to each sink follows exactly one flow path. A flow is called *splittable* if the total flow to each sink can use multiple paths.

Theorem 13.4.1 *Given an instance of the unsplittable flow problem with $d_i | d_j$ or $d_j | d_i$ for each $1 \leq i, j \leq k$, there exists an unsplittable flow that violates the capacity constraint on any arc by at most $d_{max} = \max_{1 \leq i \leq k} d_i$, with total* *cost at most the optimal cost of any splittable flow that satisfies all the capacity constraints.*

A similar but weaker theorem holds without any assumption on the demands (see the exercises). We prove Theorem 13.4.1 by an iterative relaxation algorithm. The underlying integral problem is the min-cost circulation problem, and we will use Theorem 13.3.1.

13.4.1 Linear programming relaxation

We obtain the following linear programming formulation, denoted by $LP_{unsplit}$, for the minimum cost unsplittable flow problem, by casting it as a minimum cost circulation problem. Here $b_v = -d_v$ for each $v \in T$ and $b_s = \sum_{v \in T} d_v$ and $b_v = 0$ for each $v \in V \setminus (T \cup s)$.

$$\text{minimize} \qquad \sum_{a \in A} c_a x_a$$

$$\text{subject to} \qquad x(\delta^{out}(v)) - x(\delta^{in}(v)) = b_v \qquad \forall \, v \in V$$

$$0 \leq x_a \leq u_a \qquad \forall \, a \in A$$

Since the linear program is the same as LP_{circ}, we obtain the same characterization as in Lemma 13.3.2 as well as in Corollary 13.3.3.

13.4.2 Iterative algorithm

We present in Figure 13.4 the iterative algorithm proving Theorem 13.4.1. The main idea is to relax the capacity constraints on the arcs so that Theorem 13.3.1 can be applied.

13.4.3 Correctness and performance guarantee

In each step, when a flow is routed to some sink v, Theorem 13.3.1 implies that each arc carries flow that is at least $d_v = d_{min}$. Thus, it is possible to route d_{min} flow on this path as required by the algorithm. The optimality of the cost follows from a standard inductive argument, since at each step we only relax the capacity constraints. We now show that the capacity on each arc is violated by at most d_{max}, completing the proof of Theorem 13.4.1.

Lemma 13.4.2 *The iterative algorithm for the minimum cost unsplittable flow problem returns an unsplittable flow such that the capacity on each arc is violated by at most d_{max}.*

Iterative Minimum Cost Unsplittable Flow Algorithm

(i) Initialization $F \leftarrow \emptyset$.

(ii) While $V(G) \neq \emptyset$ do

  (a) Let $d_{min} = \min\{d_v : v \in T\}$. Round up u_a to the closest multiple of d_{min} for all arcs $a \in A$.

  (b) Find an optimal extreme point solution x to $LP_{unsplit}$, and remove all arcs with $x_a = 0$.

  (c) Find a path from s to $v \in T$ where $d_v = d_{min}$. Route the flow to v on this path. Update $T \leftarrow T \setminus \{v\}$ and reduce capacities on the arcs on the path by d_{min}.

(iii) Return the set of flow paths discovered.

Figure 13.4 Minimum cost unsplittable flow algorithm.

Proof The routed flow is unsplittable by construction. The capacities are violated in Step (ii)a when they are rounded up. Let the demands be $d_1 \leq d_2 \leq \cdots \leq d_k$ in increasing order. Observe that $d_1 | d_2 | \ldots | d_k$. We now show by induction that when the demands $d_1, \ldots, d_i$ have been routed, the capacity on each arc is at most d_i more than its initial capacity and is a multiple of d_i for each $1 \leq i \leq k$. The claim clearly holds for $i = 1$. By the induction hypothesis we assume the claim is true for $i - 1$ (i.e., the capacity is violated by at most d_{i-1} and is a multiple of d_{i-1}). While routing d_i, the capacity is increased to a multiple of d_i. Since $d_{i-1} | d_i$, the increase in the ith step is bounded by $d_i - d_{i-1}$ which bounds the total violation at the end of ith step by d_i as required. $\square$

13.5 Bin packing

In this section, we show the Karmarkar–Karp algorithm for the bin-packing problem. This is one of the earliest and is still one of the most sophisticated instances of using the iterative technique for an approximation algorithm. In an instance I of the one-dimensional bin-packing problem, we are given n items each of which has a size between 0 and 1. The objective is to pack the items into a minimum number of unit-size bins. Let $\text{OPT}(I)$ denote the number of bins required in an optimal solution to instance I. We present the following theorem due to Karmarkar and Karp.

Theorem 13.5.1 *There is a polynomial time algorithm that returns a solution with at most* $\text{OPT}(I) + O(\log^2 \text{OPT}(I))$ *bins.*

13.5.1 Linear programming relaxation

A natural linear programming relaxation is to require that each item is put in
at least one bin and each bin can pack items of total size at most one, but
this relaxation has a (multiplicative) integrality gap of 2 (see exercises). To
obtain an additive approximation, we need a so-called *configuration* linear
programming relaxation for the problem. Consider an instance I of the bin-
packing problem with $n(I)$ items of $m(I)$ different types. For $1 \leq i \leq m(I)$, let
b_i be the total number of items of type i and s_i be the common size of these
items. Let $T_1, \ldots, T_N$ be all the possible configurations in which a single bin can
be packed:

$$\{T_1, \ldots, T_N\} := \{(k_1, \ldots, k_{m(I)}) \in \mathbb{Z}_+^m : \sum_{i=1}^m k_i s_i \leq 1\}.$$

Note that N can be exponential in $n(I)$ and $m(I)$. Let $T_j = (t_{j1}, \ldots, t_{jm(I)})$ where
t_{ji} denotes the number of items of type i in configuration j. The configuration
linear programming relaxation for the bin-packing problem is as follows.

$$\text{minimize} \quad \sum_{j=1}^N x_j$$

$$\text{subject to} \quad \sum_{j=1}^N t_{ji} x_j \geq b_i \qquad \forall 1 \leq i \leq m(I)$$

$$x_j \geq 0 \qquad \forall 1 \leq j \leq N$$

where the constraints ensure that the configurations chosen contain at least
b_i items for each type i. This linear programming has exponentially many
variables, but there is a polynomial time algorithm to compute a fractional
solution differing from the optimum by at most δ. Consider the dual of the
linear program.

$$\text{maximize} \quad \sum_{i=1}^{m(I)} b_i y_i$$

$$\text{subject to} \quad \sum_{i=1}^{m(I)} t_{ji} y_i \leq 1 \qquad \forall 1 \leq j \leq N$$

$$y_i \geq 0 \qquad \forall 1 \leq i \leq m(I)$$

The dual program has m variables but exponentially many constraints, but if
there is a polynomial time separation oracle to determine if a given y is a feasible

solution, then the dual program can be solved by the ellipsoid algorithm. The separation problem for the dual linear program is to determine, given y, if there exists a configuration $T = \{t_1, t_2, \ldots, t_m\}$ so that $\sum_{i=1}^{m(I)} t_i y_i > 1$. This is equivalent to the following maximization problem on the variables t_i. Recall that s_i denotes the size of items of type i.

$$\text{maximize} \quad \sum_{i=1}^{m(I)} y_i t_i$$

$$\text{subject to} \quad \sum_{i=1}^{m(I)} s_i t_i \leq 1$$

$$t_i \in \mathbb{Z}_+ \qquad\qquad \forall 1 \leq i \leq m(I)$$

where the constraint is the definition of a configuration. This is a knapsack problem where s_i and y_i correspond to the size and profit of item i, respectively. So the separation problem is equivalent to a knapsack problem, which is NP-hard to solve optimally. Nevertheless, if there is a polynomial time *weak* separation oracle to determine whether a given y is a feasible dual solution with error at most δ on the dual objective function or y is an infeasible dual solution, then the dual program can be approximated by the ellipsoid algorithm with an error at most δ.

In the following, we sketch how to obtain an approximate solution to the (primal) configuration linear program using the ellipsoid algorithm. For the dual program, we can solve the weak separation problem by rounding each y_i down to the nearest rational number that is a multiple of $\frac{\delta}{2n}$, and then use a dynamic programming algorithm to solve the resulting knapsack problem optimally in polynomial time. Using the ellipsoid algorithm with the weak separation oracle, we can then obtain a solution y^* to the dual problem with $y^*b \geq \text{OPT}_{dual} - \delta$, where b is the vector of the number of items of each type and OPT_{dual} is the optimal value of the dual program. Let $T_1', T_2', \ldots, T_{N'}'$ be the bin configurations that appeared as a separating hyperplane during the execution of the ellipsoid algorithm, where N' is bounded by a polynomial in $n(I)$ and $m(I)$. Consider the dual program restricted to the constraints that correspond to $T_1', \ldots, T_{N'}'$ and let the optimal value of this restricted dual program be OPT'_{dual}. Then $y^*b \geq \text{OPT}'_{dual} - \delta$, since the weak separation oracle can always give the same answer as for the original problem. To obtain an approximate solution to the primal program, we obtain an optimal solution to the restricted primal program in which we use only the variables that correspond to the configurations in $T_1', \ldots, T_{N'}'$ and delete all other variables; in other words, we obtain an optimal solution to the dual of the restricted dual program. Since there are only polynomially many variables and constraints, this resticted primal program can be solved optimally in polynomial time. Let OPT'_{primal} be the optimal value of the restricted primal program. Then we have

$$\text{OPT}'_{primal} - \delta = \text{OPT}'_{dual} - \delta \leq y^*b \leq \text{OPT}_{dual} = \text{OPT}_{primal}.$$

Therefore, an optimal solution to the restricted primal program is an approximate solution to the primal program with additive error at most δ.

13.5.2 Characterization of extreme point solutions

The following lemma is a direct consequence of the Rank Lemma.

Lemma 13.5.2 *Given any extreme point solution to the configuration linear program, there are at most $m(I)$ nonzero variables, where $m(I)$ is the number of different types of items in instance I.*

To illustrate the use of Lemma 13.5.2, we show a very simple algorithm with a good performance guarantee when the number of different types of items is small. Let $\text{LIN}(I)$ denote the optimal value of the configuration LP associated with instance I. Let $\text{SIZE}(I) = \sum_{i=1}^{m(I)} s_i b_i$ be the sum of the sizes of all the items in instance I.

Lemma 13.5.3 $\text{OPT}(I) \leq \text{LIN}(I) + \frac{m(I)+1}{2}$.

Proof Let x be an optimal extreme point solution of the configuration LP for instance I. Then, by Lemma 13.5.2, x has at most $m(I)$ nonzero variables. We open $\lfloor x_j \rfloor$ bins with configuration j for each j. The remaining items form an instance I'. Let $f_j = x_j - \lfloor x_j \rfloor$. Then $\text{SIZE}(I') \leq \text{LIN}(I') = \sum_j f_j$. We now find a packing for instance I' of cost at most $\text{SIZE}(I') + \frac{m(I)+1}{2}$. A packing for instance I' of cost at most $m(I)$ can be constructed by using one new bin for each configuration j with nonzero f_j, and then removing excess items (the items that appear in more than one configuration). On the other hand, any greedy packing algorithm will give a solution for instance I' of cost at most $2\text{SIZE}(I') + 1$, since each bin, except possibly one, will be at least half full. Hence, the better of these two packings has cost at most the average, which is $\text{SIZE}(I') + \frac{m(I)+1}{2} \leq \sum_j f_j + \frac{m(I)+1}{2}$, which in turn gives a packing for instance I with cost at most $\sum_j \lfloor x_j \rfloor + \sum_j f_j + \frac{m(I)+1}{2} = \text{LIN}(I) + \frac{m(I)+1}{2}$, proving the lemma. $\square$

13.5.3 Defining residual problems: Grouping and elimination

Given Lemma 13.5.3, one would like to reduce the number of distinct item sizes of the input instance. The idea of grouping is to divide the items into groups of similar sizes, and create a residual problem by increasing the sizes of each item to the largest item size in its group, so as to decrease the number of distinct item sizes in the residual problem. By doing so, however, the total item size of the residual problem and hence the optimum of the residual problem increases, and so there is a tradeoff in choosing the parameters. The main idea of the Karmarkar–Karp algorithm is to define the residual problem iteratively, so that in each iteration the number of distinct item sizes decrease by a constant factor, while the optimum in the residual problem increases by only an extra $O(\log(\text{OPT}))$ number of bins. Applying this procedure inductively will lead to Theorem 13.5.1.

The following is a simple method to bound the optimum of the residual problem. Let I and J be two bin-packing instances. We write $I \preceq J$ if there is an injective function f mapping items in I into items in J so that $\text{SIZE}(a) \leq \text{SIZE}(f(a))$ for each item $a \in I$, where $\text{SIZE}(a)$ is the size of item a. Clearly, if $I \preceq J$, then $\text{OPT}(I) \leq \text{OPT}(J)$, $\text{LIN}(I) \leq \text{LIN}(J)$, and $\text{SIZE}(I) \leq \text{SIZE}(J)$. This method will be used throughout to analyze the performance of the grouping techniques.

13.5.3.1 Linear grouping

The following process is called linear grouping with parameter k. Let I be an instance of the bin-packing problem and let k be a positive integer. Divide the set I into groups $G_1, G_2, \ldots, G_q$ so that G_1 contains the k largest items, G_2 contains the next k largest items, and so on. Hence $G_1 \succeq G_2 \succeq \cdots \succeq G_q$ and $|G_i| = k$ for all groups except the last group. Let G_i' be the multiset of items obtained by increasing the size of each item in group G_i to the maximum size of an item in that group. Then $G_1 \succeq G_2' \succeq G_2 \succeq \cdots \succeq G_q' \succeq G_q$. Let $J := \cup_{i=2}^{q} G_i'$ and $J' := G_1$. Then $J \preceq I \preceq J \cup J'$. Note that the items in J' can be trivially packed in k new bins, by using one new bin for each item. Therefore, we have the following after linear grouping.

Lemma 13.5.4 *After linear grouping with parameter k, we have*

- $\text{OPT}(J) \leq \text{OPT}(I) \leq \text{OPT}(J) + k,$
- $\text{LIN}(J) \leq \text{LIN}(I) \leq \text{LIN}(J) + k,$
- $\text{SIZE}(J) \leq \text{SIZE}(I) \leq \text{SIZE}(J) + k.$

13.5.3.2 Geometric grouping

The following refinement of linear grouping is called geometric grouping with parameter k. This is the key idea in the Karmarkar–Karp algorithm to reduce the number of distinct item sizes iteratively.

Let I be an instance of the bin-packing problem. Let $\alpha(I)$ denote the size of the smallest item in instance I. For $0 \leq r \leq \lfloor \log_2 \frac{1}{\alpha(I)} \rfloor$, let I_r be the instance consisting of those items from I whose sizes are in the interval $[2^{-(r+1)}, 2^{-r})$. Let J_r and J'_r be the instances obtained by applying linear grouping with parameter $k \cdot 2^r$ to I_r. Let $J := \cup_r J_r$ and $J' := \cup_r J'_r$.

Lemma 13.5.5 *After geometric grouping with parameter k, we have*

- $\text{OPT}(J) \leq \text{OPT}(I) \leq \text{OPT}(J) + k \lceil \log_2 \frac{1}{\alpha(I)} \rceil$,
- $\text{LIN}(J) \leq \text{LIN}(I) \leq \text{LIN}(J) + k \lceil \log_2 \frac{1}{\alpha(I)} \rceil$,
- $\text{SIZE}(J) \leq \text{SIZE}(I) \leq \text{SIZE}(J) + k \lceil \log_2 \frac{1}{\alpha(I)} \rceil$,
- $m(J) \leq \frac{2}{k} \text{SIZE}(I) + \lceil \log_2 \frac{1}{\alpha(I)} \rceil$.

Proof From Lemma 13.5.4, it follows that $J_r \preceq I_r \preceq J_r \cup J'_r$ and thus $J \preceq I \preceq J \cup J'$. Hence, $\text{OPT}(J) \leq \text{OPT}(I) \leq \text{OPT}(J \cup J') \leq \text{OPT}(J) + \text{OPT}(J')$. Note that $\text{OPT}(J') \leq \sum_r \text{OPT}(J'_r)$. Each J'_r contains at most $k \cdot 2^r$ items each of size less than 2^{-r}. Hence J'_r can be packed into at most k bins. Thus, $\text{OPT}(J') \leq k \lceil \log_2 \frac{1}{\alpha(I)} \rceil$, and therefore $\text{OPT}(J) \leq \text{OPT}(I) \leq \text{OPT}(J) + k \lceil \log_2 \frac{1}{\alpha(I)} \rceil$. The proofs of the next two inequalities are similar.

For each r, since we apply linear grouping with parameter $k \cdot 2^r$, all except the last group in J_r have $k \cdot 2^r$ items, and the items in each group are of the same size. Also, each item in I_r has size at least $2^{-(r+1)}$, and thus we have

$$\text{SIZE}(I_r) \geq 2^{-(r+1)} \cdot n(I_r) \geq 2^{-(r+1)} \Big((m(J_r) - 1) \cdot k \cdot 2^r \Big).$$

Therefore, $m(J_r) - 1 \leq \frac{2}{k} \text{SIZE}(I_r)$, and thus

$$m(J) \leq \frac{2}{k} \text{SIZE}(I) + \lceil \log_2 \frac{1}{\alpha(I)} \rceil.$$

$\square$

13.5.3.3 Elimination of small items

In the geometric grouping process, the performance depends on the smallest item size. In the following, we show that we can eliminate items of small sizes without affecting the approximation performance ratio much. Let I be an instance of the bin-packing problem. Let g be a real number between 0 and 1.

Iterative Bin-Packing Algorithm

(i) Eliminate all small items of size at most g.

(ii) While $\text{SIZE}(I) > 1 + \frac{1}{1-\frac{2}{k}}\lceil \log_2 \frac{1}{g} \rceil$ do

   (a) Perform geometric grouping with parameter k to create instance J and J'. Pack J' using at most $k\lceil \log_2 \frac{1}{g} \rceil$ new bins.

   (b) Compute an optimal extreme point solution x to the configuration LP on instance J with error at most 1.

   (c) For each j with $x_j \geq 1$, create $\lfloor x_j \rfloor$ bins with configuration j and remove the items packed from the problem.

(iii) Pack the remaining items using at most $2 + \frac{2}{1-\frac{2}{k}}\lceil \log_2 \frac{1}{g} \rceil$ bins.

(iv) Insert the small items eliminated in Step 1, using new bins only when necessary.

Figure 13.5   Karmarkar–Karp bin-packing algorithm.

We say an item is *large* if its size is larger than $\frac{g}{2}$ and *small* otherwise. Consider a process that starts with a given packing of large items into bins, and then inserts the small items, using a new bin only when necessary. If the cost of the given packing of the large pieces is C, then the cost of the packing resulting from the process is at most $\max\{C, (1+g)\text{OPT}(I) + 1\}$ (see the exercises).

13.5.4 Iterative algorithm

With the grouping technique developed, we present the iterative algorithm in Figure 13.5. The parameters k and g will be set as $k = 4$ and $g = \frac{1}{\text{SIZE}(I)}$.

13.5.5 Correctness and performance guarantee

To prove the correctness and the performance guarantee, we will bound the number of iterations of the algorithm (in particular it will terminate) and the number of bins used by the algorithm. Let t be the number of iterations of the algorithm. For $1 \leq i \leq t$, let I_i be the instance at the beginning of iteration i, and J_i, J_i' be the instances resulting from geometric grouping on I_i, and let X_i and Y_i be the number of bins created in Step (ii)c and Step (ii)a in iteration i of the algorithm.

Lemma 13.5.6 *The iterative algorithm will terminate in at most $O(\ln n)$ iterations.*

Proof Note that the total size of the residual problem decreases geometrically:

$$\text{SIZE}(I_{i+1}) \leq \text{LIN}(I_{i+1}) \leq \sum_j (x_j - \lfloor x_j \rfloor) \leq m(J_i) \leq \frac{2}{k}\text{SIZE}(I_i) + \left\lceil \log_2 \frac{1}{g} \right\rceil$$

where the second last inequality follows from Lemma 13.5.2 and the last inequality follows from Lemma 13.5.5. Therefore,

$$\text{SIZE}(I_{i+1}) \leq \left(\frac{2}{k}\right)^i \text{SIZE}(J) + \lceil \log_2 \frac{1}{g} \rceil \left[1 + \frac{2}{k} + \cdots + (\frac{2}{k})^{i-1} \right]$$

$$\leq \left(\frac{2}{k}\right)^i \text{SIZE}(I) + \frac{1}{1 - \frac{2}{k}} \left\lceil \log_2 \frac{1}{g} \right\rceil$$

Since $\text{SIZE}(I_t) > 1 + \frac{1}{1-\frac{2}{k}} \left\lceil \log_2 \frac{1}{g} \right\rceil$, this implies that $\left(\frac{2}{k}\right)^t \text{SIZE}(I) \geq 1$ and hence

$$t \leq \frac{\ln \text{SIZE}(I)}{\ln \frac{k}{2}} + 1 = O(\ln n).$$

Therefore, the running time of the algorithm is polynomial. □

Lemma 13.5.7 *The total number of bins used by the algorithm is at most* $\text{OPT}(I) + O(\ln^2 \text{OPT}(I))$.

Proof To bound the number of bins used by the algorithm, we note that $\text{LIN}(I_{i+1}) \leq \text{LIN}(J_i) + 1 - X_i \leq \text{LIN}(I_i) + 1 - X_i$ by Step (ii)c of the algorithm, which implies that

$$\sum_{i=1}^{t} X_i \leq \text{LIN}(I) + t.$$

By Lemma 13.5.5, we have for each $1 \leq i \leq t$

$$Y_i \leq k \left\lceil \log_2 \frac{1}{g} \right\rceil.$$

Note that Step (iii) is always possible by any greedy algorithm. The number of bins produced by the algorithm after Step (iii) is at most

$$\sum_{i=1}^{t} X_i + t \cdot Y_i + 2 + \frac{2}{1 - \frac{2}{k}} \left\lceil \log_2 \frac{1}{g} \right\rceil.$$

After inserting the small items, the total number of bins used by the algorithm is at most the maximum of $(1 + g)\text{OPT}(I) + 1$ and

$$\text{OPT}(I) + \left(\frac{\ln \text{SIZE}(I)}{\ln \frac{k}{2}} + 1 \right) \left(1 + k \left\lceil \log_2 \frac{1}{g} \right\rceil \right) + 2 + \frac{2}{1 - \frac{2}{k}} \left\lceil \log_2 \frac{1}{g} \right\rceil$$

because $\sum_{i=1}^{t} X_i \leq \mathrm{LIN}(I) + t \leq \mathrm{OPT}(I) + t$ and $t \leq \left(\frac{\ln \mathrm{SIZE}(I)}{\ln \frac{k}{2}} + 1 \right)$ and $Y_i \leq$ $k \left\lceil \log_2 \frac{1}{g} \right\rceil$. By setting $k = 4$ and $g = \frac{1}{\mathrm{SIZE}(I)} \geq \frac{1}{n}$, and noting that $\mathrm{OPT}(T) \geq$ $\mathrm{SIZE}(I)$, we see that the total number of bins is at most $\mathrm{OPT}(I) + O(\ln^2 \mathrm{OPT}(I))$, proving Theorem 13.5.1. □

13.6 Iterative randomized rounding: Steiner trees

In this section, we present a recent application of the iterative rounding method augmented with randomized rounding for the classical undirected Steiner tree problem. The Steiner tree problem is defined on an undirected graph $G = (V, E)$ with nonnegative costs c on the edges and the vertex set partitioned into terminals R and nonterminals or Steiner nodes $V \setminus R$. A Steiner tree is an undirected spanning tree that must span the terminals and can span any subset of the Steiner nodes. The Steiner tree problem is to find one of minimum cost and is known to be APX-hard. The methods from Chapter 10 give a 2-approximation algorithm for this problem (using the original method of Jain that introduced the iterative method) as well as its various generalizations.

The basic Steiner tree problem however had a simple 2-approximation algo-rithm before the iterative rounding method of Jain. First, observe that we may work with the *metric completion* of the costs on the edges in solving the prob-lem: This completion replaces the graph with a complete graph where the cost of any new edge is the cost of the shortest path under the original costs between the endpoints of the edge. It is not hard to see that edges of any optimal solution will be retained in the completion, and that any Steiner tree in the completion can be converted to one in the original graph by replacing any new edges chosen by the corresponding shortest path. Thus, we can assume that the input to the Steiner tree instance is a metric without loss of generality.

The classical 2-approximation for the Steiner tree problem starts with the metric completion restricted only to the terminal nodes in R and computes a minimum spanning tree on it. To get a feasible solution, we replace the edges in the spanning tree by the corresponding paths as above. To see that this solution is indeed a 2-approximation, it suffices to demonstrate a solution in the metric completion on R of cost at most twice the optimal. To do this, consider an optimal Steiner tree, double every edge, and take an Eulerian tour around the "perimeter" of a planar representation of this doubled tree. This walk can start at any terminal and visit every other terminal once and return to the starting terminal: Short-cutting the segments between terminals will give a cycle in the metric completion on R of cost no more than twice that of the optimal Steiner tree. Thus, we have demonstrated the existence of a solution of cost at most twice the optimal, which is a cycle on R made of $|R|$ segments. Since we only require a tree, we can discard the costliest segment and thus argue that there exists a path of cost at most $2\left(1 - \frac{1}{|R|}\right)$ times the optimal, completing the proof.

We now present an improvement to the previous algorithm based on building up the optimal solution, not using single edges denoting paths that join pairs of terminals but instead using subtrees that connect more than two terminals optimally. Such subtrees are called full components, and we start with the previous minimum spanning tree solution and identify subsets of more than two vertices that can be connected by optimal full components on them. We then include these components and discard a few redundant edges in the spanning tree and proceed until we have substantially reduced the cost of the spanning tree. The initial application of this idea was due to Zelikovsky [134] and subsequently improved in [15, 115]. We describe a recent improvement in this line of attack which chooses the full components iteratively and randomly based on an LP relaxation.

13.6.1 Linear programming relaxation

A *full component* on a subset K of the terminals is a tree whose leaf set is K and internal nodes are Steiner vertices. Note that the edges of any Steiner tree can be partitioned in a unique way into full components. The goal of the following LP relaxation is to describe the Steiner tree problem as the choice of its optimal full components. Note that a set of full components on sets $K_1, K_2, \ldots, K_r$ forms a Steiner tree exactly when the hypergraph formed by these subsets as hyperedges on R is a hyperspanning tree: namely, no pair of them has an intersection of more than one terminal, and there is a path between any pair of terminals following hyperedges. This leads to the following hypergraphic LP relaxation: Let $F(K)$ denote the minimum cost full component for terminal set $K \subset R$, and let C_K be its cost. The hypergraphic relaxation for minimum cost Steiner tree below is similar to the subtour LP for spanning trees in its design.

$$\text{minimize} \qquad \sum_K C_K x_K$$

$$\text{subject to} \qquad \sum_{K:K \cap S \neq \emptyset} x_K(|K \cap S| - 1) \leq |S| - 1 \qquad \forall \emptyset \neq S \subseteq R$$

$$\sum_K x_K(|K| - 1) = |R| - 1$$

$$x_K \geq 0 \qquad \forall K$$

An integral feasible solution of the above LP gives the full components of a Steiner tree. Our goal is to bound the integrality gap of the above relaxation.

Theorem 13.6.1 *The integrality gap of the hypergraphic relaxation for undirected Steiner tree is at most* $1 + \frac{\ln 3}{2}$.

To convert the proof of the theorem into a rounding algorithm, one needs to use the methodology of arguing that by restricting oneself to sufficiently large full components in the preceding description, one can get sufficiently close to the LP value: Formally, to get a $(1 + \epsilon)$-approximation to the previous LP relaxation, it suffices to use full components of size bounded by a (large) constant for every fixed constant $\epsilon > 0$. The details of this claim form the basis of the r-restricted full component method, which are nontrivial and can be found in [66].

Finally, we need to show that the earlier formulation, even with bounded-size full components, is polynomially solvable. For this, we can devise a separation oracle for a given fractional solution. We build an auxiliary multigraph on the terminal set R as follows: For every full component set K with positive value of x_K in the support that is supplied to the separation oracle, we add the edges of an *arbitrary* spanning tree on the nodes of K to this auxiliary graph and give each of these edges a fractional value of x_K. We now claim that the resulting fractional multigraph solution is feasible for the subtour relaxation for a spanning tree on the nodes of R if and only if the supplied solution x is feasible for the hypergraphic relaxation. The proof of this claim is very similar to that of the proof of the Bridge Lemma 13.6.2 and is deferred to the exercises.

13.6.2 Iterative randomized rounding

To describe the algorithm, we need some notation first. Define the *loss* of full component $F(K)$ on $K \subset R$, denoted by $LOSS(K)$ to be the minimum cost subset of $F(K)$'s edges that connect the Steiner nodes in it to the terminals. We use $loss(K)$ to denote the cost of the edges in $LOSS(K)$. The *loss-contracted full component* of K, denoted by $TLC(K)$, is obtained from $F(K)$ by contracting the edges in $LOSS(K)$, or (using the contract notation, we have $TLC(K) = F(K)/LOSS(K)$). Note that $TLC(K)$ is a spanning tree on the terminal set K and its edges do not correspond to edges in the original graph. For clarity we denote the edge set $E(F(K)) \setminus LOSS(K)$ by $LC(K)$. Since the edges in $TLC(K)$ are precisely the edges remaining in $LC(K)$, there is a natural bijection between these two edge sets. We emphasize that we use two different notations for them only to distinguish that $TLC(K)$ is an auxiliary spanning tree on the

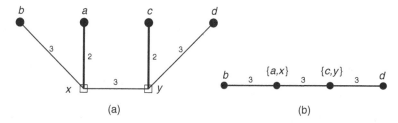

Figure 13.6   (a) Graph $F(K)$ is a full component with terminals $K = \{a, b, c, d\}$ and Steiner vertices $\{x, y\}$. The bold edges $\{a, x\}$ and $\{y, c\}$ form $LOSS(K)$. (b) Graph $TLC(K)$ is shown obtained after contracting $LOSS(K)$.

Iterative Randomized Loss Contraction Algorithm

(i) Initialization $T_1 \leftarrow MST(R)$.

(ii) Let x be an optimal solution to the hypergraphic LP relaxation. Let M be the smallest value that is at least $\sum_K x_K$ such that $t = M \ln 3$ is an integer.

(iii) For $1 \leq i \leq t$ do

    (a) Sample K_i with probability $\frac{x_K}{M}$ for each full component K (and choose no tree with probability $(1 - \sum_K x_K / M)$).

    (b) $T_{i+1} \leftarrow MST(T_i \cup TLC(K_i))$.

(iv) Return any Steiner tree in $ALG = T_{t+1} \cup \bigcup_{i=1}^{t} LOSS(K_i)$.

Figure 13.7   Iterative randomized rounding algorithm for Steiner tree.

set K while $LC(K)$ is a subset of edges with endpoints in the full component of K including some Steiner nodes. See Figure 13.6 for an example.

Since contraction is involved in several stages of the algorithm in Figure 13.7, we may have different auxiliary edges between a pair of terminals (due to loss contraction of different full components) but we retain all such edges as parallel edges in the analysis.

The idea of the iterative randomized algorithm is to start with a MST on the terminals and iteratively choose a full component on K with probability proportional to the value of its choice variable, and add all of its $LOSS(K)$ edges and some of the remaining loss-contracted edges $LC(K)$ to the final solution. An auxiliary spanning tree on the whole terminal set R is used to track which portion of the loss-contracted edges from each iteration are retained in the final solution. The candidates for inclusion in this auxiliary tree are precisely the auxiliary edges induced in $TLC(K)$. Furthermore, as we start retaining some of these intermediate loss-contracted edges, we can drop some original spanning tree edges, which reduce the cost of the MST that is retained. This auxiliary spanning tree that records the drop in the value of the initial solution is denoted T_i at iteration i in the algorithm (Figure 13.7). This charging device allows us to formulate a clean recurrence for the reducing value of T_i in expectation, and hence bound the total cost of the solution in the end. The algorithm is shown in Figure 13.7.

In the last step, when we refer to edges in T_{t+1}, notice that this may include some auxiliary edges from $TLC(K_i)$ for some iteration in Step (iii)b. However, due to the bijection between these edges and the corresponding real edges in $LC(K_i)$, we actually include the real edges in $LC(K_i)$ in this step.

We argue that $T_{t+1} \cup \bigcup_{i=1}^{t} LOSS(K_i)$ contains a Steiner tree on R. In particular, we argue that for every pair of terminals joined by an edge in T_{t+1}, there is a path between them in the union of the real edges corresponding to the auxiliary edges in this tree plus the edges in $\bigcup_{i=1}^{t} LOSS(K_i)$. Note that if an edge in T_{t+1} is an original edge from T_1, there is nothing to prove. Else, it is a new auxiliary edge introduced as part of some $TLC(K_i)$. However, the corresponding real edge in $LC(K_i)$ along with the edges in $LOSS(K_i)$ contain a path between these two endpoints by construction, proving our claim.

13.6.3 Correctness and performance guarantee

The main idea of the analysis is to bound the cost of the set of edges ALG in expectation over the random component choices of the algorithm, by its constituent parts of the final spanning tree T_{t+1} plus the loss values of the components contracted on the way. We do this in two steps. The cost of the spanning tree is tracked using a recursion relating the cost of the tree T_{i+1} to that of the tree in the previous iteration T_i, and then telescoping the result using a key lemma termed the Bridge Lemma. The expected loss is bounded by a simple argument relating it to the cost of the full components from which it is contracted. Together, these two bounds give the final bound on the expected cost of the edges in ALG.

13.6.3.1 Preparations

We start by defining the drop of a full component K with respect to a terminal spanning tree T (i.e., a tree spanning exactly the terminals). Recall from the definition of node contraction that T/K denotes the (multi)graph obtained by identifying the terminals spanned by K into a single node. Define

$$DROP_T(K) = E(T) \setminus E(MST(T/K))$$

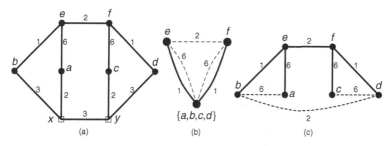

Figure 13.8 (a) Terminal spanning tree T on the terminals $\{a,b,c,d,e,f\}$ with edges $\{ea,eb,ef,fc,fd\}$ along with a full component on $K = \{a,b,c,d\}$ with edges $\{xa,xb,xy,yc,yd\}$. (b) Dashed edges form $DROP_T(K)$. (c) Graph $TDROP_T(K) \cup E(T)$ where the $TDROP_T(K)$ edges are dashed. Observe that each edge $f \in TDROP_T(K)$ is the heaviest edge in the unique cycle in $T \cup \{f\}$.

and let $drop_T(K)$ be the cost of the edges in $DROP_T(K)$. Note that these are precisely the edges in T that can now be dropped given an alternate means of connecting the terminals in K via a full component on them, hence the name. See Figure 13.8 for an illustration.

The Bridge Lemma lower bounds the expected drop.

Lemma 13.6.2 *Given a terminal spanning tree T and a feasible solution x to the hypergraphic LP formulation,*

$$\sum_K x_K drop_T(K) \geq c(T).$$

Proof The proof of this lemma uses the close relation between the hypergraphic relaxation and the subtour elimination LP we encountered in Chapter 4 for spanning trees, presented again here.

minimize $\displaystyle\sum_{e\in E} c_e z_e$

subject to $z(E(S)) \leq |S| - 1$ $\forall \emptyset \neq S \subset V$

              $z(E(V)) = |V| - 1$

                  $z_e \geq 0$ $\forall e \in E$

The proof idea is to convert the solution x for the hypergraphic relaxation into a solution z for the subtour LP on the vertex set of terminals R. For this we introduce some auxiliary edges on the vertex set R. In particular, for each full component K such that $x_K > 0$, contracting the edges in $E(T) \setminus DROP_T(K)$ and retaining the labels of the terminals in K in the contracted graph, we get a spanning tree $TDROP_T(K)$ on the node set K. Moreover, there is a bijection between the edges of this spanning tree and the edges in $DROP_T(K)$ (just as was the case between $TLC(K)$ and $LC(K)$). Give each of these edges in $TDROP_T(K)$ (now running between nodes of K) a z-value of x_K, making parallel edges between pairs of terminals as needed. Let this set of auxiliary multiedges that are given z-values be F. We see that

$$\sum_{e \in F} c_e z_e = \sum_K x_K drop_T(K).$$

Note that we introduced exactly $|K| - 1$ edges for each full component K, and for any $S \subseteq R$, at most $|S \cap K| - 1$ of these edges in F have both ends in S since these edges form a tree on K. Therefore, x being feasible for the hypergraphic relaxation implies that z is feasible for the subtour relaxation. Thus, the left-hand quantity in the lemma has cost that of a feasible solution to the subtour relaxation on the graph of the auxiliary edges. Note that the auxiliary edges corresponding to full components of size two generate the original edges of T in this auxiliary graph as well.

By Theorem 4.1.1, since the subtour relaxation is the convex hull of integral spanning trees in the graph made of the edges in $E(T) \cup F$, the cost of any tree is at least that of the minimum-cost spanning tree in this auxiliary graph. But consider any edge $f \in F$, which corresponds to some auxiliary edge in $TDROP_T(K)$ for some full component K, and hence corresponds to an edge in $DROP(K)$. By the definition of $DROP(K)$, the edge f was dropped from the original tree T in choosing $MST(T/K)$, and hence was the costliest edge in some cycle in T/K. Thus, when we add this auxiliary edge f between its endpoints in $TDROP_T(K)$ in the tree T, it still continues to be a maximum cost edge in the unique cycle formed in $T \cup f$. Since this is true for every $f \in F$, the minimum cost tree in $E(T) \cup F$ is T itself. See Figure 13.8c for an illustration. This completes the proof.   □

We need two more observations before we commence the proof.

Lemma 13.6.3 *The value of $T_1 = MST(R)$, the initial terminal spanning tree, is at most twice the optimal value of the hypergraphic LP relaxation for Steiner tree.*

The proof of this lemma follows the short-cutting argument in the beginning of this section, but on the full components in the optimal fractional solution for the hypergraphic relaxation, and showing that this doubled short-cut solution is feasible for the subtour LP relaxation for spanning trees in the metric completion of R. The details are left as an exercise.

Lemma 13.6.4 *For any full component K, we have $loss(K) \leq C_K/2$.*

Proof First, we assume without loss of generality that every internal Steiner node has degree three in K (else we can make it so by splitting higher degree nodes into degree-three nodes and connecting them in a tree-like fashion with zero-cost edges). Now root the tree at an arbitrary leaf and let every internal node choose the cheapest of its two children. These chosen edges give paths from every Steiner node to a terminal leaf and have cost at most twice that of the full component, proving the lemma. ☐

13.6.3.2 Inductive analysis

We now give the proof of Theorem 13.6.1.

Proof We bound the cost of the terminal spanning tree T_{i+1} based on that of T_i. One way to derive this spanning tree is to add in edges of $LC(K_i)$ and drop the edges in $DROP_{T_i}(K_i)$. Thus, we have

$$c(T_{i+1}) \leq c(T_i) - drop_{T_i}(K_i) + c(LC(K_i)).$$

By linearity of expectation, we can derive the expected value based on the distribution from which K_i is drawn as follows:

$$E[c(T_{i+1})] \leq E[c(T_i)] - \frac{1}{M}\sum_K x_K drop_{T_i}(K) + \frac{1}{M}\sum_K x_K c(LC(K)).$$

Let $lp^* = \sum_K x_K C_K$ and $loss^* = \sum_K x_K loss(K)$, and since $LC(K) = C_K - loss(K)$, we have

$$E[c(T_{i+1})] \leq E[c(T_i)] - \frac{1}{M}\sum_K x_K drop_{T_i}(K) + (lp^* - loss^*)/M.$$

Applying the Bridge Lemma 13.6.2 to bound the second term, we get the following:

$$E[c(T_{i+1})] \leq \left(1 - \frac{1}{M}\right)E[c(T_i)] + (lp^* - loss^*)/M.$$

By induction, we can unravel this recurrence as follows:

$$E[c(T_{i+1})] \leq \left(1 - \frac{1}{M}\right)^t E[c(T_1)] + (lp^* - loss^*)\left(1 - \left(1 - \frac{1}{M}\right)^t\right).$$

Now we use the bound from Lemma 13.6.3 to get the following bound:

$$E[c(T_{i+1})] \le lp^* \left(1 + \left(1 - \frac{1}{M}\right)^t\right) - loss^* \left(1 - \left(1 - \frac{1}{M}\right)^t\right).$$

This takes care of the first component of the edges in ALG. For the second component, namely the edges in $\cup_{i=1}^t LOSS(K_i)$, we have the following bound:

$$\sum_{i=1}^t E[loss(K_i)] = \sum_{i=1}^t \sum_K x_K loss(K)/M = \sum_{i=1}^t loss^*/M = t \cdot loss^*/M.$$

Adding the two components, we get

$$\begin{aligned}
E[c(ALG)] &= E[c(T_{t+1})] + t \cdot loss^*/M \\
&\le lp^* \left(1 + \left(1 - \frac{1}{M}\right)^t\right) + loss^* \left(\frac{t}{M} + \left(1 - \frac{1}{M}\right)^t - 1\right) \\
&\le lp^* \left(1 + \left(1 - \frac{1}{M}\right)^t\right) + \frac{lp^*}{2} \left(\frac{t}{M} + \left(1 - \frac{1}{M}\right)^t - 1\right) \\
&\le lp^* \left(\frac{1}{2} + \frac{3}{2}\left(1 - \frac{1}{M}\right)^t + \frac{t}{2M}\right) \\
&\le lp^* \left(\frac{1}{2} + \frac{3}{2}e^{-t/M} + \frac{t}{2M}\right) \\
&\le lp^* \left(1 + \frac{\ln 3}{2}\right).
\end{aligned}$$

Here the second inequality uses Lemma 13.6.4, and the last inequality follows from the fact that $\frac{1}{2} + \frac{3}{2}e^{-x} + \frac{x}{2}$ is minimized at $x = \ln 3$ taking on value $1 + \frac{\ln 3}{2}$. This is also why we chose $t = M \ln 3$. $\square$

13.7 Notes

The discrepancy theorem is due to Beck and Fiala [12]. Our presentation of the Steinitz's result follows that of Bárány [10], who attributes this proof to Grinberg and Sevastyanov [65]. Steinitz's original proof [127] also used linear dependencies and gave constant $2d$ instead of d. Steinitz's result has many applications in mathematics (see e.g., [10]), as well as in designing approximation algorithms for scheduling problems (see e.g., [11] and the references in [10]). Some other problems about sums of ± 1 signs can also be solved by a similar iterative method, see [10].

The single source unsplittable flow problem was first introduced by Kleinberg [81], who gave a constant factor approximation algorithm for the unweighted problem. This was improved by Dinitz, Garg, and Goemans [33], who gave an algorithm for the unweighted problem which finds an unsplitting flow that violates the arc capacities by at most d_{max}. Kolliopoulos and Stein [82] used the iterative relaxation idea to obtain a bicriteria approximation algorithm for the weighted problem, which returns a solution with cost at most twice the optimum and the arc capacities at most thrice that of the splittable flow. This is improved by Skutella [123] to get an approximation algorithm with optimal cost and the same guarantee on the arc capacities.

The bin-packing result is from the work of Karmarkar and Karp [77], which builds on the asymptotic PTAS by Fernandez de la Vega and Lueker [42] and develops the iterative relaxation technique for the configuration linear program of the problem.

Our description of the Steiner tree approximation algorithm is based on the work of Bryka et al. [20]; we closely followed the treatment due to Chakrabarty, Könemann, and Pritchard [24].

Exercises

13.1 (Bednarchak and Helm [13]) The bound on the Beck–Fiala theorem can be improved to $2d - 3$. Can you prove this improved bound by refining the iterative method?

13.2 (Skutella [123]) Given any instance of the unsplittable flow problem, let f be a minimum cost splittable flow. Give an efficient algorithm that returns an unsplittable flow with cost at most that of f such that the total flow on each arc a is at most $2f_a + d_{max}$. (*Hint*: Reduce the general problem to the problem in Theorem 13.4.1.)

13.3 Show that the natural LP relaxation for the bin-packing problem has a multiplicative integrality gap approaching two. On the other hand, show how a greedy bin-packing algorithm achieves a packing of instance I into at most $2\text{SIZE}(I) + 1$ bins.

13.4 Show that the greedy procedure to pack small items defined in Section 13.5.3.3 uses at most $\max\{C, (1 + g)\text{OPT}(I) + 1\}$ bins.

13.5 Show that the bin-packing problem is a special case of the single source unsplittable flow problem.

13.6 Show that the generalized assignment problem is a special case of the single source min-cost unsplittable flow problem.

13.7 Prove Lemma 13.6.3 by showing that an optimal solution to the hyper-graphic LP relaxation for Steiner trees can be doubled and converted to a feasible solution to the subtour relaxation for the minimum spanning tree problem on the terminals of the Steiner tree problem.

13.8 Prove that the hypergraphic LP relaxation for Steiner trees with full components of up to a fixed constant size can be solved in polynomial time. Use the method outlined in the chapter of converting this to testing separation of a corresponding point in the subtour elimination formulation for spanning trees on an auxiliary multigraph on the terminal set, as in Lemma 13.6.2.

14

Summary

We have described an iterative method that is versatile in its applicability to showing several results in exact optimization and approximation algorithms. The key step in applying this method uses the elementary Rank Lemma to show sparsity of the support of extreme point solutions for a wide variety of problems. The method follows a natural sequence of formulating a tractable LP relaxation of the problem, examining the structure of tight constraints to demonstrate an upper bound on the rank of the tight subsystem defining the extreme point, using the Rank Lemma to imply an upper bound on the support, and finally using this sparsity of the support to find an element in the support with high (possible fractional) value.

The two key steps in the method are upper bounding the rank of the tight constraints and using the sparsity of the support to imply a high-valued element. Various uncrossing techniques in combinatorial optimization are very useful in the first step. However, new ideas are typically required in the second step, which can be usually carried out with a "token charging" argument to prove by contradiction the presence of a high-value element in the support: Assign a set number, k, of tokens to each support variable (now assumed to be low valued for contradiction) and redistribute these tokens so as to collect k tokens per tight constraints and show some leftover tokens for the contradiction. While there is no unified way to arrive at the specific token redistribution argument, some insight can be gained by looking at the structure of tight independent constraints and their differences as was done in the case of spanning trees, network matrices, submodular flows, and the survivable network design and STSP problems. Furthermore, these token charging arguments can involve integral redistributions or a fractional redistribution based on the values in the extreme point; several examples of both types of token redistributions were presented (e.g., in the chapters on spanning trees).

We believe the iterative method can be used to prove integrality of even more general classes of problems. Indeed, recent research [7] continues to push the envelope of such proofs to such general classes as lattice polyhedra. Other recent results [83, 110] have been obtained also using the iterative method and its variants. Some promising areas for future investigation include an alternate proof of integrality of totally unimodular matrices starting from their definition based on the bicoloring characterization due to Ghila-Houri [120], as well as exploring the relation of the techniques used in the iterative method to the characterization of totally dual integral systems.

The iterative method is versatile, but it is much less so than the other classical methods to prove integrality of polyhedral relaxations such as Total Unimodularity and Total Dual Integrality. All the results on exact optimization in this book are re-derivations of the results achieved by these two methods. An intriguing open question is to more formally derive a relation between the iterative method and these other more powerful methods for proving integrality. Nevertheless, a key advantage of the iterative method is its adaptability to designing approximation algorithms for the base problems augmented with complicating constraints.

On the approximation algorithms front, the iterative method belongs in the class of techniques for designing approximation algorithms based on a linear programming relaxation of the problem, such as deterministic rounding, randomized rounding, the primal-dual method [1,73], and methods based on Lagrangean relaxations. Like the primal-dual method, this method shares a rich intersection with the set of polynomial-time solvable exact characterizations that can be proven using the method, as we demonstrated in many of the earlier chapters. Looking ahead, the iterative method might offer new insights into the design of improved approximation algorithms for the traveling salesperson problems and its many variants, given their close connection to degree-bounded spanning tree problems. Some initial connections in this direction have already been explored [107] but much more remains to be done in this direction.

We close with the hope that our monograph will add the iterative method to the set of general techniques in the toolkit for the design of exact and approximation algorithms based on linear programming characterizations. We also hope that it will encourage a unified presentation of many of these beautiful results at an elementary level for the setting of undergraduate classrooms as well as for self-study by inspired enthusiasts of combinatorial optimization.

Bibliography

[1] A. Agrawal, P. Klein, R. Ravi, *When trees collide: An approximation algorithm for the generalized Steiner problem on networks*, in Proceedings of the Twenty-Third Annual ACM Symposium on Theory of Computing (STOC), 134–144, 1991.

[2] N. Alon, J. Spencer, *The probabilistic method*, 3rd edition, Wiley Series in Discrete Mathematics and Optimization, 2008.

[3] N. Andelman, Y. Mansour, *Auctions with budget constraints*, in Proceedings of 9th Scandinavian Workshop on Algorithm Theory (SWAT), 26–38, 2004.

[4] S.A. Andrea, E.T. Wong, *Row rank and column rank of a matrix*, Mathematics Magazine, 34(1), 33–34, 1960.

[5] E.M. Arkin, R. Hassin, *On local search for weighted k-set packing*, Mathematics of Operations Research, 23(3), 640–648, 1998.

[6] Y. Azar, B. Birnbaum, A. Karlin, C. Mathieu, C. Nguyen, *Improved approximation algorithms for budgeted allocations*, in Proceedings of 35th International Colloquium on Automata, Languages and Programming (ICALP), 186–197, 2008.

[7] N. Bansal, R. Khandekar, J. Konemann, V. Nagarajan, B Peis, *On generalizations of network design problems with degree bounds*, in Proceedings of Integer Programming and Combinatorial Optimization (IPCO), 2010.

[8] N. Bansal, R. Khandekar, V. Nagarajan, *Additive guarantees for degree bounded directed network design*, in Proceedings of the Fourtieth Annual ACM Symposium on Theory of Computing (STOC), 769–778, 2008.

[9] R. Bar-Yehuda, *Using homogenous weights for approximating the partial cover problem*, in Proceedings of the 10th Annual ACM-SIAM Symposium on Discrete Algorithms (SODA), 71–75, 1999.

[10] I. Bárány, On the power of linear dependencies, In *Building Bridges*, Grötschel and Katona, editors, Springer, 31–45, 2008.

[11] I. Bárány, *A vector-sum theorem and its application to improving flow shop guarantees*, Mathematics of Operations Research, 6, 445–452, 1981.

[12] J. Beck and T. Fiala, *"Integer-making" theorems*, Discrete Applied Mathematics, 3, 1–8, 1981.

[13] D. Bednarchak, M. Helm, *A note on the Beck-Fiala theorem*, Combinatorica, 17(1), 147–149, 1997.

[14] P. Berman, *A $d/2$ approximation for maximum weight indepedent set in d-claw free graphs*, in Proceedings of the 7th Scandinavian Workshop on Algorithms Theory (SWAT), 31–40, 2000.

[15] P. Berman, V. Ramaiyer, *Improved approximations for the Steiner tree problem*, In Proceedings of the Third Annual ACM-SIAM Symposium on Discrete Algorithm (SODA), 554–563, 1992.

[16] G. Birkhoff, *Tres observaciones sobre el algebra lineal,* Universidad Nacional de Tucuman Revista, Serie A, 5, 147–151, 1946.

[17] J.A. Bondy, U.S.R. Murty, *Graph Theory with Applications*, available online from www.ecp6.jussieu.fr/pageperso/bondy/books/gtwa/gtwa.html.

[18] O. Boruvka, *O jistém problému minimálním (About a certain minimal problem)* (in Czech, German summary), Práce mor. prírodoved. spol. v Brne III 3: 37–58.

[19] S.C. Boyd, W.R. Pulleyblank, *Optimizing over the subtour polytope of the travelling salesman problem*, Mathematical Programming, 2, 163–187, 1990.

[20] J. Byrka, F. Grandoni, T. Rothvoß, L. Sanità, *An improved LP-based approximation for Steiner trees*, in Proceedings of the 42nd Symposium on the Theory of Computing (STOC), 583–592, 2010.

[21] N. Bshouty, L. Burroughs, *Massaging a linear programming solution to give a 2-approximation for a generalization of the vertex cover problem*, in Proceedings of the 15th Annual Symposium on the Theoretical Aspects of Computer Science (STACS), 298–308, 1998.

[22] M.C. Cai, X. Deng, W. Zang, *A min-max theorem on feedback vertex sets*, Mathematics of Operation Research, 27, 361–371, 2002.

[23] D. Chakrabarty, G. Goel, *On the approximability of budgeted allocations and improved lower bounds for submodular welfare maximization and GAP*, in Proceedings of the 49th Annual Symposium on Foundations of Computer Science (FOCS), 687–696, 2008.

[24] D. Chakrabarty, J. Könemann, D. Pritchard, *Integrality gap of the hypergraphic relaxation of Steiner trees: a short proof of a 1.55 upper bound*, arXiv:1006.2249v1, June 2010.

[25] Y.H. Chan, W.S. Fung, L.C. Lau, C.K. Yung, *Degree bounded network design with metric costs*, in Proceedings of the 49th Annual IEEE Symposium on Foundations of Computer Science (FOCS), 125–134, 2008.

[26] Y.H. Chan, L.C. Lau, *On linear and semidefinite programming relaxations for hypergraph matching*, in Proceedings of the 21st Annual ACM-SIAM Symposium on Discrete Algorithms (SODA), 1500–1511, 2010.

[27] B. Chandra, M. Halldórsson, *Greedy local improvement and weighted set packing approximation*, in Proceedings of the 10th Annual ACM-SIAM Symposium on Discrete Algorithms (SODA), 169–176, 1999.

[28] J. Cheriyan, S. Vempala, A. Vetta, *Network design via iterative rounding of setpair relaxations*, Combinatorica 26(3), 255–275, 2006.

[29] V. Chvatal, *Linear Programming*, Freeman, 1983.

[30] W.J. Cook, W.H. Cunningham, W.R. Pulleyblank, A. Schrijver, *Combinatorial Optimization*, John Wiley and Sons, 1998.

[31] W.H. Cunningham, *Testing membership in matroid polyhedra*, J. Combinatorial Theory B, 36, 161–188, 1984.

[32] W.H. Cunningham, A.B. Marsh, *A primal algorithm for optimum matching*, (in Polyhedral Combinatorics – Dedicated to the memory of D.R. Fulkerson) Mathematical Programming Study, 8, 50–72, 1978.

[33] Y. Dinitz, N. Garg, M. Goemans, *On the single-source unsplittable flow problem*, Combinatorica, 19, 1–25, 1999.

[34] J. Edmonds, *Maximum matching and a polyhedron with 0,1-vertices*, Journal of Research National Bureau of Standards Section B, 69, 125–130, 1965.

[35] J. Edmonds, *Paths, trees and flowers*, Canadian Journal of Mathematics, 17, 449–467, 1965.

[36] J. Edmonds, *Optimum branchings*, Journal of Research National Bureau of Standards Section B, 71, 233–240, 1967.

[37] J. Edmonds, *Submodular functions, matroids, and certain polyhedra*, in Proceedings of the Calgary International Conference on Combinatorial Structures and their Application, Gordon and Breach, New York, 69–87, 1969.

[38] J. Edmonds, *Matroids and the greedy algorithm*, Mathematical Programming, 1, 125–136, 1971.

[39] J. Edmonds, R. Giles, *A min-max relation for submodular functions on graphs*, Annals of Discrete Mathematics, 1, 185–204, 1977.

[40] J. Egerváry, *Matrixok kombinatorius tulajdonsagairol,* [in Hungarian: On combinatorial properties of matrices] Matematikaies Fizikai Lapok, 38, 16–28, 1931.

[41] S.P. Fekete, S. Khuller, M. Klemmstein, B. Raghavachari, N. Young *A network-flow technique for finding low-weight bounded-degree trees*, Journal of Algorithms 24(2), 310–324, 1997.

[42] W. Fernandez de la Vega, G.S. Lueker, *Bin packing can be solved within $1 + \epsilon$ in linear time*, Combinatorica, 1, 349–355, 1981.

[43] L. Fleischer, K. Jain, D.P. Williamson, *Iterative rounding 2-approximation algorithms for minimum-cost vertex connectivity problems*, Journal of Computer System and Science, 72(5), 838–867, 2006.

[44] A. Frank, *Orientations of graphs and submodular flows*, Congr. Numer., 113, 111–142, 1996. Festschrift for C. St. J. A. Nash-Williams.

[45] A. Frank, *Rooted k-connections in digraphs*, Discrete Applied Mathematics, 157, 1242–1254, 2009.

[46] A. Frank, E. Tardos, *An application of submodular flows*, Linear Algebra and Its Applications, 114/115, 329–348, 1989.

[47] A. M. Frieze, *Personal communication*, March 2007.

[48] G. Frobenius, *Über zerlegbare Determinanten*, Sitzungsber, König. Preuss. Akad. Wiss. **XVIII**, 274–277, Jbuch. 46.144, 1917.

[49] T. Fukunaga, H. Nagamochi, *Network design with weighted degree constraints*, in Proceedings of Workshop on Algorithms and Computation (WAOA), 214–225, 2009.

[50] S. Fujishige, *Submodular Functions and Optimization*, 2nd edition, Elsevier, 2005.

[51] Z. Füredi, *Maximum degree and fractional matchings in uniform hypergraphs*, Combinatorica 1(2), 155–162, 1981.

[52] Z. Füredi, J. Kahn, P. Seymour, *On the fractional matching polytope of a hypergraph*, Combinatorica, 13(2), 167–180, 1993.

[53] M. Fürer, B. Raghavachari, *Approximating the minimum-degree Steiner tree to within one of optimal*, Journal of Algorithms, 17(3), 409–423, 1994.

[54] H.N. Gabow, *On the L_∞-norm of extreme points for crossing supermodular directed network LPs*, in Proceedings of Integer Programming and Combinatorial Optimization (IPCO), 392–406, 2005.

[55] H.N. Gabow, *Upper degree-constrained partial orientations*, In Proceedings of the 17th Annual ACM-SIAM Symposium on Discrete Algorithm (SODA), 554–563, 2006.

[56] M.R. Garey and D.S. Johnson, *Computers and Intractability: A Guide to the Theory of NP-Completeness*, Freeman, 1979.

[57] R. Garg, V. Kumar, V. Pandit, *Approximation algorithms for budget-constrained auctions*, in Proceedings of Approximation Algorithms for Combinatorial Optimization (APPROX), 102–113, 2001.

[58] N. Garg, V.V. Vazirani, M. Yannakakis, *Multiway cuts in directed and node weighted graphs*, in Proceedings of the 21st International Colloquium on Automata, Languages, and Programming (ICALP), 487–498, 1994.

[59] M.X. Goemans, *Minimum bounded-degree spanning trees,* in Proceedings of the 47th Annual IEEE Symposium on Foundations of Computer Science (FOCS), 273–282, 2006.

[60] M.X. Goemans, D.P. Williamson, The primal-dual method for approximation algorithms and its application to network design problems, *Approximation Algorithms for NP-Hard problems*, PWS Publishing Co., 1996.

[61] R.L. Graham, P. Hell, *On the history of the minimum spanning tree problem*, Annals of the History of Computing, 7, 43–57, 1985.

[62] R. Gandhi, S. Khuller, A. Srinivasan, *Approximation algorithms for partial covering problems*, in Proceedings of the International Colloquium on Automata, Languages, and Programming (ICALP), 225–236, 2001.

[63] M. Ghodsi, H. Mahini, K. Mirjalali, S.O. Gharan, A.S. Sayedi-Roshkhar, M. Zadimoghaddam, *Spanning trees with minimum weighted degrees*, Information Processessing Letters, 104(3), 113–116, 2007.

[64] F. Grandoni, R. Ravi, M. Singh, *Iterative rounding for multi-objective optimization problems*, in Proceedings of European Symposim on Algorithms, 95–106, 2009.

[65] V.S. Grinberg, S.V. Sevastyanov, *The value of the Steinitz constant*, Funk. Anal. Prilozh., 14, 56–57, 1980. (in Russian)

[66] C. Gröpl, S. Hougardy, T. Nierof, H.J. Proömel, Approxiamtion algorithms for the Steiner tree problems in graphs, in X.C. Heng and D.Z. Du, editors, *Steiner Trees in Industries*, 253–279, Kluwer Academic, 2001.

[67] M. Grötschel, L. Lovasz, A. Schrijver, *The ellipsoid method and its consequences in combinatorial optimization*, Combinatorica, 1, 169–197, 1981.

[68] M. Grötschel, L. Lovasz, A. Schrijver, *Corrigendum to our paper "The ellipsoid method and its consequences in combinatorial optimization"*, Combinatorica, 4, 291–295, 1984.

[69] I. Hajirasouliha, H. Jowhari, R. Kumar, R. Sundaram, *On completing Latin squares*, in Proceedings of the 24th International Symposium on Theoretical Aspects of Computer Science (STACS), 524–535, 2007.

[70] M. Held, R.M. Karp, *The traveling-salesman problem and minimum spanning trees*, Operations Research, 18, 1138–1162, 1970.

[71] F.S. Hillier, G.J. Lieberman, *Introduction to Operations Research*, (6th edition), Mcgraw-Hill, 1995.

[72] C.A.J. Hurkens, A. Schrijver, *On the size of systems of sets every t of which have an SDR, with an application to the worst-case ratio of heuristics for packing problems*, SIAM Journal on Discrete Mathematics, 2(1), 68–72, 1989.

[73] S. Iwata, *Submodular function minimization*, Math. Programming, Ser. B, 112(1), 45–64, 2008.

[74] S. Iwata, L. Fleischer, S. Fujishige, *A combinatorial strongly polynomial algorithm for minimizing submodular functions*, Journal of the Association for Computing Machinery (JACM), 48, 761–777, 2001.

[75] K. Jain, *A factor 2 approximation algorithm for the generalized Steiner network problem*, Combinatorica, 21, 39–60, 2001. (Preliminary version in *Proc. 39th IEEE FOCS*, 1998.)

[76] N. Karmarkar, *A new polynomial-time algorithm for linear programming*, Combinatorica, 4, 373–395, 1984.

[77] N. Karmarkar, R. Karp, *An efficient approximation scheme for the one dimensional bin-packing problem*, in Proceedings of the 23rd Annual Symposium on Foundations of Computer Science (FOCS), 312–320, 1982.

[78] L.G. Khachian, *A polynomial algorithm in linear programming*, Dokl. Akad. Nauk SSSR 244, 1093–1096, 1979. (English translation in Soviet Math. Dokl. 20, 191–194, 1979.)

[79] S. Khanna, J. Naor, F.B. Shepherd, *Directed network design with orientation constraints*, SIAM Journal on Discrete Mathematics, 19(1), 245–257, 2005.

[80] T. Király, L.C. Lau, M. Singh, *Degree bounded matroids and submodular flows*, in Proceedings of the 13th Conference on Integer Programming and Combinatorial Optimization (IPCO), 259–272, 2008.

[81] J.M. Kleinberg, *Single-source unsplittable flow*, in Proceedings of the 37th Annual IEEE Symposium on Foundations of Computer Science (FOCS), 68¡V77, 1996.

[82] S.G. Kolliopoulos, C. Stein, *Approximation algorithms for single-source unsplittable flow*, SIAM Journal on Computing, 31(3), 916–946, 2001.

[83] J. Könemann, O. Parekh, D. Pritchard, *Max-weight integral multicommodity flow in spiders and high-capacity trees*, in Proceedings of Workshop on Approximation and Online Algorithms (WAOA), 1–14, 2008.

[84] D. König, *Gráfok és mátrixok*. Matematikai és Fizikai Lapok 38: 116—119, 1931.

[85] M. Krivelevich, *On a conjecture of Tuza about packing and covering of triangles*, Discrete Mathematics, 142, 281–286, 1995.

[86] J.B. Kruskal, *On the shortest spanning subtree of a graph and the traveling salesman problem*, in Proceedings of the American Mathematical Society, 7(1), 48–60, 1956.

[87] H.W. Kuhn, *The Hungarian Method for the assignment problem*, Naval Research Logistic Quarterly, 2, 83–97, 1955.

238   *Bibliography*

[88] L.C. Lau, S. Naor, M. Salavatipour, M. Singh, *Survivable network design with degree or order constraints*, in Proceedings of the 40th ACM Symposium on Theory of Computing (STOC), 651–660, 2007.

[89] L.C. Lau, M. Singh, *Additive approximation for bounded degree survivable network design*, in Proceedings of the 41st ACM Symposium on Theory of Computing (STOC), 759–768, 2008.

[90] J.K. Lenstra, D.B. Shmoys, E. Tardos, *Approximation algorithms tor scheduling unrelated parallel machines*, Mathematical Programming, 46, 259–271, 1990.

[91] J.H. Lin, J.S. Vitter, ϵ-*approximations with minimum packing constraint violation*, in Proceedings of the 24th Annual ACM Symposium on the Theory of Computing (STOC), 771–782, 1992.

[92] A. Louis, N.K. Vishnoi *Improved algorithm for degree bounded survivable network design problem*, in Proceedings of 12th Scandinavian Symposium and Workshops on Algorithm Theory (SWAT), 408–419, 2010.

[93] L. Lovász, *On two minimax theorems in graphs*, Journal of Combinatorial Theory, Series B, 21, 96–103, 1976.

[94] L. Lovász, *Submodular functions and convexity*, in A. Bachem, M. Grötschel, and B. Korte, ed., *Mathematical Programming – The State of the Art*, Springer, 235–257, 1983.

[95] C.L. Lucchesi, D.H. Younger, *A minimax theorem for directed graphs*, Journal of the London Mathematical Society, 17(2), 369–374, 1978.

[96] J. Matoušek, J. Nešetřil, *An Invitation to Discrete Mathematics*, Oxford University Press, 2nd edition, 2008.

[97] V. Melkonian, E. Tardos, *Algorithms for a network design problem with crossing supermodular demands*, Networks, 43(4), 256–265, 2004.

[98] K. Menger, *Zur allgemeinen kurventheorie*, Fund. Math. 10, 96–115, 1927.

[99] M. Molloy, B. Reed, *Graph Colouring and the Probabilisitc Method*, Springer Series in Algorithms and Combinatorics 23, 2002.

[100] J. Munkres, *Algorithms for assignment and transportation problems*, Journal of the Society for Industrial and Applied Mathematics, 5, 32–38, 1957.

[101] H. Nagamochi, T. Ibaraki, *A note on minimizing submodular functions*, Information Processing Letters, 67, 239–244, 1998.

[102] H. Nagamochi, T. Ibaraki, *Polyhedral structure of submodular and posi-modular systems*, Lecture Notes in Computer Science 1533, Springer-Verlag, Kyung-Yong Chwa and Oscar H.Ibara (Eds.), Algorithms and Computation, 9th International Symposium (ISAAC), 169–178, 1998.

[103] V. Nagarajan, R. Ravi, M. Singh, *Simpler analysis of LP extreme points for traveling salesman and survivable network design problems*, Operations Research Letter, 38(3), 156–160, 2010.

[104] C.St.J.A. Nash-Williams. *Edge disjoint spanning trees of finite graphs*, J. London Math. Soc., 36, 445–450, 1961.

[105] G.L. Nemhauser, L.E. Trotter, *Vertex packings: structural properties and algorithms*, Mathematical Programming, 8, 232–248, 1975.

[106] G.L. Nemhauser, L.A. Wolsey, *Integer and Combinatorial Optimization*, Wiley-Interscience, 1999.

[107] T. Nguyen, *A simple LP relaxation for the asymmetric traveling salesman problem*, in Proceedings of International Workshop on Approximation Algorithms for Combinatorial Optimization (APPROX), 207–218, 2008.

[108] Z. Nutov, *Approximating directed weighted-degree constrained networks*, in Proceedings of International Workshop on Approximation Algorithms for Combinatorial Optimization (APPROX), 219–232, 2008.

[109] M.W. Padberg, M.R. Rao, *Odd minimum cut-sets and b-matchings*, Mathematics of Operations Research, 7, 67–80, 1982.

[110] D. Pritchard, *Approximability of sparse integer programs*, in Proceedings of European Symposium of Algorithms (ESA), 83–94, 2009.

[111] R. C. Prim, *Shortest connection networks and some generalisations,* in Bell System Technical Journal, 36, 1389–1401, 1957.

[112] M. Queyranne, *Minimizing symmetric submodular functions*, Mathematical Programming, 82, 3–12, 1998.

[113] R. Ravi, M.X. Goemans, *The constrained minimum spanning tree problem*, in Proceedings of Fifth Scandinavian Workshop on Algorithm Theory (SWAT), 66–75, 1996.

[114] H.E. Robbins, *A theorem on graphs with an application to a problem of traffic control*, American Mathmatics Monthly, 46, 281–283, 1939.

[115] G. Robins, A. Zelikovsky, *Tighter bounds for graph Steiner tree approximation*, SIAM Journal on Discrete Mathematics, 19(1), 122–134, 2005.

[116] B. Saha, A. Srinivasan, *A new approximation technique for resource-allocation problems*, in Proceedings of First Annual Symposium on Innovations in Computer Science (ICS), 342–357, 2010.

[117] P. Sasatte, *Improved approximation algorithm for the feedback set problem in a bipartite tournament*, Operations Research Letters 36(5), 602–604, 2008.

[118] A. Schrijver, *A combinatorial algorithm minimizing submodular functions in strongly polynomial time*, J. Combin. Theory Ser. B, 80, 346–355, 2000.

[119] A. Schrijver, *On the history of combinatorial optimization (till 1960)*, Handbook of Discrete Optimization, 24, Eds. K. Aardal, G.L. Nemhauser and R. Weismantel, 2005.

[120] A. Schrijver, *Theory of Linear and Integer Progamming*, Wiley, 1998.

[121] A. Schrijver, *Combinatorial Optimization - Polyhedra and Efficiency*, Springer–Verlag, New York, 2005.

[122] D. Shmoys, E. Tardos, *An approximation algorithm for the generalized assignment problem*, Mathematical Programming, 62(3), 461–474, 1993.

[123] M. Skutella, *Approximating the single-source unsplittable min-cost flow problem*, Mathematical Programming B, 91(3), 493–514, 2002.

[124] M. Singh, *Iterative Methods in Combinatorial Optimization*, Ph.D. thesis, Carnegie Mellon University, 2008.

[125] M. Singh, L.C. Lau, *Approximating minimum bounded degree spanning tress to within one of optimal*, in Proceedings of 39th ACM Symposium on Theory of Computing (STOC), 661–670, 2007.

[126] A. Srinivasan, *Budgeted allocations in the full-information setting*, in Proceedings of International Workshop on Approximation Algorithms for Combinatorial Optimization Problems, 247–253, 2008.

[127] E. Steinitz, *Bedingt konvergente Reihen und konvexe Systeme*, J. Reine Ang. Mathematik, 143, 128–175, 1913, ibid., 144, 1–40, 1914, ibid., 146, 1–52, 1916.

[128] M.A. Trick, *Scheduling multiple variable-speed machines*, in Proceedings of the 1st Conference on Integer Programming and Combinatorial Optimization (IPCO), 485–494, 1990.

[129] W.T. Tutte, *Lectures on matroids*, Journal of Research National Bureau of Standards Section B, 69, 1–47, 1965. [reprinted in D. McCarthy, R.G. Stanton, editors, *Selected Papers of W.T. Tutte* vol. II, Charles Babbage Research Centre, 439–496, 1979].

[130] A. van Zuylen, *Linear programming based approximation algorithms for feedback set problems in bipartite tournaments*, Conference on Theory and Applications of Models of Computation, 2009.

[131] R. J. Vanderbei, *Linear Programming: Foundations and Extensions*, 3rd edition, Springer, 2007.

[132] V. Vazirani, *Approximation Algorithms*, Springer, 2001.

[133] S.J. Wright, *Primal-Dual Interior-Point Methods,* SIAM Publications, 1997.

[134] A. Zelikovsky, *An 11/6-approximation algorithm for the network Steiner problem*, Algorithmica, 9, 463–470, 1993.

[135] C. Zhang, G. Wang, X. Liu, J. Liu, *Approximating scheduling machines with capacity constraints*, in Proceedings of 3rd International Workshop on Frontiers in Algorithms (FAW), 283–292, 2009.

Index

$E(X,Y)$, 19
$\delta(S)$, 19
$\delta(v)$, 19
$\delta^{in}(S)$, 20
$\delta^{in}(v)$, 20
$\delta^{out}(S)$, 20
$\delta^{out}(v)$, 20
$d^{in}(S)$, 20, 24
$d^{out}(S)$, 20, 24
coreq(S), 167
$d(S)$, 20, 21
$d^{in}(v)$, 20
$d^{out}(v)$, 20
$i(S)$, 23
$r(S)$, 66

arborescence, 20, 88
assignment problem, 1

basic feasible solution, 15
biset, 96
bisupermodular function, 99
bicriteria approximation, 102, 173
bilaminar family, 99
bin packing, 212
bipartite matching, 1, 28, 71
bipartite tournament, 194
budgeted allocation problem, 35

chain, 68
corequirement, 167, 177
complementary slackness conditions, 18

connected, 20
    strongly connected, 20
    weakly connected, 20
connectivity requirement function, 25
contraction, 20
cross-free family, 113, 115
crossing family, 111
crossing sets, 23
cut function, 21
    directed, 24
    undirected, 21

directed cut, 117
directed cut cover, 117

extreme point solution, 4, 13

feedback arc set, 119
feedback vertex set, 194

general assignment problem, 32, 36
graph orientation, 122

hypergraph, 155, 203
hypergraph discrepancy, 203
hypergraph matching, 155

induced edge function, 23
integral solution, 13
intersecting bisets, 98
intersecting sets, 23, 51
iterative randomized rounding, 220
iterative relaxation, 5, 7
iterative rounding, 5, 7

laminar family, 51, 91, 151
linear programming, 1, 12
  algorithms, 16
  duality, 17
  duality theorem, 18
local ratio method, 157, 159

matching
  bipartite matching, 28
  general matching, 145
  hypergraph matching, 155
matroid, 65
  graphic matroid, 66
  linear matroid, 66
  partition matroid, 66
  rank function, 66
matroid basis, 67, 139
matroid intersection, 71, 120, 140
  of k matroids, 82
Menger's theorem, 20
minimum arborescence, 71, 88
minimum bounded degree arborescence, 101
minimum bounded degree matroid basis, 77
minimum bounded degree spanning tree, 57, 77, 81
minimum bounded degree Steiner network, 173
minimum bounded degree submodular flow, 124
minimum cost circulation, 110, 208
minimum cost flow, 110
minimum cost unsplittable flow, 210
minimum crossing spanning tree, 80
minimum spanning tree, 46, 67
multicriteria approximation, 187
multicriteria spanning tree, 187

network matrix, 75, 76, 117, 131, 132
node multiway cut, 197

partial Latin sqaure, 160
partial vertex cover, 184

rank function, 66
rank lemma, 4, 14
rearrangments of sums, 206
rooted connectivity, 95

separation oracle, 6, 17
  weak separation oracle, 214
spanning subgraph, 20
spanning tree, 20
Steiner network, 164
submodular flow, 112, 113, 142
submodular function, 21
  crossing submodular function, 23, 111
  intersecting submodular function, 23
  strongly submodular function, 22, 165
submodular function minimization, 25
subtour elimination LP, 47
supermodular function, 23
  bisupermodular function, 99
  skew supermodular function, 24, 165

tight odd-set, 147
totally unimodular matrix, 132
traveling salesman problem, 47, 164
tree, 20
triangle cover, 191

uncrossing technique, 50, 68, 75, 90, 98, 113, 117, 146, 166
unsplittable flow, 210

vertex cover, 40, 182
  bipartite graphs, 40
  partial vertex cover, 184

Printed in the United States
by Baker & Taylor Publisher Services